THE FUTURE AS CATASTROPHE

THE FUTURE AS CATASTROPHE

IMAGINING DISASTER IN
THE MODERN AGE

EVA HORN

TRANSLATION BY VALENTINE PAKIS

Columbia University Press
New York

Columbia University Press
Publishers Since 1893
New York   Chichester, West Sussex
cup.columbia.edu
Copyright © 2018 Columbia University Press
Originally published in German as *Zukunft als Katastrophe*
(Frankfurt: Fischer, 2014).
All rights reserved

Library of Congress Cataloging-in-Publication Data
Names: Horn, Eva author. | Pakis, Valentine A. translator.
Title: The future as catastrophe : imagining disaster in the modern age / Eva Horn;
[translated by Valentine Pakis].
Other titles: Zukunft als Katastrophe. English
Description: New York : Columbia University Press, 2018. |
Includes bibliographical references and index.
Identifiers: LCCN 2018008908 (print) | LCCN 2018022545 (ebook) |
ISBN 9780231547956 (e-book) | ISBN 9780231188623 (cloth) |
ISBN 9780231188630 (pbk.)
Subjects: LCSH: Fiction—History and criticism. | Disasters in literature. |
Future, The, in literature. | Disaster films—History and criticism. |
Future, The, in motion pictures.
Classification: LCC PN3352.D57 (ebook) | LCC PN3352.D57 H6713 2018 (print) |
DDC 809/.933582—dc23
LC record available at https://lccn.loc.gov/2018008908

Cover design: Noah Arlow
Cover image: © Peder Norrby

CONTENTS

Acknowledgments vii

INTRODUCTION 1

1. LAST MEN 21

2. CATASTROPHE WITHOUT EVENT:
IMAGINING CLIMATE DISASTER 55

3. SURVIVAL:
THE BIOPOLITICS OF CATASTROPHE 89

4. THE FUTURE OF THINGS:
ACCIDENTS AND TECHNICAL SAFETY 134

5. THE PARADOXES OF PREDICTION 174

CONCLUSION 227

Notes 239
Bibliography 261
Index 275

ACKNOWLEDGMENTS

The idea of dealing with our sense that the future that is headed toward disaster first came to me in 2008, in the moment of the financial crisis. I was struck by the feeling that we were all waking up to a future that was less and less predictable and that we could not ever prepare for. As a literary scholar, I wanted to know more about the cultural history of this feeling—and found that it had been there all along, accompanying modernity's trust in an ever-brighter future like a dark shadow. Many friends and colleagues, students, and interlocutors have left their traces in this book, in the form of arguments and objections, encouragements, challenges, or generously offered ideas.

Early on, Nitzan Lebovic invited me to a conference in Tel Aviv on the Politics of Time, giving me an occasion to present some rough ideas on the aporias of foreknowledge. He also pointed out to me the biopolitical subtext of many disaster movies. Friedrich Balke had me come to Weimar to discuss some of these ideas further within the context of film and media theory. Michèle Lowrie invited me to a conference on Security at NYU in 2009, where I discussed my reading of *12 Monkeys* and was introduced to John Hamilton's ideas on the topic. Three years later, Michèle gave me the occasion to discuss my thoughts on Byron at the University of Chicago with her, Eric Santner, David Wellbery, and Anselm Haverkamp, who gave me a better understanding of the darkness of Byron's anthropology. An early encouragement to write on the future from a humanities perspective came from Harald Welzer. Ulrich Bröckling, whose ideas on prevention were crucial for parts of this book, gave me an excellent commentary on chapter 5. The first reader of the book's German manuscript was Isak Winkel Holm in 2013, who was so knowledgeable on the entire subject that, having met him only late in the writing process, I briefly wished to start all over again. He saved me from that impulse by giving me a brilliant and thorough commentary on my early manuscript. Pál Kelemen and his students, by inviting me to Budapest during the last stages of writing in 2013, helped me strengthen the general outline of my book. My students in Vienna, accompanying the development of my book at various stages, forced me to clarify many details of my readings and the book's historical narrative. Through his continuing encouragement and insistence, my editor at Fischer Verlag, Alexander Roesler, was crucial in eventually getting the book to the finish line. My assistant, Martina Süess, brought the manuscript into a shape that finally started resembling a book.

This is a shortened and updated translation of my book *Zukunft als Katastrophe*, which came out in German in 2014. I wish to thank Wendy Lochner for her confidence in me as an author new to Columbia University Press. I am grateful to the two anonymous reviewers who made excellent suggestions on how to change the manuscript for the English edition. Ben Robinson oversaw my editing and secured the image rights. His comments helped make the English version a shorter, more concentrated version of the German edition.

Writing about the future as catastrophe is challenging, intellectually and otherwise. I dedicate this book to those who have taught me how to dwell in the present: my friends.

THE FUTURE AS CATASTROPHE

INTRODUCTION

THE WORLD WITHOUT PEOPLE

A man is speeding through Manhattan in a sports car, racing down Fifth Avenue toward Midtown. Although it is daytime, the streets are empty. Cars are parked on the side of the road, but otherwise nobody is there. A suspicious amount of grass is growing through the cracks in the asphalt. The camera pans high above the rooftops, and we see that the man is the only person in the city and that his car is the only thing moving, its motor's distant humming the only sound. In Times Square, the grass is shoulder high, and deer are grazing. What was once a flurry of crowds, advertisements, and chaotic traffic is now overgrown, peaceful in the afternoon light of an Indian summer.

The opening credits of the film *I Am Legend* (2007) are like the fantasy of a weary city dweller: a deserted metropolis, plants overrunning the eternally busy streets. Complete silence.[1] The last living person in this empty city, Dr. Robert Neville (Will Smith), suddenly has the entire city to himself. He is free of the burdens imposed by incessant social contact and by a civilization whose familiarity with plants and animals was limited to parks and household pets. Yet the film is not about an idyllic return to nature. It is about the ultimate catastrophe—the end of humanity. Neville is the lone survivor of a manmade epidemic that has depopulated almost the entire world. He is the Last Man, both a witness to and a victim of the

FIGURE 0.1 New York after the end of humankind: Fifth Avenue overgrown with plant life.

Source: Still from *I Am Legend* (2007).

FIGURE 0.2 Humans go, the wilderness returns. The last man, Dr. Robert Neville (Will Smith), hunting deer in Midtown Manhattan.

Source: Still from *I Am Legend* (2007).

end of the human species. Nevertheless, this image of a quietly decaying, empty New York is more than just a horrifying scenario (fig. 0.1). It is also a secret desire: an image of postapocalyptic peace that can only come when mankind has finally vanished (fig. 0.2).

In recent years, the image of a world without people has gained a symptomatic popularity.[2] In his nonfiction bestseller *The World Without Us*

(2007), Alan Weisman has imagined the future decay of cities and infrastructure in the wake of mankind's extinction. Weisman's book was so popular that it inspired the television series *Life After People* (History Channel). The book describes locations abandoned by humanity, showing how quickly houses and prominent architectural landmarks deteriorate after the departure of the humans who maintain them. Concrete will crumble; steel cables, snap; and bridges, fall apart. Weeds will grow rampant, and animals will shelter in our high-rises. Weisman presents a picture of a world finally "relieved" of the pressure placed on it by humanity:

> Look around you, at today's world. Your house, your city. The surrounding land, the pavement underneath, and the soil hidden below that. Leave it all in place, but extract the human beings. Wipe us out, and see what's left. How would the rest of nature respond if it were suddenly relieved of the relentless pressures we heap on it and our fellow organisms?[3]

Weisman's scenario of a future without man where nature has taken over is also one of a return to the origins *before* mankind—just as Manhattan in *I Am Legend* gradually comes to resemble the overgrown rocky promontory that, just four centuries ago, was known as Mana-hatta. The narrative of humanity's sudden (and slightly miraculous) disappearance is strangely comforting. Once humans are gone from the earth, their vestiges will soon vanish. Its natural balance restored, the world will bloom and flourish again, a Garden of Eden, a return to the beginning. This is a narrative of sickness and healing, of pressure and its release—told by the very being that was the sickness. Humankind blissfully dreams of its own extinction.

The same story can also be told from a slightly different point of view. One hundred million years from now, a spaceship with a crew of alien paleontologists lands somewhere on the "Great Northern Continent" of the Earth. In a deep canyon, they come across a broad stratum of rock in which they discover metal and stone artifacts: signs of an ancient and long-extinct civilization. In the same stratum, however, they also find traces of a great catastrophe that must have drastically altered the living conditions on the planet. What the alien researchers are analyzing are the remains of humanity, preserved for millions of years.

This story is told by the geologist Jan Zalasiewicz in his book about the long-term archaeological traces that human beings will leave on the face of the earth.[4] Zalasiewicz's posthuman narrative is used to introduce the geological term "Anthropocene." The Anthropocene designates the current epoch, in which it has become clear that humans will leave an indelible geological impression: "Since the start of the Industrial Revolution, Earth has endured changes sufficient to leave a global stratigraphic signature distinct from that of the Holocene or of previous Pleistocene interglacial phases, encompassing novel biotic, sedimentary, and geochemical change."[5] Humanity, in other words, is not just a fleeting disease on the planet. Its impression will not simply be obscured beneath plants and sediment but will last for millions of years. While Zalasiewicz focuses on our geological agency and everlasting effect on the planet, Weisman emphasizes the transient nature of human achievement and structures. But both narratives are based on an apocalyptic fiction in which humankind will have vanished and all that will remain of it are scraps or a geological stratum.

Both narratives are symptomatic of the present relationship to the future. They adopt an impossible postapocalyptic standpoint: Humankind looks back upon itself *after* its end. It is a gaze in the future perfect, a future that *will have been*. This perspective, that is, a gaze looking back on the future *as past*, is emblematic of our current relation to the future. And this relation to the future seems to be inevitably dependent on narratives, fictions, or fictional modes of thought—even in the most nonfictional genres. Given Zalasiewicz's diagnosis that humans have entered the epoch of the Anthropocene, it is somewhat ironic that humans are dreaming of their own extinction in the very epoch named for the indelible trace they will have left in the geohistory of the planet. Remarkably, however, both postcatastrophic stories are strangely discreet about the event that has wiped out humankind. Weisman speculates briefly about a *Homo sapiens*–specific virus that could kill everyone in a single stroke, but his book makes no mention of what happened to the seven billion corpses. Humans are just magically gone.[6] Tellingly, both thought experiments are about a catastrophe without disaster, death, and destruction, as though we were looking back at our demise from a distant future, as alien witnesses to our own end.

THE FUTURE AS CATASTROPHE

The fiction of a world without people is symptomatic of a currently pervasive apocalyptic fantasy. It extends from mainstream movies to scientific nonfiction and from philosophical essays to the novel. Clearly, this fantasy participates in the breakdown of the modern order of time, recently analyzed by Aleida Assmann. She describes the disintegration of a temporal order in the modern age in which the future was still an "auratic key concept," a space of hope and planning, a locus of utopia.[7] Today's conceptions of the future could not be further removed from such optimism. Their tense is the future perfect, and their object is the future as catastrophe. This fantasy—its contents, sources, political functions, and epistemological implications—is the topic of the present book. The fantasy of the future as catastrophe is the emblem of a new, highly ambivalent attitude toward the future, marked by a strange fixation with catastrophe as a moment when an ultimate truth is revealed.

Images of catastrophe and its aftermath have taken hold of today's popular imagination. The "apocalyptic tone"[8] of the 1980s has been revived in a wide variety of media and genres: in film (from Roland Emmerich to Lars von Trier), in literature (from Cormac McCarthy and Paolo Bacigalupi to Michel Houellebecq), in popular works of nonfiction, in computer games, in sociological and philosophical discussions (from Ulrich Beck and Peter Sloterdijk to Timothy Morton and Bruno Latour), in the natural sciences (from geology to climatology), and even in the notoriously optimistic and growth-oriented field of economics. Sociology describes our current society as a "risk society" marked by self-generated yet widely distributed dangers. The German sociologist Ulrich Beck has analyzed a "global risk society" in which threats are delocalized and incalculable.[9] Jared Diamond's study of collapsing societies became a bestseller, as did Harald Welzer's bleak prognosis of imminent "climate wars" and resource conflicts.[10] James Hansen, one of the earliest scientists to warn about the threat of climate change, recently corrected his own prognosis with the following words: "I was too optimistic."[11] James Lovelock, who in the 1970s developed the "Gaia hypothesis" about the biosphere as a macro-organism, has lately turned to foretell "Gaia's revenge."[12] Almost every month sees a new movie imagining a more or less spectacular end of the world (*2012, Melancholia, Seeking a Friend for the End of the World, 4:44: End of the World*), contemplating the extinction of the human race (*Oblivion, World War Z, Contagion*), or taking place in a deserted world after the disappearance of humankind (*9, Wall-E, The Book of Eli, After Earth*). Other movies explore the dissolution of social order (the Mad Max series, *Time of the Wolf, Hell, The Road*). The apocalyptic obsession of current cinema has even become the object of parody, as in *This Is the End* from 2013. The grimmest postapocalyptic novel of recent years, Cormac McCarthy's *The Road*, won the Pulitzer Prize and was made into a prominent film starring Viggo Mortensen and Charlize Theron.

The present feels as though it is stumbling toward an end. Today's idea of the future has been succinctly put into words by a position paper from the reinsurance company Swiss Re: "The future is not a question of distance in time. The future is what radically differs from the present."[13] We see the future as a radical disruption with regard to the present, something we can hardly anticipate or prevent. It might consist of a nuclear meltdown the day after tomorrow or an end of the world in millions of years—either way, it will be radically different from everything we know in the present.

The term for such unforeseeable disruption is old, and it initially referred to the realm of literature. The Greek word καταστροφή (*katastrophē*) is a compound made up of the preposition κατά (*kata*) "down, downward" and the verb στρέφειν (*strephein*) "a turning." Literally, "catastrophe" thus denotes a "sudden downward turn." Aristotle referred to it as a *peripeteia*, a reversal in which a situation turns into its opposite, from fortune to misfortune.[14] In poetic theories after Aristotle, however, *katastrophē* came to denote not the turning point but rather its *result*. In this sense, "catastrophe" is the final part of the plot (the denouement), when everything has taken its ultimate course—for better or for worse.[15] It is an ending, a conclusion—something that *will have come*. This does not necessarily have to be an unhappy ending. Only at the end is it possible to survey and make sense of a given story. The poetological term eventually made its way into theology and the natural sciences in the early-modern period, where it came to designate a purely negative event.[16] For theologians, a catastrophe is an act of divine retribution; for historians, a political revolution; and for scientists, it implies the "decay, corruption, and dissolution of nature," as David Hume put it.[17]

During the twentieth century, the term "catastrophe" eventually transformed into a "ubiquitous category of crisis that gradually came to denote a process instead of an event."[18] It thus became a keyword for a modern historical sense of the present, the sense of looming danger. "Something is taking its course," as it is put in Beckett's *Endgame*.[19] The present is seen as marked by an imperceptible process of doom. This feeling was captured most succinctly by Walter Benjamin: "The concept of progress is to be grounded in the idea of the catastrophe. That things 'just go on' *is* the catastrophe. It is not that which is approaching but that which is. Strindberg's thought: Hell is not something which lies ahead of us,— but *this life here*. Redemption looks to the small fissure in the ongoing catastrophe."[20] Benjamin's understanding of the term is thus the opposite of its original meaning as a sudden turn of events. For him, the catastrophe is that *there is no longer any event*. What is horrifying is the continuity, the fact that the present keeps on unfolding into the future—its inexorable perpetuation.

The present consciousness of an imminent yet entirely unpredictable catastrophe combines precisely these two opposed conceptions: on the one hand, the sense of a break from the present, which derives from poetics but continues to inform even the concept of the future used by insurance companies; on the other, the idea formulated by Benjamin that the true catastrophe is the continuation of the here and now. The idea of the future as catastrophe is a combination of continuity and discontinuity, the notion that the very perpetuation of the present is heading toward a disastrous turn.

Today, the most common metaphor for this is the "tipping point." It signifies the point at which a previously stable condition suddenly becomes unstable, tips over, and turns into something qualitatively different. Malcolm Gladwell has described the tipping point as the moment of achieving a critical mass, when a slow swelling gives way to exponential proliferation. According to Gladwell, the tipping point of social processes involves the introduction of something entirely new simply by means of a few well-connected people beginning to spread, for example, a virus, a brand, or a particular form of social behavior.[21] Such turning points, however, are not restricted to social dynamics. They are crucial elements of any complex system, such as financial markets, the climate, or the ecosystem. Here, the tipping point represents the threatening possibility that, through the simple accumulation of small steps and minute acts, a situation can go out of balance. Impending tipping points of this sort can be observed nearly everywhere: in the climate, the ecosystem of the oceans, the welfare state, financial markets, logistic systems, and consumer behavior.

The problem is that such systemic turning points are hard to predict. Since self-regulating systems (like ecosystems, markets, or societies) can keep themselves in balance for a long time before they suddenly reach the dangerous point in question, they may seem stable while actually heading for a crisis. The concept of the tipping point means that, at some point, self-regulation will no longer work, that a system will become "saturated" (as the phenomenon is called in chemistry), or that (to borrow an expression from physics) a "critical mass" will be reached. Tipping points are thus not caused by human decisions. Rather, they are phenomena of spontaneous emergence. A critical change in conditions will develop out of a barely noticeable tendency, out of an accumulation of tiny steps. Inevitably, such changes are hard to predict as they are brought about by minuscule quantitative growth or seemingly negligible side effects. They are veiled by an appearance of stability suggesting that everything will go on as before.

Today's awareness of the future as catastrophe consists in the feeling of being at a tipping point, at a moment when simply going on with our customary lifestyles will gradually lead to catastrophe—yet one that we can hardly anticipate in its scenario and repercussions. This is why the disaster scenarios currently most discussed revolve around the collapse or disruption of highly complex systems. Global warming, which currently dominates concerns about a major destabilization of the earth's life system, can thus be understood as a name used to render this type of catastrophe representable as an object of study and concern. Climate change, to which I will devote a whole chapter, is nevertheless not the only problem at hand, as is pointed out in the current debates about the Anthropocene, which cannot be reduced to global warming. What we are dealing with is a *metacrisis* composed of many interrelated factors, dispersed into a multitude of scenarios, and distributed among many different subsystems.

As this book will argue, this novel type of catastrophe is a *catastrophe without event*. It may have many different forms of "outbreak," but it essentially (and paradoxically) consists in the sheer perpetuation of current policies, lifestyles, and modes of managing the future. It lacks identifiable agents, a precise moment in time, and a definite location in space, and it is not confined to any particular single scenario. The catastrophe without event is characterized by disparate, diffuse, and ultimately undefinable scenarios, temporalities, localities, and processes. The bleak underlying feeling today is that the continuation of the present will inevitably lead to a radical break or collapse. No one knows, however, exactly how this will come about.

CATASTROPHE AS REVELATION

The cacophony of scientific, political, and fictional depictions of catastrophe raises the question of what is at stake in them all. What compels us to imagine ourselves as the last men on earth, as in *I Am Legend*? What latent conflicts and desires are processed or brought to the surface by these fantasies? How does our predilection for disaster stories relate to our inability to make political decisions that would stall the looming dangers coming from, for example, environmental damage or high-risk technology? Which imagined disasters are inherent to our concepts of precaution, security, and safety? Imagined disasters illustrate potential dangers and risks that we cannot fully grasp. The imagination of disaster seems to shed a light through the fog of an overly complex world, to make things manageable and to promise to reveal an essential truth.

So why does the awareness of an impending crisis go hand in hand with a remarkable inability to act, both politically and individually? Why are we so eager to read books about the demise of humanity while remaining politically passive, neither protesting on the streets nor giving up our cars? Hardly anybody spends their days stocking a private bunker with groceries; we do not even take out more home insurance. We are on high alert while also lame and indecisive, repeatedly conjuring up looming catastrophes and immediately forgetting them.

The aim of this book is to decipher this ambivalent engagement with catastrophe as a symptom of the modern relation to the future. My concern is not to provide a social or psychological analysis of collective anxieties. The book aims to examine the images, narratives, and scenarios—that is, the fictions—that define and inform this relation. These fictions are part of a social dimension that has become known as the "collective imaginary." According to Charles Taylor, images, myths, stories, and symbols influence the ways in which "people imagine their social existence, how they fit together with others . . . the expectations that are normally met, and the deeper normative notions and images that underlie these expectations."[22] Shared conceptions, attributions, narratives, images, and metaphors are modes by which we understand "reality," from the basic elements of a given lifestyle to semiotic systems, the effable and ineffable, and the relations among various subsystems of society. The future and our collective and individual relation to it are part of this imaginary. Knowing and communicating about the future is impossible without stories: stories that "look back" from the future to the present or that extrapolate from past predictions about what is to come. Such narratives structure the way we anticipate and plan for the future and, above all, how we try to prevent catastrophic futures from occurring.

Our relation to the future is thus unthinkable without metaphors, images, visions, or hypothetical scenarios of potential future worlds. In this regard, Ulrich Beck has pointed out the decisive role of "staging" risks and dangers: "For only by imagining and staging world risk does the future catastrophe become present—often with the goal of averting it by influencing present decisions."[23] Fictional scenarios of the future in literature, film, popular culture, and popular nonfiction are such "stagings" as much as they are metaphors (such as "Lifeboat Earth" or "Spaceship Earth")[24] or symbols (from the mushroom cloud to the hockey-stick graph of climate change). They are also the sites for *negotiations* about the future and the measures used to securitize it, whether with optimism or alarm, with skepticism or precaution, "prepared for anything" or willing to accept risk. They inform the expectations and anxieties we have regarding the future. In doing so, they are neither mere symptoms of the collective psyche nor simply media of ideological indoctrination but epistemic tools to understand and discuss potential futures. They furnish modernity's open and plannable future with images, narratives, and affects. With their vivid images and exceptional plots and characters, they are more poignant than sociological averages or the humdrum predictions of technocrats and futurologists. Future fictions thus create not only the future but, above all, the present, that is, the reality in which we live, or at least our notion of it.

Catastrophes are perceived not just as a break from a given reality but rather as a revelation of underlying structures, the irruption of something "real" yet imperceptible in everyday life. Slavoj Žižek has remarked that notions of the "real"—that is, of a reality beneath everyday social surfaces—are themselves structured by fantasms that we encounter at the movie theater, in literature, in the rhetoric of politicians, and in popular science.[25] According to Žižek, these popular fantasms structure what we regard to be probable, possible, expectable, and authentic; they influence the imaginary patterns and cognitive schemes through which we perceive and interpret reality. This notion of the "real," which tends to come to our attention in emergency situations, unanticipated turns of events, moments of civil unrest, and the collapse of social institutions, is thus itself an imaginary construct. As such, it is something to be analyzed on the basis of its fictional sources and stages.[26] Examples of such fantasms include discussions of "emergencies" in which different social rules ought to be applied for the sake of survival; the notion of mutually assured destruction (a.k.a. MAD); or the hope, which underlies every act of prevention, that our knowledge of the future is accurate enough to be the basis of an intervention into the course of events.

Unlike other forms of relating to the future—such as promises, plans, utopias, or hopes—future catastrophes are seen primarily in the light of their obviation or prevention. This is why every depiction of impending catastrophe claims to reveal something that *already exists in the present*. With the disaster, something that we previously just feared, suspected, imagined, or possibly even misunderstood will become an event and take on a tangible—horrific—form. Catastrophes are emergencies that suddenly claim to unveil the "true face" of everything that had *already* been looming as a danger. In predicting or imagining a catastrophe, what had existed only in hypotheses, statistical probabilities, or prognoses all of a sudden appears with a clear and palpable shape.

The epistemic effect of catastrophe scenarios lies in the promise of revelation. In this sense, they are always *apocalyptic*—that is, revelatory: They expose a hidden "truth" about humanity, both about the inner essence of individuals and about the bonds that constitute the texture of society. Disasters thus illuminate society under stress and reveal the collective or individual reactions to this stress, from self-sacrifice and solidarity to the reckless fight for survival. Catastrophes test human beings, their strength and resilience, the sustainability of their bonds, and the ability of their social institutions to withstand a crisis. They show what people are made of beyond the cocoon of intact civilization. Imagined catastrophes thus produce a specific form of anthropology by creating exceptional situations for decision making, both individual and collective. They thereby reveal which values and possessions really count, which communities are sustainable, and which are fragile. The basic idea is that, when push comes to shove, the true essence of our existence will come to light.

ABOUT THIS BOOK

This book is neither a psychological study nor a cultural history of catastrophic visions of the future. It is rather a historical analysis of how imaginative depictions of future catastrophes have structured collective realities. Such realities are contingent and subject to historical change. The catastrophic imaginary traced in this book emerges in Romanticism with the figure of the Last Man, shapes the fantasies of the end of humankind in the Cold War, and still haunts current disaster fiction. The historical span this book is concerned with—from 1800 to the present—is best framed by two literary texts that, though written nearly two hundred years apart, depict almost identical catastrophic scenarios: Byron's poem "Darkness" (1816) and Cormac McCarthy's novel *The Road* (2006). They mark the beginning and provisional end point of a specifically modern notion of catastrophe. In their radical view of humanity and of nature after our demise, both texts combine a sharp contemporary awareness of crisis with an insight into the ethical dimensions of catastrophes. They show how a disaster might affect not only our environment but also the essence of humanity.

Tellingly, both McCarthy's and Byron's texts revolve around a collapse of the climate. They portray a world gone dark and cold, a world after the end. In the chill of a final winter, all of life has come to a halt except for a few last survivors, who struggle in despair to postpone their death. The point of both works is that the end of nature is also an end to that which makes human beings what they are. The catastrophe exposes the inherent fragility of the world and humankind: "The frailty of everything revealed at last," as McCarthy's novel puts it.[27] Byron, too, develops an anthropology of catastrophe that denudes man of all his better and humane features but in an almost more radical way. Faced with disaster, Byron's last men evince no rationality, solidarity, or sympathy but rather prove to be wretched, selfish, and cruel: "All hearts / Were chill'd into a selfish prayer for light," and "no love was left."[28] What this vision of destruction demonstrates is the existential dependency of human beings on the fragile world they inhabit, exploit, and pretend to control. Both texts encapsulate their devastating anthropological diagnosis in an image of the ultimate taboo: cannibalism. Yet the image of cannibalism is perhaps not merely the epitome of human depravation in a moment of crisis. It is also an allegory for a human relationship to the world that consists primarily of consumption and waste. When the earth is no longer there to nourish it, humanity will turn on itself as the last resource to be exploited.

I will begin by offering a brief summary of the history of the catastrophic imagination. Based as it is on fictional disaster scenarios, this book is an attempt to provide, as it were, a *historical* diagnosis of our *present* relation to the future. This also means, however, that historical fissures need to be taken into account. Without understanding how the classical notion of the apocalypse, derived from the Book of Revelation, had come to an end around 1800, one might be tempted to ascribe the continuing presence of apocalyptic motifs and symbols to a continuity of an eschatological idea of history. Chapter 1 will give a brief history of the end of eschatological thought and the rise of a purely secular notion of catastrophe. Without an understanding of the specific attitude toward catastrophe and security that was developed in the nuclear age, it would be impossible to grasp the bewildering novelty of our current idea of the future as a "catastrophe without event." As Walter Benjamin remarked, history can serve to illuminate the present. The historical examples of the catastrophic imaginary serve as "constellations" in which "what has been comes together in a flash with the now."²⁹ The interpretations presented in this book are meant to reveal precisely such flashpoints, where historically contextualized texts come together with our present concerns, fears, and epistemic, moral, and political dilemmas.

The following chapters begin with two historical scenes: Romanticism and the Cold War. Whereas Romanticism dismissed the traditional theological understanding of catastrophe and thereby laid the foundation for a genuinely modern and secular conception of the future, the atomic age took into account the consequences of mankind's active and conscious self-annihilation (chapter 1). From that point on, the future as catastrophe suddenly seemed like an imminent possibility with which human beings had to contend. If the second half of the twentieth century lived under the spell of nuclear war as a politically viable disaster, today this scenario has given way to a type of catastrophe far less tangible: the looming catastrophe without event, whose most poignant—yet still uncannily opaque—image is that of climate change. My historical overview thus arrives in the present with a discussion of past and current models of the climate catastrophe (chapter 2). Climate change represents a catastrophe of an entirely new kind, one that has replaced the great historical caesura of a nuclear strike. The uncanny and hypercomplex transformation of our life-worlds that climate change brings forth has become the image of an unpredictable future composed of multiple complex and interrelated disasters.

At this point it is possible to outline three central areas of current catastrophic thinking that have arisen from the genealogy of the modern catastrophic imagination. The first raises the question of survival, more specifically, of the social, political, and individual dilemmas posed by situations of survival (chapter 3). Here I will analyze present-day survivalist movements and recent popular catastrophe films as fantasies of society in a state of emergency. Both are concerned with the biopolitics of survival, that is, with the question of who should be allowed to survive and who can, under extreme circumstances, be left to die. Second, imagined catastrophes engender regimes of safety and prevention. My final two chapters are devoted to the prevention of future catastrophes: to the matter of technical safety, on the one hand (chapter 4), and, on the other, to the paradoxes of foreknowledge, prevention, and preemption (chapter 5). In both cases, my aim is to uncover the narrative structures that underlie the models of safety and security and that inform the politics of prevention. While technical safety is nothing but the anticipation of a future accident whose "prehistory" has to be reconstructed, prevention of social disasters has to take a standpoint in a fictitious future in order to look back at the present. Yet the narratives that are at the basis of any kind of foreknowledge and prevention also give accounts of their own tragic failures. All knowledge of the future contains a degree of *nonknowledge*, a constitutive misconception inherent to any effort to shape and prevent future events. If the future can be grasped only in the form of narratives, these narratives reveal the limits of our relationship to the future.

Fictions of the future are thus models in which the inextricable link between knowledge and nonknowledge is spun out into a potential world—a world imbued with what is *not yet known.* In a present characterized by a catastrophe without event, fictions are a way of giving tangible shape to the intangible. They create something that can be narrated, represented, and experienced—a concrete and model situation in which the future can be grasped and thus emotionally processed. Narratives can turn the threatening future into the object of subjective consciousness and individual affect. Through fiction, we may not be able to master the uncanniness of looming catastrophe, but at least we are able to keep it in sight.

The material examined in this book is not restricted to conventional forms of fiction such as novels, images, or films. In a broader sense, fictions are also the figures of thought and speech used by philosophers or sociologists, figures such as "the bomb" (which haunted the Cold War), "Lifeboat Earth" (thought to be always "too full"), or the "Anthropocene" (which implies humanity's retrospective examination of its own effects on the planet). Not least, fictions are also scientific extrapolations, hypotheses, scenarios, and simulations, including, for example, Malthus's sinister calculation of a future subsistence crisis, the expectation of global cooling that haunted the nineteenth century, the Cold War doctrine of mutually assured destruction, the reports issued by the Club of Rome, the so-called nuclear winter modeled by the TTAPS team in the 1980s, and today's climate simulations of global warming. The convergence of aesthetic and scientific depictions of the future demonstrates how literature and science, fiction and politics mutually inform and comment on one another. They are forms of experimenting with and exploring a space that is inaccessible to knowledge based on experience or observation. To juxtapose literature, images, or films alongside scientific scenarios and political metaphors is also to gain a clearer view of the nature of these experiments and thus a better understanding of the collective imaginary. Unlike scientific scenarios, which are created within specialized academic disciplines, aesthetic fictions are not limited to a particular object or epistemological method. Rather, they are interested in multiple perspectives and forms of knowledge—and in the aporias and contradictions that thereby emerge. While science may give us the brute facts on such things as climate change, mutation rates after a nuclear strike, the etiology of large-scale accidents, resource shortages, or the destruction of ecological systems, novels and films can produce a "thick description" of their consequences both for the individual and for humanity at large.[30] They can provide internal *and* external perspectives—a dual viewpoint of both the observer and the victim of a catastrophe.

This dual perspective of involvement and reflection—of subjection and distance—is most clearly embodied in the image of the Last Man, a figure from Romanticism that persisted throughout the Cold War and into the present. This literary figure is the expression of an aesthetic representation that always and simultaneously demonstrates the conditions of visibility and effability. Literary disasters do not present "facts" about catastrophes but rather make transparent the schematics through which we *perceive* disasters or in which potential disasters can be *imagined*. To borrow a term from Richard Grusin, they are "premediations" of disasters that are only accessible to us in the specific forms of their conveyance.[31] It is in the *form* of fictions that the underlying ratio of blindness and insight can be elucidated, a ratio inherent in all forms of foreknowledge. Fictions illuminate not only what we know about the future but also the *conditions* of such knowledge and the misconceptions that necessarily accompany it. Fictions thus design narratives that explore the relationship between knowledge and nonknowledge, certainty and uncertainty, plannability and loss of control. In doing so, they translate the abstractness of these epistemic aporia into concrete narratives, perceptions, and affects. It is only on the basis of fictions that we are able to access the difficulties of our relation to the future as individuals, discuss them collectively, and deal with them politically.

ANALYZING SCENARIOS

One concept that has proven to be especially useful in my analysis is the *scenario*, which despite its origins in screenwriting has not been a common term in literary and film criticism. A scenario is an instrument for exploring possible futures. The technique of scenario analysis was developed by the strategist Herman Kahn during the Cold War in order to simulate the options and potential developments of a nuclear war, a type of conflict entirely novel at the time and that did not allow for any experimentation. Even if scenarios are invented worlds, they are conceived as *possible* processes with a given starting point in known reality; as potential courses of events, they are meant to clarify which factors might play important roles in deciding on the situation's outcome. Kahn defines scenarios as follows:

> A scenario results from an attempt to describe in more or less detail some hypothetical sequence of events. Scenarios can emphasize different aspects of future history.... The scenario is particularly suited to dealing with several aspects of a problem more or less simultaneously. By the use of a relatively extensive scenario, the analyst may be able to get a feel for events and the branching points dependent upon critical choices. These branches can then be explored more or less systematically. The scenario is an *aid to the imagination*.[32]

Clearly, scenarios, which became one of the most important tools of futurology, are neither prognoses nor visions of the future; rather, they are analytic explorations of *possibilities*. If a situation *x* should arise, what would be the best course of action in response (*a*, *b*, or *c*)? What might the possible consequences of these responses be? Which factors will determine how this situation might unfold? What difficulties might emerge? How large would their role be in relation to other factors? At what points will decisions have to be made, and what consequences will they have? The scenario technique is an experimental form of storytelling that allows possible courses of action to be "tested." Consequently, there is not one "scenario" in the singular but only "scenarios"—multiple divergent processes or "alternative futures." They ask: *What would happen if . . . ?* and answer with a set of narratives that are both accurately fact based and, at the same time, have to be necessarily hypothetical and highly creative. Their epistemological advantage over abstract models of the future lies in their ability to go into detail, offering a thick description of the future that is meant to analyze and understand the complexity of its often simultaneous and interrelated aspects. Moreover, they highlight the branching points created by critical choices. By enabling decision makers to understand these crucial branching points and their diverging outcomes, scenarios have been important tools in anticipating, planning, and shaping the future ever since the Cold War.

In situations where experimentation is impossible (for which the nuclear war was a paradigmatic example), scenarios open up a different, *third* realm of knowledge, a realm in which experiments and experiences can be worked through without causing harrowing repercussions in reality. They thus serve as a paradigmatic case of the way in which our relation to the future depends on narrative structures, be it in the form of foreknowledge, planning, precaution, or safety measures. Narratives do this not only in literature but also in scientific or technical analyses of the future—basically in any kind of hypothetical narrative that serves to explore potential sequences of events. As media of time-axis manipulation, narratives can unfurl a sequence of events retrospectively, from a future perspective that represents the branching points where decisions are made in favor of one future over another. Unlike prophecies or visions, which always predict a single outcome, hypothetical narratives underscore the contingency of future knowledge by calling attention to the critical decision points or "bifurcations" (as Jorge Luis Borges called them) that will determine which sort of future might actually occur.

In terms of methodology, this entails a slight but decisive shift in my treatment of fictions. The following chapters are *not* primarily concerned with plots and narrative structures, metaphors and motifs, characterizations, stylistics, or the many language games literature plays, from rhetorical figures to style. My focus will rather lie on the *margins* and *backgrounds* of the fictional worlds presented. I read these worlds as *scenarios*. This means concentrating more intently on the backgrounds than on the foregrounds of the texts I read: not so much on the plot but on the world in which it is set, not so much on the characters but on the implicit conditions that make them act as they do. In the field of narratology, this world of action is called "diegesis" and is treated as something distinct from the story. According to Étienne Souriau, it is a "totality of beings, things, facts, events, phenomena, and contents within a spatio-temporal framework,"[33] or, in Gérard Genette's words, it is "a universe rather than a train of events (a story)."[34] What interests me are the parameters of these fictive universes. How did they come about? Such questions require an investigative approach and an eye for details—small clues in the background of the actual plot (such as weather conditions), the material objects that are being used, references to historical technologies, fragments of backstories, minor characters, and so on. In the case of scenarios, storyline is less important than the *conditions of possibility* that allow things to take place as they do. This will be the focus of my readings.

To analyze scenarios is thus to observe the preconditions that enable the world of action. It demands that we treat the imagined universe of a literary text, image, or film *as though it materially existed* and that we approach it not only with historical and cultural knowledge but also with practical knowledge of the world. This is not a matter of plumbing the elements of this world for their symbolic or metaphorical meaning but rather of accepting them as diegetic realities—only in order to marvel at them all the more. To "enter" a diegesis, a fictional universe, is to tap into its context, just as we explore unfamiliar worlds in our everyday lives—not, that is, to understand them as signs or symbols that in turn refer to something outside of this world (in the abstract realms of literary history, philosophy, theology, and so on). To comprehend the scenario of a potential world is not merely to illuminate it with historical knowledge but *also* to do so with a sort of heuristic naivety that is oriented toward descriptions, literal meanings, and "basic" understandings.

This may even mean applying personal experiences and practical knowledge to a world that, having never existed, can never really be known. It is an alien world that alters and shifts our view of the world in which we actually live. Only in such a way can we understand the strange universes of fiction as *possibilities* for our real environment. Just such a possibility is the world presented in McCarthy's *The Road*. The uncanny and horrifying scenario the novel depicts eventually closes with a puzzling image: that of a trout with labyrinthine patterns on its back, a fish that smells like moss in one's hand, a fish that no longer exists. It stands for a world that, as expressed in the last lines of the novel, "could not be put back. Not be made right again."[35] Surely this passage would not have made such an impression on me had I never held a live trout—slimy, cold, and strange, yet with incredibly sensitive, shimmering marbleized skin. Reading McCarthy's book, I was reminded of feeling the cold, twitching fish in my hand, and today I think of it as a token of the world's strangeness and familiarity—and of its fragility. My aim in this book is to retrace the intricate contours of this fragility.

1

LAST MEN

THE END OF THE WORLD, OLD AND NEW

The end of the world is one of mankind's most ancient fantasies. It marks a moment of ultimate futurity, an end of history and of human existence, and it is often depicted in lurid, highly symbolic imagery. For the Christian version of this end, biblical prophecies, most notably the Revelation of St. John, have provided what one could call the classic model of occidental apocalypse. The Revelation casts the end of the world in a sequence of steps that can be summed up, very briefly, as the destruction of the earth, a violent struggle between the forces of good and evil, followed by a universal judgment of the living and the dead and, ultimately, the establishment of a new eternal order, the New Jerusalem. This classic model is marked by a concept of futurity best expressed in the Latin word *adventus*: "that which comes toward us," "that which arrives." In this eschatological understanding of history, the future is part of God's plan for human history, and thus it already exists and "comes toward the present." The future is thus what is revealed in the Revelation, a future of destruction and divine reckoning but also an end of times that will bring forth a new, eternal world. The prophecies paint the process of destruction in the form of enigmatic figures, lurid imagery, and allegories in need of interpretation in order to apply them to explain present events. However, the truth thus revealed lies not so much in St. John's visions and their symbolism but in the destruction meticulously depicted in them. The catastrophe itself has revelatory power, as indicated in the Greek word ἀποκάλυψις (*apocalypsis*, "uncovering, lifting the veil, revealing"). What is revealed by the apocalypse is the true value and the true power of everything and everyone. The end of the world is the *unmasking of all things*, the manifestation of their true essence. The political value of the biblical prophecies therefore lay directly in the images of the downfall of empires, the shattering of the emblems of earthly power, and the punishment of the mighty. This destruction is a promise that mundane power will end, that the current world will be subject to a final reckoning, and that those who, at present, are powerless and virtuous will eventually be rewarded. The end of the world, no matter how dire it will be, thus implies a promise for the future: the advent of supreme justice, where evil will be punished and virtue rewarded. This is why destruction, within the model of classic apocalypse, always contains a perspective of hope. Within the catastrophe, a final truth will emerge, and the value of every being and every thing will eventually be revealed.

The presence of the apocalyptic imagery in the modern age and even in the present, as documented by, for example, Eugen Weber, should not create the illusion of a simple continuity of apocalyptic thought and its concept of a future as *adventus*.[1] The modern age keeps taking recourse to apocalyptic rhetoric and comparisons, but modernity, as many historians have argued, has left behind the idea of an eschatological model of history planned by divine providence and of a future as fixed within this plan.[2] The idea of a history that can inform the present based on a fundamental continuity of experience and expectation, as in Cicero's formula of *historia magistra vitae* (history as the instructor of life), has been dismissed in the modern age.[3] Since the Enlightenment, human history is open to change and progress toward radical new forms of existence and knowledge. The course of the future is subject to human decision and intervention but also to chance. Time is, as a story by Jorge Luis Borges aptly put it, "a garden of forking paths."[4] The future therefore can—and must—be planned and shaped by human decisions or prevented by human foresight. As the future in the modern age is a product of human decisions but also of chance, it has become obscure and unpredictable. No prophet, no seer, and no god can reliably see into the course of time.

Humans can only attempt to perceive trends and develop hypotheses or assumptions about the future. As modernity starts developing a whole range of foresight techniques, from the philosophy of history to statistics and eventually computer simulations, from utopias to science fiction, these visions of futurity can only conceive of *possible* futures, of potential outcomes that have no certainty. In the modern age, the future is never anything but a possibility, yet it is a possibility that charges human beings with the endless task of foreseeing, planning, and providing for the futures to come.

The future's openness and its obscurity call for imagination, extrapolation, experimentation, and projection as to what the world and humankind could and will be. As human actors cease to conceive of themselves as the passive recipients of events coming toward them and begin to see themselves as the *authors* of their own future, a contingent future opens before them, a future both of hope and anxiety. The future is not just the space for utopian promises and humanity's progress; it also opens up a catastrophic imaginary—the expectation of an abrupt change, a sudden disruption of all existing things. The long tradition of seeing futurity as a space for human progress, a space of hope and improvement, has, throughout modernity, been counterbalanced and undermined by a line of thought that sees a catastrophe looming. This pessimistic basso continuo underlies modernity's well-established and highly effective optimism, its faith in progress, growth, and the human ability to shape its own fate. Darkly woven into the dreams and wishes for the times to come is a discourse of doom, a discourse calling for vigilance and the prevention of future dangers but also conjuring wild nightmares of disaster and end times.

Within this modern catastrophic imaginary, the idea of apocalypse—of the end of the world—changes profoundly. It ceases to be imagined as an ultimate judgment and a new beginning; rather, as the German philosopher Günther Anders and others have pointed out, it turns into a "naked" or "truncated" apocalypse, an end without any hope for a new beginning.[5] There is, however, one element that the modern catastrophic imaginary has in common with the classical model of apocalypse: its *revelatory* nature. Modern catastrophes are seen as situations that cast a light on the present and bring forth a specific kind of knowledge. While limited disasters may put communities to the test of their resilience and social coherence, the end of the world produces an ultimate anthropological knowledge about humans as a species and as historical beings, an anthropology of disaster. This knowledge is based on the specific temporal form of *futurum perfectum*, the accomplished future, a gaze backward to understand an ultimate truth that can only be revealed in hindsight, at the very end of days. The anthropology of disaster can only appear from the vantage point of an (anticipated) end, the moment when humankind *will have been*. As we look "backward" from a future finitude onto everything existing in the present, the essence of things is uncovered. The end of the world as a narrative thought experiment casts a cold and revealing light on all things human, a light that brings out not only the quality and worth of individuals but also the stability of political institutions and social bonds and even the usefulness or uselessness of objects and things.

The protagonist of this genuinely modern narrative is the "Last Man." The last human survivor of an end of humanity, like Dr. Neville in *I Am Legend*, is the figure of an ultimate truth about humankind, which is only revealed to this very last specimen. The Last Man is in the paradoxical situation of being both the victim of the ultimate catastrophe and its last surviving witness and spectator. He is thus in a position both to live through *and* reflect upon the ultimate truth that only disaster brings to light. This position of "lastness" is the specific epistemological perspective adapted to a modern understanding of an open future. Only at the end will a final truth about humanity be revealed. The Last Man will be the only one to see what is left of humankind when it is stripped of the bonds and protections of civilization, when communities are put to an ultimate stress test, when social bonds are strained under the horrors of a fight for survival, or when the regimes designed to secure a human future become the instruments of its own demise. The Last Man may—in his numerous fictional and visual versions—evoke motifs of the classical apocalypse, and he might resemble the visionary in the Revelation, but, in fact, he is a genuinely modern invention. As we will see, he is the protagonist of an apocalypse without God, without the idea of ultimate judgment, and without the hope for a new world after the end of the world. Unlike the visionary, he is deeply involved in the ultimate disaster: he is not just a spectator but the last victim of extinction. He is a "naked man" deprived of the protections of civilization, of social bonds, and of resources for survival. He is subject to a disaster that is no longer part of an eschatological course of history. Melancholic or anxious, he wanders through the ruins of civilization and human culture and looks at what remains after the end of the word.

Yet he is also a figure of recognition and understanding regarding what brought about the end. The position of "lastness" reveals not only the essence of what it means to be human, as we will see in literary figures from Byron to Beckett to McCarthy. The gaze of "lastness" casts a light on a form of society and its culture and technology that have made the end of the world a highly effective form of political and military leverage. "Lastness" is the (fictional) position—at once inside and out—from which to analyze a cultural and political setting. It can therefore reveal the internal logic but also the blind spots, the taboos, and obscene desires that govern or are latent in the present order of things. The Last Man is a figure of melancholy but also of precaution. He is an allegory of the paradoxes of hindsight: an understanding of the present from a fictional viewpoint, which will eventually reveal that this future was not fate. He is the one to understand that this future—which amounts to the very destruction of future—might have been prevented had humankind known what he, the Last Man, has come to know. So even at the end, the Last Man personifies the contingency of this end, the lack of any divine providence or eschatological scheme.

This chapter will look at two epochs that are, in an exemplary way, involved with this idea of "lastness" as an epistemological perspective. First, Romanticism dreams up the Last Man as an emblematic figure of a new, secular understanding of catastrophe and of an equally secular and disillusioned gaze upon human history. Second, the Cold War is an epoch that conceives of the present as an end time, given the technical possibility of a global nuclear apocalypse. Although they are profoundly different in their understanding of the technicalities of the world's end, both epochs are steeped in a deep pessimism about the future. Both epochs envision a future as catastrophe. In so doing, they develop essential modes of thinking about the unthinkable, of analyzing disastrous trends, and of developing narratives of "lastness" that are essentially meant to stave off the end of days.

ROMANTIC DARKNESS

The figure of the Last Man emerges in Romanticism, both in literature and in painting. European Romanticism from France to Germany and England abounds with apocalyptic imagery and Last Men, from the French author François Xavier Cousin de Grainville's *Le dernier homme* (1805), Byron's poem "Darkness" (1816), Thomas Campbell's poem "The Last Man" (1823), and their many imitators, to Mary Shelley's roman à clef *The Last Man* (1826) and John Martin's paintings of lonely men contemplating the destruction of cities and palaces and looking upon a depopulated earth.[6] The Romantic apocalyptic imagination can be seen as both grappling with and ultimately dismissing the classical apocalyptic model. It is a form of "working through" the classical apocalypse. For unlike the narrator of St. John's visions, who only envisions the apocalyptic disaster without being directly involved, the Romantic Last Man is both witness to and victim of the catastrophe. While the Book of Revelation does not mention a single individual victim, the Romantic Last Man is an individual both subject to the catastrophic events and in a position to reflect on them. Hence his central role for a modern catastrophic imaginary that originates in the Romantic engagement with both the Christian eschatological tradition and Enlightenment philosophy and anthropology. It is not by chance that the Last Man has a history that reaches far beyond the Romantic period. Born around 1800 but with a career throughout the nineteenth century,[7] the figure still keeps haunting twentieth- and twenty-first-century postapocalyptic fiction and film, including George Stewart's *Earth Abides* (1949), about the few survivors of a global pandemic; Richard Matheson's *I Am Legend* (1954) and its many movie adaptations;[8] and Arno Schmidt's *Schwarze Spiegel* (1951), where a lonely yet well-read misanthrope roams the deserted landscape of the Lüneburger Heide in Germany after a global nuclear war. Recently, the Last Man has been revived in Cormac McCarthy's Pulitzer Prize–winning novel *The Road* (2006).

The Last Man is the emblematic incarnation of a modern form of subjectivity facing disaster. If the end of the world is no longer a demonstration of God's might, the Last Man represents the human not as a creature of God but as a natural living being. In the figure of the Last Man, two positions are inextricably intertwined: subjection and contemplation.

What starts here is the genuinely modern tradition of thinking of the end of the world as a radically secular event, an event in which we are involved yet that we try to contemplate, imagine, represent, and, if possible, prevent. In the ultimate disaster, the human being is cast as a living body that both suffers and beholds its own extinction.

One of the earliest and most radical examples of the Romantic confrontation with the classical model of apocalypse is a short text by the German author Jean Paul, "Speech of the Dead Christ down from the Universe That There Is No God" ("Rede des toten Christus vom Weltgebäude herab, daß kein Gott sei," 1796). The text, a parenthesis inserted in his novel *Siebenkäs*, quickly became popular throughout Europe via a French translation by Madame de Staël. The text presents itself as an experimental glance into the mind of an atheist. Imagining a world without God, the narrator dreams of waking up in a churchyard at the very moment of the Last Judgment. The sun has disappeared, the graves have opened, and the dead have risen to await their judgment. Yet nothing happens. Jesus Christ appears and reveals to the crowd awaiting its judgment that God does not exist:

> I traversed the worlds, I ascended into the suns, and soared with the Milky Ways through the wastes of heaven; but there is no God. I descended to the last reaches of the shadows of Being, and I looked into the chasm and cried: "Father, where art thou?" But I heard only the eternal storm ruled by none, and the shimmering rainbow of all living beings stood without sun to create it, trickling above the abyss.[9]

At the moment that is supposed to reveal God's power, Jean Paul converts apocalypse into the revelation of his absence. For the first time in the history of an occidental imagination of the world's end, this end is definite, an end with no judgment, no salvation, no New Jerusalem. Man is abandoned by God, an "orphan."[10]

Man's metaphysical and eschatological abandonment—his "godforsakenness"—not only cancels out the possibility of salvation but also calls into question human nature. Humans are no longer children of God but only natural living beings subject to nothing but the laws of nature. Jean Paul's Christ decries the void, the "cold nothingness."[11] Anticipating Nietzsche by almost a hundred years, this literary thought experiment already draws the consequence of the death of God. The universe is no longer ruled by divine providence but by the blind power of natural forces, including mere chance: "Mute inanimate Nothing! Chill eternal Necessity! Insane Chance! Know ye that which lieth beneath ye? . . . Is that beside me a human being still? Thou poor man! Thy little life is Nature's sigh, or but its echo."[12] From this secular perspective (deplored by Jean Paul as the desperate worldview of an atheist), humans are reduced to nothing more than a thing of nature. Jean Paul's idea of a secular end of the world thus is not just theological; it also has profound anthropological consequences. The merely "natural" definition of man ("Nature's sigh") calls into question a traditional understanding of humanity as a creature of God: "Is that beside me a human being still?" Each human is now subject to "chill eternal necessity" and "insane chance." Jean Paul's disconcerting version of an apocalypse without God shows the Last Man as a figure of radical abandonment. But it is exactly in this abandonment that humanity's nature is redefined. What is revealed at the end of times is a view of the human race as part of nature. Mankind has no metaphysical dimension but is just "bare" material life, a living body, and a soul bereft of a divine Father.

While deconstructing the classical model's core elements of apocalypse, Jean Paul's text nevertheless echoes the intense visual qualities of the Book of Revelation. His dream is full of symbols: somber depictions of the sinking sun, a fingerless clock, the dead rising from their graves, black midnight. The strongest visual element in the text is *darkness*—the eclipse of the sun, seemingly echoing Revelation 16:10: "And the fifth angel poured out his vial upon the seat of the beast; and his kingdom was full of darkness; and they gnawed their tongues for pain." But Jean Paul's darkness is not an angel's work. The sun symbolizes God, and his absence not only stops time—hence the fingerless clocks—but plunges the world into a darkness both physical and metaphysical.

Darkness is thus the visual scenery that surrounds the Last Man in the Romantic imagination. This apocalyptic blackout tinges Romantic poetry of the end of the world and marks Romantic paintings of that subject. While Caspar David Friedrich's famous painting *Monk by the Sea* (1808 or 1810) might be the most famous visual expression of man's metaphysical abandonment, it does not explicitly deal with the end of the world as such. While vaguely alluding to Friedrich's famous staging of a lonely

FIGURE 1.1 John Martin, *The Last Man* (1849), oil on canvas, 214 × 138 cm.

Source: Walker Art Gallery, Liverpool (Board of Trustees of the National Museums and Galleries on Merseyside).

beholder within a wide dark space, the image that most explicitly tries to represent Romantic darkness is John Martin's painting *The Last Man* (1849). The British painter's work was obsessed with scenes of apocalyptic destruction and the end of the world. Famous for his so-called blockbuster paintings in huge formats, with spectacular subjects and stark chiaroscuro effects, Martin focused much of his work on biblical disasters such as the Flood, the destruction of Sodom and Gomorrah, and the Last Judgment (fig. 1.1).[13]

Martin's painting shows a figure in biblical garments, lost in a vast, desolate landscape, gazing from a ledge in the foreground onto a scene of destruction beneath him. His loneliness is emphasized by the emptiness of the landscape, covered with rocks, ruins, and, on closer scrutiny, the corpses of humans and animals. The scenery brings together the topics invoked in a modern aesthetics of the sublime: an immense vastness that seems to exceed the grasp of the human mind and a horror that goes beyond human comprehension. The spectator, however, seems to be watching all this from a safe distance. Martin obviously, as in many of his other paintings, tries to combine a modern aesthetics of the sublime with motifs from the classical apocalypse. Next to the man lie the lifeless bodies of a woman and a small child. His family has already succumbed to whatever disaster has brought forth the end of all living beings. He raises his hands toward the sky, in a futile gesture of entreaty or rage directed toward (an invisible, absent) God.

What is most striking about Martin's painting, however, is the darkness that overshadows the entire scene. The sun is sinking spectacularly in crimson red, but it seems to shed not light but darkness, scarcely illuminating the ruins and the female corpse lying beside the Last Man. Martin aims at a visual paradox: he paints darkness using color and light, as if darkness, just like light, were an active force. Instead of light, darkness seems to "shine" on the scene in which the Last Man is set. He stands under the obscure sky of destruction, the ultimate beholder of mankind's final extinction. He is the incarnation of a human reflection on our own end as a species, the incarnation of a human victim and witness to the catastrophe. As such, I would like to suggest, he is also the figuration of the beholder's gaze on the painting—set into the painting. He sees what theoretically only the beholder (or God, who is strikingly absent) is able to see: the destruction of the very instance of observation. The picture thus shows an impossible, paradoxical viewpoint emblematic for the modern catastrophic imaginary: the gaze of a human being witnessing the extinction of humanity. In this paradox lies the marker of the picture's fictional character. Like Jean Paul's vision, which is framed as a thought experiment, Martin's pictorial vision can only be regarded as a hypothesis that displays its imaginary character.

When Martin painted his *Last Man* paintings in 1826 (now lost), 1833, and 1849, the topic was already fashionable in the extreme. "Last Man" poems and novels abounded. But what is at stake in this topic goes beyond the Romantic attempt both to revive and overcome the biblical model of apocalypse. As we saw in Jean Paul and John Martin, it offers a perspective on the future that is both involved in and distanced from the events about to happen. The Romantic Last Man is more than a reflection on the finitude of human existence. The Last Man is an anthropological test case: a subject in an intricate thought experiment on the nature and potential of humankind—of humans seen precisely as biological beings, the "bare life" already addressed by Jean Paul.

A poem by Lord Byron takes this a step further. Not surprisingly, the poem is titled "Darkness." Byron's poem envisions a particularly dramatic setting: the sun has died, and the world lies in coldness and gloom. Unlike Jean Paul, Byron's poem is almost entirely devoid of references to the biblical model, and, unlike Martin's paintings, it lacks an individual protagonist to suffer and witness the ultimate destruction. With an astute yet distanced tone, Byron depicts the different stages of despair and chaos:

> I had a dream, which was not all a dream.
> The bright sun was extinguish'd, and the stars
> Did wander darkling in the eternal space,
> Rayless, and pathless, and the icy earth
> Swung blind and blackening in the moonless air;
> Morn came and went—and came, and brought no day,
> And men forgot their passions in the dread
> Of this their desolation; and all hearts
> Were chill'd into a selfish prayer for light:
> And they did live by watchfires—and the thrones,
> The palaces of crowned kings—the huts,
> The habitations of all things which dwell,
> Were burnt for beacons; cities were consum'd,
> And men were gather'd round their blazing homes
> To look once more into each other's face;
> Happy were those who dwelt within the eye
> Of the volcanos, and their mountain-torch:
> A fearful hope was all the world contain'd;
> Forests were set on fire—but hour by hour
> They fell and faded—and the crackling trunks
> Extinguish'd with a crash—and all was black.
> The brows of men by the despairing light
> Wore an unearthly aspect, as by fits
> The flashes fell upon them; some lay down
> And hid their eyes and wept; and some did rest
> Their chins upon their clenched hands, and smil'd;
> And others hurried to and fro, and fed
> Their funeral piles with fuel, and look'd up
> With mad disquietude on the dull sky,

The pall of a past world; and then again
With curses cast them down upon the dust,
And gnash'd their teeth and howl'd: the wild birds shriek'd
And, terrified, did flutter on the ground,
And flap their useless wings; the wildest brutes
Came tame and tremulous; and vipers crawl'd
And twin'd themselves among the multitude,
Hissing, but stingless—they were slain for food.
And War, which for a moment was no more,
Did glut himself again: a meal was bought
With blood, and each sate sullenly apart
Gorging himself in gloom: no love was left;
All earth was but one thought—and that was death
Immediate and inglorious; and the pang
Of famine fed upon all entrails—men
Died, and their bones were tombless as their flesh;
The meagre by the meagre were devour'd,
Even dogs assail'd their masters, all save one,
And he was faithful to a corpse, and kept
The birds and beasts and famish'd men at bay,
Till hunger clung them, or the dropping dead
Lur'd their lank jaws; himself sought out no food,
But with a piteous and perpetual moan,
And a quick desolate cry, licking the hand
Which answer'd not with a caress—he died.
The crowd was famish'd by degrees; but two
Of an enormous city did survive,
And they were enemies: they met beside
The dying embers of an altar-place
Where had been heap'd a mass of holy things
For an unholy usage; they rak'd up,
And shivering scrap'd with their cold skeleton hands
The feeble ashes, and their feeble breath
Blew for a little life, and made a flame
Which was a mockery; then they lifted up
Their eyes as it grew lighter, and beheld
Each other's aspects—saw, and shriek'd, and died—

> Even of their mutual hideousness they died,
> Unknowing who he was upon whose brow
> Famine had written Fiend. The world was void,
> The populous and the powerful was a lump,
> Seasonless, herbless, treeless, manless, lifeless—
> A lump of death—a chaos of hard clay.
> The rivers, lakes and ocean all stood still,
> And nothing stirr'd within their silent depths;
> Ships sailorless lay rotting on the sea,
> And their masts fell down piecemeal: as they dropp'd
> They slept on the abyss without a surge—
> The waves were dead; the tides were in their grave,
> The moon, their mistress, had expir'd before;
> The winds were wither'd in the stagnant air,
> And the clouds perish'd; Darkness had no need
> Of aid from them—She was the Universe.

While declaring his vision "a dream," Byron is quick to point out that it was "not all a dream." His catastrophe is not just a pure act of invention but what one today would call a "worst-case scenario," a detailed depiction of a potential catastrophe of global scale. Byron sketches out all the potential consequences this event could entail. In this daydream (or daymare), humanity is placed in a disaster scenario as if it were an experimental setting, as R. J. Dingley has remarked: "At the very least mankind seems to be failing a kind of ultimate test."[14] "Darkness" is the poetic account of a hypothetical anthropological stress test.

The poem's scenario—the total and definitive extinguishing of the sun—is not new. As a possible cosmic event it had already been discussed in Fontenelle's *Entretiens sur la pluralité des mondes* (1686).[15] Yet Byron gives this scenario a totally different twist by turning the cosmic disaster into a social catastrophe. This catastrophe proceeds by stages, described by Byron in a plodding blank verse and enumerated in a monotonous, paratactic syntax: "and … and … and …"

First, people plunge into panic and selfishness. They burn everything that can give them light and heat—the forests, the "habitations of all things which dwell," destroying nature and culture alike. Next, the symbols of power and wealth, "palaces" and "thrones," are used as combustibles.

While the institutions of social order disappear, humans crumble under the stress of panic and despair. Some weep, some fall into a hysterical frenzy, some simply await their death in silence. What is strikingly absent from this drab scenario is any sign of rational thinking: there is no empathy, no solidarity, no mutual aid.

The poem mentions no single individual and their fate. Human beings are only addressed as an anonymous "they," a plural that erases any kind of individual perspective. Byron links the stages of disaster to one another, an endless litany of horrors. The text establishes a cold, distanced glance on the horrors it depicts, throwing a merciless light on the progress of human distress. To emphasize the desperate and clueless behavior of humans, Byron juxtaposes it to that of the animals, which simply stop being able to follow their "natural" behavior. The birds are unable to fly, the vipers unable to "sting," just as humans are unable to reason or to act. Once deprived of light and heat, man is simply one more living creature madly and recklessly trying to survive. While Jean Paul's godless apocalypse subjects everything to the ineluctable laws of nature, Byron even denatures nature. Both men and animals have lost what was attributed to them "by nature": instincts or, on the part of humans, reason. What is left of them are living bodies on the verge of extinction.

In the next step, humans revert to a Hobbesian state of nature, a war of all against all: "And War, which for a moment was no more, / Did glut himself again: a meal was bought / With blood, and each sate sullenly apart / Gorging himself in gloom: no love was left." No "love," that is, no solidarity, no cooperation, no empathy is left among the starving humans. Under the pressure of catastrophe, humans lose all humaneness. In one last step, man even violates the ultimate taboo and reverts to cannibalism. "The pang / Of famine fed upon all entrails—men / Died, and their bones were tombless as their flesh; / The meagre by the meagre were devour'd." It is obvious that Byron's imagery is not taken from the old apocalyptic symbols, which are surprisingly scarce in the poem.[16] The text displays no references to the eschatological model of world's end; it is interested solely in the catastrophe's social and moral consequences. This means looking at dying humankind as a purely secular, biological entity reduced to its bodily needs and overwhelming fears. What his imaginary stress test reveals is a human nature stripped of any impulse toward empathy, altruism, compassion, or solidarity. Under duress, human life is nothing but an existence ridden by selfishness, fear, and perverse brutality epitomized by cannibalism and the "hideousness" of the last two men.

Through this depiction of mankind in the catastrophe, "Darkness" mordantly does away with the image of humankind that Enlightenment anthropology had composed. Rousseau had declared "pity," that is, compassion, the chief human quality.[17] Other philosophers of the eighteenth century, such as Gotthold Ephraim Lessing, Johann Gottfried Herder, the Marquis de Condorcet, and the British philosopher of the Enlightenment William Godwin had outlined a history of humankind built on the idea of man's infinite potential for moral and intellectual perfection and progress.[18] While the Enlightenment had seen empathy, friendship, and rationality as the chief human virtues, in "Darkness" these virtues have disappeared without a trace. The poem targets this optimistic anthropology, revealing a different face of humanity under the terror of the ultimate end, one more brutal, egoistic, and ruthless than the beasts. Humans—not the animals—kill and devour one another to survive for a few more days in the darkness. Strikingly, the only "humane" figure in the poem (also the only individual "actor" addressed in the text) is a dog who faithfully guards his master's corpse until his own death. Nothing of the sort can be said of human beings.

THE FUTURE AS FAMINE: MALTHUS

In the face of the ultimate catastrophe, Byron clearly discards not only the Enlightenment's optimistic anthropology; he also does away with a model of history that projects moral and material progress into the future. In the bleak future he envisions for the end of times, humankind will fall back into a senseless, cruel, and selfish state. This anthropological and historical criticism of Enlightenment anthropology and philosophy of history seems to be taken from a contemporary of Byron who also started out as a vehement critic of Enlightenment optimism: Thomas Robert Malthus. With his disconsolate image of catastrophe, Byron seems to draw on Malthus's highly controversial yet immensely popular *Essay on the Principle of Population*. Its first edition was published in 1798 and was mainly a violent polemic against the historical optimism of Godwin and

Condorcet. Later, substantially revised versions of the *Essay* came out in 1803 (the second edition, which Malthus considered a totally new work), 1806, 1807, 1817, and 1826. Byron's poem, I suggest, is, especially with its cold survey of humanity as an anonymous population, profoundly marked by Malthus's economic perspective, though it never explicitly refers to its key words or its author. Like "Darkness," Malthus's essay portrayed an image of human futurity that was more than dire.

Aimed at disproving the idea of a morally, intellectually, and economically progressing humanity, Malthus's fundamental intellectual move lies in arguing that what is seen as "progress" is actually not a positive development but a path to doom. While for hundreds of years population growth had been seen as an indicator of a nation's wealth and well-being—and thus as an indicator of a brighter future—Malthus is one of the first thinkers to argue that this "progress" will eventually undermine its own basis and lead to catastrophe. His basic argument is well known: as the agricultural production of food can only progress in a linear fashion, it cannot keep pace with population growth, which proceeds in an exponential way. Mankind was thus, Malthus argued, headed toward a catastrophic subsistence crisis. As long as the reproduction rate of the European populations was exceeding the rate of increase in food production, sooner or later these populations would suffer more and more food shortages, soaring wheat prices, and consequently hunger, child mortality, and epidemics:

> Supposing the present population [of the entire globe] equal to a thousand millions, the human species would increase as the numbers 1, 2, 4, 8, 16, 32, 64, 128, 256, and subsistence as 1, 2, 3, 4, 5, 6, 7, 8, 9. In two centuries the population would be to the means of subsistence as 256 to 9; in three centuries as 4096 to 13; and in two thousand years the difference would be almost incalculable.[19]

Taking his point of departure not from a philosophical but from an economic analysis, Malthus essentially criticized the central tenets of Enlightenment anthropology, mainly the idea of the perfectibility of human society as laid out, for example, in Condorcet's *Sketch for a Historical Picture of the Progress of the Human Mind* (1794), which argued that humans have, in the past, progressed morally, culturally, and technologically and thus are more than likely to do so in the future. More than his projection, which was based on relatively crude statistics, Malthus's innovation and his influence on Byron lies in his shift of anthropological focus. Malthus's argument is based not on man's moral and intellectual capacities but on man *as a living being*, as a biological existence. This body has two conflicting qualities: on the one hand, it consumes certain resources (such as food, combustibles, habitations, space); on the other hand, it procreates and thereby multiplies the demand for these resources. The ratios of these two human needs, Malthus concluded, are in a dramatic disproportion that would eventually prove catastrophic.

Methodologically, Malthus came to this conclusion by an act of extrapolation: he took the British birth statistics of the last decades of the eighteenth century as his sample and extrapolated his findings to larger numbers and bigger time frames, that is, the globe and the future of humanity. This is exactly what makes Malthus a genuinely modern thinker. His view of humans as living entities, as bodies that consume and multiply, makes Malthus one of the godfathers of what Michel Foucault calls modern biopolitics. Biopolitics addresses the human not as the bearer of rights or of intellectual capacities but as a living being. Foucault put it this way: "For millennia, man remained what he was for Aristotle: a living animal with the additional capacity for a political existence; modern man is an animal whose politics places his existence as a living being in question."[20] Humans are bodies, but these bodies are *political bodies*, bodies subject to political interventions into their health, demographic structure, work productivity, reproduction rates, etc. Modern biopolitics makes humans' physical existence—fertility, consumption, ability to work, need for recreation, pathologies, and accidents—the object of political control and regulation. It also—and in this respect Malthus's economic approach is all the more exemplary—addresses humans not just as bodies (instead of "souls") but from the viewpoint of *large numbers*, that is, of statistics.[21]

The burgeoning discourse of modern economic thought addresses the human species as a collective singular, a statistical entity. This perspective will be essential for any kind of social or economic forecast in the modern age. It starts, in the middle of the eighteenth century, with the German economist and statistician Johann Peter Süssmilch. Süssmilch developed the first statistical laws that govern the rates of deaths and births and the consumption and production rates of certain goods.[22] What he discovered is the surprising *stability* in the statistics of such unsettling human events as birth and death; what Malthus discovers is the latent *instability* present in the statistical regularities, their potential drift toward catastrophe.

The controversy provoked by Malthus stems in part from the icy tone he uses in his—initially highly polemical—essay. Malthus simply accepts starvation as a law of nature: "It has appeared, that from the inevitable laws of our nature some human beings must suffer from want. These are the unhappy persons who, in the great lottery of life, have drawn a blank."[23] According to Malthus, life is a lottery of survival. His economic take on human life gives a specific meaning to what Jean Paul called "chill eternal necessity" and "insane chance." Human survival, human future and well-being, are subject to a statistical calculus, that is, "insane chance." This calculus also informs Malthus's dismal forecast of humanity's future:

> Famine seems to be the last, the most dreadful resource of nature. The power of population is so superior to the power in the earth to produce subsistence for man, that premature death must in some shape or other visit the human race. The vices of mankind are active and able ministers of depopulation. They are the precursors in the great army of destruction; and often finish the dreadful work themselves. But should they fail in this war of extermination, sickly seasons, epidemics, pestilence, and plague, advance in terrific array, and sweep off their thousands and ten thousands. Should success be still incomplete, gigantic inevitable famine stalks in the rear, and with one mighty blow levels the population with the food of the world.[24]

Following this logic for the future of the species, humanity is heading toward a crushing subsistence crisis unless its reproduction rate is—as Malthus proposes—"checked" by political intervention. He suggests laws that prescribe late marriage and premarital chastity, aided by—if need be—prostitution and abortion. Extrapolating from the birth rates of the past twenty years in relation to the food supply, his forecast is dire. If population is not regulated in relation to existing resources, he predicts, it will be diminished by nature's own form of population control: famine.

Global famine is the essence of Malthus's forecast for the future of humanity.

It now becomes clearer why Malthus might have been an important yet hidden reference for Byron's catastrophic imaginary. "Famine," Malthus's evil bottom line of human futurity, is also the bottom line of Byron's catastrophe. In its most sinister episode, "Darkness" depicts the encounter of the two Last Men as the confrontation of two hungry beasts in sheer terror of each other: "The crowd was famish'd by degrees; but two / Of an enormous city did survive, / . . . Their eyes as it grew lighter, and beheld / Each other's aspects—saw, and shriek'd, and died— / Even of their mutual hideousness they died, / Unknowing who he was upon whose brow / Famine had written Fiend. The world was void." Just as Malthus predicted, famine is the human condition of the future, the essence of the secular apocalypse that will await the Last Man. Byron's last survivors die out of fear of one another, terrorized by an enmity that is nothing but a brutal battle for resources. The end of humankind will be a hunger war that leads us to violate the greatest taboo of occidental culture.

What is striking in "Darkness," however, is not only this scathing diagnosis of man's anthropological essence; it is also the text's lack of empathy and its distanced perspective on the unfolding disaster. Through this distance, Byron casts exactly the same view on human beings as Malthus's statistical gaze. This is why the text only speaks about "men" or "they" as the abstract totality of the entire human population. The poem adopts this, as it were, statistical perspective on mankind as an anonymous collective. Byron shares Malthus's economic epistemology, fleshing it out in a lurid vision even more terrible than Malthus's famines. Like John Martin's dark sun, Byron's "Darkness" sheds a gloomy, excoriating light on human nature. On the somber test site of Romantic apocalypse, the Enlightenment's humanist optimism is discarded along with its idea of infinite progress toward a future ever brighter than the present. What is left is a much older conception of the human: *homo homini lupus*. Byron's Last Man is the wolf that devours his neighbor.

If this is a dream, it is not all a dream. Byron's scenario of a planet plunged in darkness can be traced to a specific historical event. The poem was written in July or August 1816 on the shores of Lac Léman, close to Geneva, Switzerland. Byron spent the summer with friends, among them Percy Shelley and Mary Godwin, soon to be Shelley's wife. The most famous product of this sojourn is Mary Shelley's *Frankenstein*. The group was confined inside because of the exceptionally bad weather in Switzerland, with constant rains and flooding around the lake, crop failures, and freezing temperatures even in July.[25] Byron later recalled that he wrote his poem "at Geneva, when there was a celebrated dark day, on which the fowls went to roost at noon, and the candles were lighted as at midnight."[26] The reason for this extreme weather was an incident of acute global climate disaster, arguably the biggest in recorded history. In April 1815, the volcano Tambora on the island of Sumbawa (Dutch East Indies, today Indonesia) had erupted, ejecting immense amounts of ash and sulfur into the upper atmosphere. The ash floated around the globe and filtered the sunlight for the next four years, causing intense climatic aberrations in the entire Northern Hemisphere, from China to Canada. The year 1816 became famous as the "Year Without a Summer" and as one of the great subsistence crises in the Western world and Asia.[27] The distress the eruption caused came at a particularly difficult historical moment in Europe. After more than twenty years of war in the wake of the French Revolution, the food crisis in Western Europe added to existing social and economic problems and triggered local poverty riots in England and Germany.

The poem bears witness to these events only in an indirect way.[28] Yet how it does so casts light on Byron's poetic technique. While talking about a future that could not be further away in time—the end of the world—Byron actually refers to the reality in which he is living. As Jonathan Bate observes, "the poem is as contemporary as it is apocalyptic."[29] Byron's poetic technique essentially consists in an imaginary extrapolation of a particular and local crisis into a maximal catastrophe scenario. While there was fog and unusually cool weather in Geneva, in the poem there is total darkness and freezing cold; while there are hunger riots in Europe, in the poem there is a gory war for food; and while there is a food shortage in Switzerland, in the poem global famine reigns. Byron's end of the world is an extrapolation in the mathematical sense. Byron blows the contemporary social and economic crisis up into a global apocalyptic scenario. Extrapolation means estimating an uncertain value based on a small known sample—just like Malthus's method of deducing global overpopulation and famine from the sample of late-eighteenth-century British demographic statistics.

Byron proceeds on an epistemological path that runs parallel to Malthus's statistical method. From a local and limited disaster of cool and gloomy weather, Byron envisions an apocalyptic scenario of a cold and dark end of the world. For both Byron and Malthus—albeit by totally different means of representation, poetry for one, statistics for the other—the catastrophic future is an extrapolation from what can already be observed in the present. This technique was to become one of the most important techniques of modern forecasting, based on large numbers and their statistics. The gaze on humanity according to the "law of large numbers" cancels out individual intentions, affects, or emotions. As such, it will also be one of the most important tools for the modern management of human future in the form of modern biopolitics (see chapter 4). In their violent dismissal of a humanist and progressive view of the future, that is, in the projection of a future as catastrophe, Malthus and Byron both offer a counterweight to modernity's insistence on a future that can and must be changed for the better by planning, forecasting, prevention, and precaution. Within progress, according to the Malthusian figure of thought, lies demise. Malthus introduces an inherent paradox within the idea of progress—the idea that what is taken as a sign of progress may actually be the harbinger of disaster. Ever since Romanticism, this darkness runs like a countercurrent against modernity's guiding idea of a future open to infinite improvement and hope.

Romantic darkness dismisses a model of eschatological history and of the end of the world as a moment of divine judgment. It casts catastrophe as a purely secular event. This entails the invention of an epistemic figure that is both a witness to and a figure of reflection upon the end, the Last Man. The Last Man is the personification of a modern relation to futurity, a catastrophic futurity that only becomes visible from an impossible yet heuristically highly productive perspective: the position of lastness. The Last Man looks back on what is left of humankind and its demise, grasping not only an anthropological truth but also understanding the mechanisms and human flaws that brought about this demise. The Last Man is a personification of the temporal structure attached to an understanding of the future in the modern age. As the future is seen as an open horizon of expectations, it can only be anticipated from the fictional position of a *future perfect*: "this is how things will have been," "this is how the world will have ended." This end is always a revelation: in what can be called an anthropology of catastrophe, it reveals an understanding of the human in the extremity of disaster. Human beings are no longer creatures subject to divine justice but to the blind chance of natural laws—the laws of subsistence.

While the nineteenth century would further develop fantasies of a secular end of the world, for instance, of a freezing-over of the planet along the lines of Romantic darkness, the twentieth century takes the idea of the future as catastrophe one step further by envisioning that humans will bring the end of the world upon themselves. At the beginning of the century, an idea starts to spread that will be materialized in the atomic bomb: the idea of a weapon so disastrous that it will forestall any future possibility of war, a "war to end all wars." The possibility of human self-annihilation is cast as a means to secure a human future. The end of the world of man's own making not only generates novel techniques for calculating conflict options but henceforth becomes epistemologically highly productive in forecasting and analyzing the future in general. It also generates a new catastrophic imaginary and a new kind of Last Man who aptly illustrates the blind spots of irrationality and madness in a doctrine that sees itself as the epitome of rationality and intelligibility. A remote offspring of the Romantic protagonist, the Cold War's Last Man personifies a newer version of the anthropology of catastrophe: a strange conjunction of hyper-rationality and the complete and utter failure of rational thinking.

NUCLEAR APOCALYPSE

The second half of the twentieth century was under the spell of an apocalyptic vision that was claimed to be both absolutely real and imminent. Like Romantic darkness, this vision found its expression in a sublime image of destruction, this time not darkness but light: a radiant flash, "brighter than a thousand suns," as Robert J. Oppenheimer put it. With the atomic bomb, of which Oppenheimer was one of the fathers, the destruction of life on earth had become a human option. In this sense, "the Bomb," as the massive arsenal of nuclear warheads was usually called, represented both an imminent future and the potential loss of all future.

In 1958, the German philosopher Karl Jaspers summarized this apocalyptic scenario as follows:

> Today, the atomic bomb is more threatening to the future of mankind than anything else. Up to this point, only imaginary conceptions of apocalypse existed.... Yet right now we are facing the real possibility of an end of the world. Not any longer a fictional apocalypse, actually not an apocalypse at all. It is the killing of all life on the whole surface of the earth that has become the possible reality with which we have to reckon from now on. And—given the increasing speed of all developments—we may have to face this already in the near future.[30]

To highlight the novelty and singularity of this danger, Jaspers draws a couple of distinctions: no longer a classical apocalypse but mere extermination (which is not so new, as we have seen); the idea of a distant end of times is replaced by an imminent threat, total nuclear annihilation. And the destruction of the world, according to Jaspers, is no longer a mere literary fiction but a "real possibility." Jaspers's formula is exemplary for the consciousness of the nuclear age, which saw itself as an epoch of lastness, a "last age."

Besides the sublime imagery of explosion, an image suggested by the physicist Edward Teller grasps the consciousness of the nuclear threat in a particularly apt way: the Doomsday Clock, which had been on the cover of the *Bulletin of the Atomic Scientists* since 1947 (fig. 1.2). The image of the clock face indicates not only the feeling of imminent threat but also the irreversible nature of the new military technology—as irreversible as the course of time. What has been invented, as Günther Anders put it, cannot be uninvented: "Our age is the Last Age. The possibility of our self-extinction cannot be taken back and cannot end—except by the end itself."[31] In the over seventy years since its inception, the clock's hands have oscillated between fifteen (1995) and two minutes to midnight (1953). The clock now not only indicates nuclear-threat levels but also reflects dangerous technologies, political events, and, since 2007, factors contributing to climate change. It indicates a feeling that has revived in the modern age: the feeling of living in the end times.

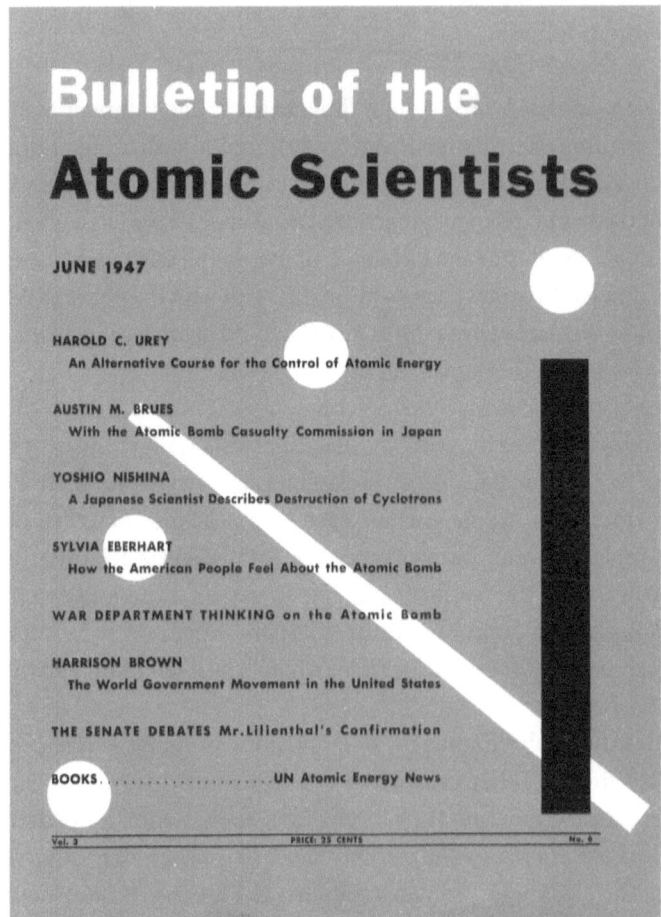

FIGURE 1.2 The Doomsday Clock, depicted for the first time on the cover of the *Bulletin of the Atomic Scientists*, June 1947. Design: Martyl Langsdorf.

Source: *Bulletin of the Atomic Scientists*.

In contrasting "*fictional* apocalypse" and "*the real* possibility of an end of the world," Jaspers, however, gets it slightly wrong. It would be more accurate to say that the Cold War was a reality superseding what previously was only a fiction. It was a conflict based on a fiction that became politically effective. The Bomb was not operative by being used but by its *potential use being imagined*, simulated, anticipated, and narrated. This is why not only the scenarios of nuclear strategy developed by think tanks and the military but also literature and film played crucial roles in thinking about the future during the Cold War.

In a certain way, even the emblematic weapon itself was a product of literature decades before it was ever built by engineers.[32] Already in 1914, just before the start of the First World War, H. G. Wells published a futuristic novel entitled *The World Set Free*. In this book, mankind makes nuclear fission accessible as an energy source, develops nuclear engines, and builds a bomb made from "Carolinum," a fictional version of plutonium. Characterized by continuous explosions, this bomb proves to be a weapon against which no defense is possible. In the course of a fictional world war during the 1950s, the weapon destroys major cities, and huge parts of Europe are reduced to rubble.

With this vision of a future weapons technology, Wells actually had his finger on the pulse of the contemporary research on radioactivity, boldly extrapolating its technological and military potential. He owed his knowledge about nuclear materials both as energy source and as possible weapon to the chemist Frederick Soddy, who in 1903 had published a popular scientific treatise on radium. In this early article, Soddy already pointed out the powerful and highly destructive potential of this new energy form. Soddy noted that the earth is "a storehouse stuffed with explosives, inconceivably more powerful than any we know of, and possibly only awaiting a suitable detonator to cause the earth to revert to chaos."[33] Accordingly, Wells's novel describes the uncontrollable power of destruction of the new weapon in graphic fashion:

> Once launched, the bomb was absolutely unapproachable and uncontrollable until its forces were nearly exhausted, and from the crater that burst open above it, puffs of heavy incandescent vapour and fragments of viciously punitive rock and mud, saturated with Carolinum, and each a centre of scorching and blistering energy, were flung high and far. Such was the crowning triumph of military science, the ultimate explosive that was to give the "decisive touch" to war.[34]

In Wells's novel, the bomb's disastrous power, however, eventually deploys a peacemaking potential prophetic of the Cold War's conflict structure. The war with the ultimate weapon turns into a "war to end all wars." Traumatized and disabused by the unprecedented destruction, the survivors establish a global government ensuring continuous peace. Even though the First World War—welcomed by Wells—proved this fantasy wrong, thirty years later it still shaped the ideas about the use and function of the actual nuclear bomb. The young Hungarian-born physicist Leo Szilard was a keen reader of Wells's novels and was reminded of *The World Set Free* immediately after his first experiments on nuclear chain reactions, in the 1930s in London.[35] A decade later, Szilard became the driving force behind the funding and development of the Manhattan Project. He essentially followed Wells's idea of peace guaranteed by an ultimate weapon.

The nuclear bomb is thus science fiction. From its first inception in literary fiction, it was considered an apocalyptic and global weapon. It epitomized both the possibility and the risk that, by a single human decision, huge numbers of humans could be wiped out, possibly even all life on earth. In 1946, the military strategist Bernard Brodie coined the expression "absolute weapon." The absolute weapon is no longer seen as an instrument to win wars but to prevent war by deterrence.[36] In this sense the Bomb was a fantasy made operative to provide leverage in international politics. It became the center of an apocalyptic rhetoric that would always refer to "the whole world," "the survival of mankind," and "continued existence on earth." In this sense, the nuclear bomb is in fact an imaginary bomb, just as the Cold War is—at least in hindsight—seen as an "imaginary war,"[37] "neither war nor peace,"[38] frozen by weapons that could not reasonably be used. This imaginary nature of the Bomb has been conjured up time and again, in fiction and politics, philosophy and strategic planning: It posed a challenge to a future of mankind (Günther Anders), it served to imagine and quantify mankind's extermination (Herman Kahn), it became the pivot of rational-choice strategies of security (Leo Szilard), and it became the chief metaphor of an obscure desire for self-destruction (Stanley Kubrick, Sidney Lumet).

NO FUTURE

The way in which the Bomb became operative as a political option profoundly changes how the future is conceived of and, accordingly, the practices of "managing" it, such as planning, decision making, prevention, and securitization. But the Bomb also changes the idea of a man-made future in an even more fundamental way. It changes the status of the future. Instead of being open to different and contingent possible worlds, a "garden of forking paths," the future itself becomes merely an option, a possibility—the alternative is that *there might be no future at all*. Anders saw this new status of the future as the result of the human inability to anticipate the consequences of one's own productions and decisions. Human beings, Anders argues, produce technologies whose potential they cannot control. Even if the weapons are not used, the human relation to the future is profoundly shaken by their invention, as this invention can never be taken back:

> The future no longer "comes"; we no longer think of it as "coming," rather we are making it. And we make it in such a manner that it includes its own alternative: the possibility of its disruption, of possible futurelessness. Even if this disruption does not occur as soon as tomorrow—by means of what we are doing today, it can occur the day after tomorrow, or in the generation of our great-grandsons or in the "seventh generation." Insofar as the effects of the things that we do today will persist, this future already exists today. That is to say, in a pragmatic sense, this future is already present. Present in the sense in which an enemy is "present," if he is, though absent in a formal sense, already within the reach of our weapons, and so can be struck by us. . . . Our deeds accomplish more than our powers of comprehension. Short-sighted as we are, our projectiles go further than we can even see.[39]

To act against this "short-sightedness" or, as he writes elsewhere, "apocalypse-blindness" (*Apokalypse-Blindheit*),[40] Anders suggests humans use their imagination and visualize the end of the world as a given possibility. As a philosopher, he thus acts very much in the role of a prophet: he warns of looming danger by predicting a desperate future in the hope of being proven wrong. Looking ahead into the future—or, rather, into the apocalyptic absence of futurity—is supposed to educate and warn in an attempt to secure the future against the dangers of the nuclear threat. "Fantasy," "imagination," and "creativity" thus became the keywords of an (especially European) peace movement that emphasized the concreteness of nuclear destruction in order to keep it at bay. The antinuclear peace movement was also the cradle of a branch of futurology that, instead of emphasizing technological and economic progress, called for a change in policy and social structure, spearheaded by Robert Jungk, a disciple of Anders. European futurology sought to switch from an apocalyptic to a utopian perspective by using, in the words of Jungk, "social fantasy" and a "futurology of mankind."[41]

However, imagination and creativity could also be used in an entirely different way. American think tanks such as the RAND Corporation or the Hudson Institute emphasized the use of creativity and imagination to elaborate the options and consequences of nuclear war in all its lurid details. On the one hand, they investigated the strategic options for the use of nuclear arms, asking questions such as: What would be the types of crises where a nuclear strike might become necessary? Which forms of deterrence are convincing enough yet would not escalate the conflict? What would the death toll look like? Which kinds of civil defense would be reasonable? On the other hand, they sought to illuminate the concrete consequences of nuclear war. In 1960, RAND's chief strategist, Herman Kahn, published *On Thermonuclear War*.[42] Its first chapter analyzes in detail the state of the country after a nuclear attack: Will the survivors envy the dead? How much tragedy is "acceptable"? What kinds of genetic damage will a nuclear strike cause?

Some of these questions made Kahn famous—and infamous: by calculating the differences of various scenarios of civil defense he casually juggled with death rates between five and ninety million people.[43] In a RAND strategic objectives committee, he merrily recommended a strategy by stating it would involve a death toll of *"only* two million" people.[44] What sounds like cynicism is actually at the core of Kahn's approach. He was interested in a *quantification* of the disaster.[45] As no experience with the types of nuclear weapons was available, and since political experiments were out of the question, this quantification would be entirely hypothetical. War was a hypothesis, one that could be rendered into numerical data and computed. "War," Kahn wrote, "is a terrible thing, but so is peace. The difference seems to be a quantitative one of degree and standards."[46]

Kahn's intention, however, was clearly antiapocalyptic. Unlike the peace movement and its futurologists, he focused on the *feasibility* of a limited war, which, under certain circumstances, could be accepted as a risk. Ironically, hardly any other planner of the nuclear war has fueled apocalyptic visions more than Herman Kahn, with his hypothetical death tolls in the millions. He became the model for the military scientists in *Dr. Strangelove* and *Fail-Safe*. Yet Kahn might have been closer to fiction than he realized. Given the impossibility of gaining experience with the H-bomb in an actual war theater, fiction—both in strategic scenario planning and in literature and film—was the only way to play out the options and observe the consequences of nuclear warfare. Strategic planners thus read novels such as Peter George's *Red Alert* (1958), the novel on which *Dr. Strangelove* was based, "to stimulate [their] reason and imagination *to cope with history before it happens*."[47]

Thinking about the future in the Cold War meant fictionalizing the future: it included thought experiments on military outcomes, strategic options, but also worst-case scenarios. It meant imagining apocalypse in order to prevent it (as in the pacifist versions of futurology) or fleshing out nuclear options in favor of a limited, and thus feasible, war. What all of these approaches have in common is that they try to make fictional modes of thinking—from thought experiments to entertainment novels—operative within a political conflict stabilized by these very fictions. Writing in the early 1980s, Jacques Derrida noted that apocalypse is a "rhetorical figure," an "invention" or a "fiction"—yet a fiction that reached directly into the "reality" of the conflict.[48]

The crucial doctrine of security and stability during the Cold War, the strategy of mutually assured destruction (MAD), was based not on facts and reality, on existing stockpiles of weapons or military supremacy. It was based on hypotheses about the enemy's options and potential actions or reactions in the future, and these hypotheses were developed not by generals or politicians but by mathematicians. In 1953, the mathematician and philosopher Albert Wohlstetter designed the first draft of a strategy of "second-strike capability" for the RAND Corporation. "Second-strike capability" was based on the possibility of deterring the enemy from an attack by maintaining the capability to strike back even after having suffered a disastrous attack.[49] Bernard Brodie elaborated this idea into a new strategy of deterrence.[50] The stability of MAD is based on the prospect of a retaliatory strike that would make a first strike extremely risky for the aggressor. Security, the doctrine claimed, is only possible if striking first remains highly dangerous because it would still have devastating consequences for the aggressor. This kind of reasoning follows the abstract logic of risk assessment. The same logic also implies that it would be dangerous to disarm, even when this might be reasonable in economic or sociopolitical terms. The Cold War was "frozen" in a fiction that stabilized it and stalled any kind of exit from this logic of mutual deterrence.

THE OBSCENE DESIRE FOR APOCALYPSE: *DR. STRANGELOVE* AND *FAIL-SAFE*

MAD is based on the assumption that both sides are able to assess their own and their opponent's options logically. The foundation for this approach was provided by game theory, a form of conflict modeling that assumes that both sides in a given conflict try to take minimum risk.[51] This entails speculating deeply on the opponent's options and motivations. Does he expect a profit if he strikes first? Is the risk of a retaliatory strike low enough for him? It was precisely at this point that the apocalyptic vision of nuclear war became the driving force behind the Cold War's dynamic military buildup. As political stability was understood to depend on the plausibility of a retaliatory strike, the stakes needed to be raised progressively. The more disastrous the consequences of a potential nuclear strike, the more effective the deterrence.

Based on the assumption of both opponents' absolute rationality, the apocalyptic spell was as intelligible as it was fragile. What if the other side did not understand its own best interest? What if it did not act rationally? The most pervasive fear was thus that of a first strike caused unintentionally, which would then escalate into an all-out war, given the escalatory logic of MAD. The eruption of irrationality or unintentionality reveals the blind spots of MAD. And this is where literature and film take the stage. Stanley Kubrick's *Dr. Strangelove* and Sidney Lumet's *Fail-Safe*, both released in 1964, focus on this same topic—an accidental first strike. While one presents it as a tragedy (*Fail-Safe*), the other stages it as a farce (*Dr. Strangelove*). Not surprisingly, Kubrick's version was the bigger success at the box office.

Dr. Strangelove confines its narrative to three settings, an air base, a B-52 bomber, and the War Room at the Pentagon, and has a single actor playing all three main characters (Peter Sellers as liaison officer at the air base, as US president, and as his advisor Dr. Strangelove). The plot could be directly taken out of one of the worst-case-scenario textbooks for strategic planning: A paranoid US Air Force general singlehandedly launches an attack on the Soviet Union. Consequently, B-52 bombers are dispatched toward Moscow. When the US military command recalls the bombers, one of them cannot be called back because of a technical failure. In the War Room, a crisis-management group consisting of the US president, top military brass, the Russian ambassador, and the military strategist Dr. Strangelove tries to figure out a solution to avoid the imminent war. The US president calls the (not quite sober) Soviet premier. It turns out that the Russians have built a Doomsday Device that will automatically detonate as soon as the USSR is attacked—but they have forgotten to inform the Americans. At the end of the movie, despite the peace efforts of the hapless presidents, the Doomsday Device is triggered, and the world ends to the ironic tones of the World War II hit "We'll Meet Again."

No matter how ludicrous Kubrick's plot may seem, he succinctly reveals the flaw of MAD. In fact, the Doomsday Device is a logical consequence of Wohlstetter's doctrine of "second-strike capability." An automated response rules out any doubt in the "assuredness" of MAD. Herman Kahn seriously thought about the notion of a Doomsday Device but rejected it as too risky. The Soviet Union developed a system named "Perimeter," usually called "the Dead Hand," and it has been speculated that it might be still in use or could at least be activated in times of international tension.[52]

Kubrick's take on the logic of Cold War security aims at its central blind spot: the possibility that the opponent does not act as reasonably as rational-choice conflict models suggest. The movie celebrates the victory of irrationality within the balance of terror. While on the part of the Americans it is madness personified in General Jack D. Ripper, on the part of the Russians it is mere stupidity that ultimately brings about the end of the world. Kubrick's Russians simply did not understand that deterrence only works if the enemy *knows*. "The whole point is lost if you keep it a secret!" Dr. Strangelove explains.[53] Kubrick lays bare the blind spot of the rational-choice type of conflict modeling: if both opponents lack the capability to analyze the conflict rationally, there is no point in applying rational-choice models.

Nuclear apocalypse, as the film celebrates it gloriously at its end, results from the clash between a highly rational security strategy and a complete failure of rationality. The sexual imagery pervading the entire movie—beginning with a copulation of airplanes in midair and including the intentionally silly names of the characters and places (such as General Jack D. Ripper, Burpelson Air Force Base, Ambassador de Sadeski, and, not least, Dr. Strangelove)—reveals, underneath the rationalist calculation, an unavowable desire for the catastrophe actually to happen. The desire to secure the future, in the Cold War, is actually undercut by an obscene desire to end it all.

This suicidal tendency at the core of MAD is even more obvious in Sidney Lumet's attempt to stage the logic of nuclear deterrence as a tragedy. Again, a version of Herman Kahn is presented, here as Professor Groeteschele, who shocks the horrified guests at a party by explaining the advantages of a war that would cost "only" sixty million lives instead of one hundred million.[54] What warfare means in the age of nuclear weapons is demonstrated when an unknown airplane penetrates US airspace. In response, "Vindicator" bombers are dispatched toward the Soviet Union. Because of a technical fault, a "go code" is transmitted to six of these airplanes at the "fail-safe" point. As a result, the planes set course for Moscow. While five of them are eventually ordered to return, one completes its mission of bombing the Soviet capital. Whereas Kubrick emphasizes the failure of rational calculus, Lumet emphasizes the failure of communication to forestall the ultimate catastrophe. Neither a telephone call between the US president and the Soviet premier nor a call to the pilot of the fatal bomber can prevent the airstrike, since the pilot has orders not to listen to any recall once he has passed the "fail-safe" point.

In Lumet's scenario, the problem is not caused by an automated bomb but by humans who follow procedures as if they were automatons.[55] They refuse to communicate and can therefore go out of control just like machines. The pilot carries out his instructions without wavering and eventually turns off the radio when his senior commanders and his wife implore him to return. Ultimately, even the US president acts like a MAD automaton. Following a logic of "tit for tat," he can see only one option to appease the Russians: he gives the order to bomb New York, although his wife is in the city. The order has to be executed by a general whose family is also living in the city. Unlike Kubrick, Lumet interprets the apparent aporia of the logic of deterrence as the tragic necessity of self-destruction and not as a silly and obscene desire. But what both movies unveil underneath the doctrine of security as deterrence is an unavowable desire to bring about the end. Only in fiction can the apocalyptic fantasy of the "ultimate weapon" reveal the blind spots of the hyper-rational yet ultimately suicidal political logic of MAD. Deterrence secretly dreams of the catastrophe while claiming to prevent it.

Romantic darkness and nuclear apocalypse share a common focus on a future as an ultimate catastrophe, an end of the world. Unlike the biblical model of apocalypse as divine judgment, this catastrophe is not part of a divine plan but a purely secular event, an event of human making, contingent, and ultimately meaningless. This idea of a catastrophic end of human history is the dark counterpart of a modern concept of the future as open, subject to human intervention, a space for progress, growth, and hope. The catastrophic imaginary, embodied by the viewpoint of the Last Man, serves as a counterdiscourse to this optimistic and progressivist conception of the future. The position of "lastness"—both anthropological and epistemological—not only produces an insight into human nature, an anthropology of catastrophe, but also an understanding of the intricate bond between the attempt to secure the future and an underlying tendency to put this future at risk. Be it in the Malthusian model that binds growth to crisis or in the idea that security can be reached by taking ever greater risks, the Last Man is the figure of this intrinsic paradox in modernity's relation to the future. However, this can only be seen from a viewpoint after the fact, the position of lastness. Yet, lastness, the position of hindsight, implies that the catastrophe has a specific temporal structure, that it is, as the word's etymology implies, "a sudden turn downward," a caesura in time that allows for a "before" and an "after." This temporal structure is the precondition for the fantasy of the Last Man, which seems to be the emblematic position of thinking the future as catastrophe in the modern age.

Today's concept of catastrophe, however, seems to depart from this temporal setting. While Romantic darkness and the nuclear apocalypse still imply a demarcated event in time, to be witnessed by the Last Man, the current catastrophic imaginary envisions a catastrophe without an event, a catastrophe that does not take place at a specific point in time and space. The clearly defined disaster scenarios of modernity—be they natural or nuclear—are making way for a contemporary catastrophic imaginary that disintegrates into a multitude of potential disaster scenarios or into incremental processes. The "big blast" of modern catastrophe is being replaced by a much more uncanny type of disaster, one with a multitude of locations, unpredictable timings, and unforeseeable consequences. This catastrophe without an event is climate change.

2

CATASTROPHE WITHOUT EVENT

Imagining Climate Disaster

WEATHER AND CLIMATE

Weather buoys in the North Atlantic are reporting drastically sinking water temperatures, a sign of the Gulf Stream's disruption. Three enormous hurricanes are forming in the northern hemisphere. Snow is falling in New Delhi; egg-sized hail is pelting Tokyo. Los Angeles is devastated by tornados, New York pounded by a tsunami. Such is the dramatic, if scientifically untenable, scenario presented in Roland Emmerich's film *The Day After Tomorrow* (2004) about sudden global climate change (fig. 2.1).[1]

The movie's protagonist, a paleoclimatologist named Jack Hall (Dennis Quaid), keeps explaining that the *weather* catastrophe at hand is in fact a *climate* catastrophe: the beginning of a "new ice age." Yet what we see is *weather*: short-term and local meteorological events. Emmerich's weather catastrophe confirms Robert Heinlein's dictum: "Climate is what we expect; weather is what we get."[2]

Climate is hard to capture in images or stories. Unlike spectacular weather phenomena such as storms, hail, spring floods, droughts, or frosts, climate does not take the shape of an event. Yet precisely because it is so difficult to grasp and represent, climate change has come to epitomize a new type of threat that I call "catastrophe without event." It is the

FIGURE 2.1 Unusually frigid weather in New York. In Roland Emmerich's *The Day After Tomorrow* (2004), extreme weather is used to give image to the impalpable process of climate change.

Source: Still from *The Day After Tomorrow* (2004).

eventlessness of current catastrophic scenarios (even if they do not all revolve around the climate) that fundamentally distinguishes them from the scenarios imagined during the Romantic era and the Cold War. It is therefore worth taking a closer look at the history of our knowledge about the climate, the fantasies about its potential changes, and, not least, the role of human beings in its formation.

For a long time, climate stood silently in the background of human history as a stable fact of life, only occasionally making its presence felt through dramatic weather events. Today, it has become a pressing matter of concern and fear. Climate change poignantly reveals the fragility of nature—a nature that has long been regarded as the robust and immutable counterpart to ever-changing human culture. Yet climate change—as only one, but the most uncanny symptom of this destabilization of nature—does not take place as an event but rather as a slow, imperceptible shifting of states, with multiple, contradictory, and unpredictable consequences. Unlike the Cold War's threat of nuclear attack, climate change has no identifiable source or responsible agents—rather, again, a multitude of sources and agents. For this reason, climate change is at the heart of the present catastrophic imagination: a catastrophe without event. This imagination has a history of its own, a history revolving around the most fundamental parameters of human existence: our natural living conditions.

Climate knows no event, only conditions and latent processes. It consists of expectations, extrapolations, probabilities, and models based on such things as average precipitation, temperatures, solar radiation, and winds. We can conceive of climate only in the form of weather events. For centuries it was therefore the *weather*—not the climate—that served as the paradigm for a future awaited full of hope and fear.[3] The weather is the oldest object of prognosis, be it by means of weather oracles and calendars (think of Groundhog Day) or by prophesying long-term weather trends such as the seven fat and seven lean years foreseen by Joseph in Genesis 41. Weather events—and in particular storms and floods—are "the stage of the gods," their means of punishing or redeeming people (or sometimes just capriciously intervening in our destinies).[4]

The history of imagining climate catastrophes undoubtedly extends further back than the famous biblical plagues that, a few centuries after Joseph, would beset and devastate the Egyptians in the time of Moses. In this chapter, however, I would like to examine only modern climate scenarios because they specifically focus—as Byron shows—on the political, social, and epistemological dimensions of future catastrophe. Fictional climate disasters are not merely creative reinterpretations of historical climate disruptions—such as, for instance, the abnormal weather that caused the "Year Without a Summer" in 1816, the weather in the wake of the eruption of Krakatoa in 1883, or the effects of the nuclear attack on Japan in 1945. Imagined climate disasters also reflect the contemporary state of science, such as the rise of paleontology in the eighteenth century, the discovery of ice ages and Darwin's theory of evolution in the nineteenth, as well as astronomy, sociology, and the study of environmental destruction and anthropogenic climate change at the end of the twentieth century. The dreams and nightmares about unfettered climate change are not only fleshed out in novels or films but also expressed in social and political utopias as well as in cautionary tales, research projects, and even architectural designs. My aim in analyzing these climate-related fictions is not to test their validity but to outline the new understanding of nature they display and process. The question is not how "realistic" future climate scenarios have been but what their social and anthropological agendas may have been. They revolve around human beings stripped of any divine providence, living beings in the midst of a catastrophe that radically changes the very basis of their existence: their natural environment.

A COMPLICATED KNOWLEDGE

Rarely has a weather forecast been as reliable as Joseph's, and seldom has the reaction to it been as reasonable as the Pharaoh's. Despite its long mythical history, weather has always been a fleeting and incomprehensible object of human knowledge.[5] Derived from the Greek Μετεωρολογία (*meteōrologia*), meteorology is the knowledge of things "hovering in the heights," of things that move around in the air but do not belong to the mathematical realm of the stars' movements.[6] The French philosopher Michel Serres has pointed out that this type of knowledge—mainly the field of expertise of farmers and sailors—concerns phenomena that defy experimentation and calculation. It has thus been systematically excluded from the canon of modern science:

> Meteorology is the repressed content of history.... I don't mean the climate, but *meteora*: clouds, rain and waterspouts, hailstorms or showers, the direction and force of the wind, here and now. And I don't mean the prevailing wind. Meteors are accidents, occurrences.... *Meteora* bear an incredible knowledge.... Philosophers, historians, the masters of science, are concerned only with the ancient idea of the law.... The weather now and the weather to come infinitely surpass our account of them, so they are of no account. Because it is the place of disorder and the unforeseeable, of local danger, of the formless. Because it is the weather of another time.[7]

Knowledge of the weather has been ousted from a form of science based on universally applicable laws and experimentation. The weather is "here and now," a unique, unpredictable, and contingent occurrence that cannot be (re)produced or measured in a closed experimental setting. "Science is shut inside. It proceeds from its beginning, from the *meteora* to the furnace, and will never leave this closure again, which excludes chance and the uncontrollable, what today we would call hyper-complexity."[8]

Modern meteorology, of course, continues to grapple with the irregularity and hypercomplexity of atmospheric phenomena. To do so, three unrelated approaches have been developed: the theoretical study of the general laws of atmospheric physics; the empirical measurement and recording of actual weather situations, with the aim of creating a sort of climate archive; and the practical art of short- and mid-term weather forecasting, which we still enjoy today in the form of weather reports. Yet as its dynamics are so complex, it is impossible to derive reliable predictions from the laws of atmospheric physics. Knowledge of the climate cannot be gained in an experimental space. As early as 1945, a meteorologist expressed the following lament: "When attempting to measure the dependence of vapor pressure on temperature, an experimental physicist does so in spaces with constant pressure and constant humidity. In the laboratory of the meteorologist, which is the atmosphere surrounding us, every element is in constant flux. There are always new images to behold; it's like a kaleidoscope creating a new view with every turn."[9] Meteorological knowledge can thus be gained only partially through theory, in the laboratory (with respect to isolatable general regularities), or in the archive (with respect to past weather events and their regularities). A fourth form of knowledge was therefore devised: simulation, a "conjectural science" that uses mathematical models in the hope of rendering the fluidity and hypercomplexity of atmospheric phenomena calculable.[10] It is no longer just a matter of statistics (as was still the case in nineteenth-century meteorology) but rather one of gauging *potential* system behavior over a longer period of time. "Experiments" of this sort can only take place in the form of computer simulations. Their application to reality is therefore by no means simply given. For the past decade, the complicated nature and epistemological uncertainty of climate knowledge has fueled discussions about the validity of scenarios of climate change.

If weather is the "here and now" of precipitation, barometric conditions, and temperatures (and thus can now be forecast fairly well for the short term), climate, according to the National Oceanic and Atmospheric Administration, is the background system underlying weather events:

> Weather consists of the short-term (minutes to days) variations in the atmosphere. Weather is expressed in terms of temperature, humidity, precipitation, cloudiness, visibility and wind. Climate is the slowly

varying aspect of the atmosphere-hydrosphere-land surface system. It is typically characterized in terms of averages of specific states of the atmosphere, ocean, and land, including variables such as temperature (land, ocean, and atmosphere), salinity (oceans), soil moisture (land), wind speed and direction (atmosphere), and current strength and direction (oceans).[11]

Climate today is defined in terms of averages, duration and regularity, probability and recurrences. Weather and the climate thus exist in a state of epistemological tension: the event versus the average, the short versus the long term, singular events versus regularity, manifestation versus latency.

This understanding of climate as subject to change and human intervention is relatively recent and constitutes a radical conceptual shift. Unlike the volatility of weather events, climate, for centuries, was seen as the stable and predictable condition of human existence.[12] The given climate in a specific area explained the character of its inhabitants and the nature of their modes of living. This old definition of climate is ingrained in the etymology of the word, which derives from the Greek *klinein*, "to incline, bend, slant." "Climate" designates the angle at which the rays of the sun fall upon a given region, and this basically determines whether it is hotter or colder there. Originally, then, "climate" was a geographical term. Both Hippocrates and Aristotle explained the differences between human physiques, illnesses, mentalities, and social institutions in terms of the various climates in which people live.[13] Influenced by thinkers such as the French cultural historian l'Abbé Jean-Baptiste Dubos, the philosopher Charles de Montesquieu, and the German philosopher and theologian Johann Gottlieb Herder, the eighteenth century borrowed these early approaches and developed them into an anthropological theory based on climate. This climate anthropology derived the differences in social institutions from the influences of heat on human bodies and minds.[14]

As a local phenomenon, climate situated humanity in a given location while at the same time explaining the diversity of human cultures and institutions. In the ancient meaning of the term, climate thus was a concept that explains humankind in and through its environment. Thinking about the relation between cultural development and natural landscapes, Herder writes: "In one place the proximity of the sea, in another the direction of the wind, here the altitude of the land, there its vicinity to mountains, and so forth, necessitate so many local qualifications to the general law, that we frequently find the most opposite climates in places that closely border on each other."[15] Climate was thus a benchmark for measuring *regional differences* between various areas and their inhabitants.

However, seen as intricately entangled with human culture, climate was not just a factor in the shaping of human bodies, cultures, and social institutions. Early on, at the turn of the nineteenth century natural scientists such as the father of modern geology, Georges-Louis Buffon, as well as philosophers like Herder started speculating about humankind as an active factor in climate history. In this view, humans are not only formed by climate but actively change climates and landscapes in turn. Civilization, according to Herder, began when humankind endeavored to alter the climate for its own purposes:

> Since climate is a compound of forces and influences to which both plants and animals contribute, serving all that is alive within a relationship of mutual interaction, it stands to reason that man, too, has a share, nay a dominant role, in altering it through his creativity. By appropriating fire from Heaven and rendering iron obedient to his hand . . . he has in several important ways participated in changing the environmental climate. Once Europe was a dank forest. . . . The forests have been cleared and, as a result, the climate and the inhabitants underwent a change. . . . We may consider mankind, therefore, as a band of bold little giants, gradually descending from the mountains, to conquer the earth and change climates with their feeble hands. How far they are capable of going in this respect only the future will reveal.[16]

Obviously, the insight into manmade climate change is not as new as it has often been presented. As a result of agriculture, deforestation, or the draining of swamps, the modification of climate has long been an integral part of the cultural history of humankind and of an understanding of man in the tradition of Herder.

The idea of an entanglement between climate and culture, however, was eventually rejected as deterministic at the beginning of the twentieth century. As the humanities and social sciences became increasingly separated from the natural sciences throughout the nineteenth and twentieth centuries, "natural factors" such as climate had to be excluded from the analysis of human cultures and societies. Likewise, climate was separated from any relation to humans by becoming exclusively the object of the natural sciences, based on measurements and computable data. With this process, climate underwent a profound redefinition. Instead of being understood as a conglomerate of local environmental factors encompassing human cultures and natural settings, climate was now cast as the "average weather." The Austrian climatologist Julius von Hann, one of the founding fathers of modern climatology, gives the following definition in his *Handbook of Climatology* (1883): "Climate is the sum total of the weather as usually experienced during a longer or shorter period of time at any given season. An account of a climate, therefore, means a description of the average state of the atmosphere."[17]

Climate research in the nineteenth century started out as an endeavor to standardize local climate measurements. Its ultimate goal was to achieve an understanding of "global climate." Seen as a global category, climate ceases to be a local and relatively static concept. Instead, it becomes a historical predicament, albeit one observed on scales that extend well beyond the human experience of time and space. This becomes clear in the definition of climate given by the Intergovernmental Panel on Climate Change (IPCC):

> Climate in a narrow sense is usually defined as the "average weather," or more rigorously, as the statistical description in terms of the mean and variability of relevant quantities over a period of time ranging from months to thousands or millions of years. The classical period is 30 years, as defined by the World Meteorological Organization (WMO). These quantities are most often surface variables such as temperature, precipitation, and wind. Climate in a wider sense is the state, including a statistical description, of the climate system.[18]

With the focus on the temporal variations of climate, the local differences that once defined the concept are no longer central. Even though it can only be recorded *on site*, "climate" has by now become a *global* concept, with a focus on its long-term *temporality*. Once a phenomenon of overwhelming phenomenal intensity (traveling was mainly seen as a "change of climate"), the modern systemic concept of climate has withdrawn into a realm of abstraction and computation.

Climate, as defined today, has become an entity epistemically cut off from bodies and locations. Global climate, let alone global climate change, is nothing we can experience with our senses.[19] Human-induced climate change, however, makes the nineteenth-century separation of the realms of human cultures and natural entities obsolete. With the Anthropocene, a term designating the anthropogenic change of the planet's entire life system (from climate change and the changing chemistry of the oceans to ozone-layer depletion and species loss), human history and natural history uncannily converge. Global warming may be the most threatening symptom of the Anthropocene, yet it is also one particularly complicated epistemically, given the highly abstract concept of climate operative today. How can we conceive of a threat that is so ungraspable and so vast that it eludes the scales of human experience?

The discovery of anthropogenic climate change requires a new understanding of climate as a cultural force. This is why it is necessary not only to look back into the history of climate and climate change but also into the various imaginations of climate disasters in the modern age. These imaginations reflect the historical forms of knowledge about the history of the earth and of its climate, from the emerging discipline of geology at the beginning of the nineteenth century to the ice cores that today's paleoclimatology is based on. From a global perspective on climate, the surface of the planet can be read as an archive of climates past—and of climate changes. Crucially, with the discovery of a historically changing climate, the question of *future climates* arises. Climate thus, in the modern age, becomes an object of speculation and imagination. As we have already seen in the case of Lord Byron's poem "Darkness" (1816), scenarios of radically changing climate serve to envision how a different natural environment might bring forth an entirely different kind of civilization—or the end of humanity altogether.

THE GREAT COOLING

Arguably the oldest climate-disaster scenario is not global warming but that of the planet cooling. It prevailed throughout the entire nineteenth century and continued to feature in the work of climatologists well into the 1970s.[20] The scenario emerged at the end of the eighteenth century and brought forth the Romantic vision of darkening, which also marked the beginning of the modern catastrophic imagination. As we have seen, Byron's "Darkness" is one of the first documents of this trepidation. In Byron's text, the global climate crisis of 1816, the "Year Without a Summer," is projected as an apocalyptic environmental collapse. The poem depicts a pessimistic anthropology of catastrophe and was an attack on the Enlightenment's benign perception of man and optimistic account of the future. But, beyond that, the poem also offers a detailed description of a climatic worst-case scenario—a world mired in darkness and cold: "The icy earth / Swung blind and blackening in the moonless air."[21] The sun's extinction not only ushers in an ice age but also the breakdown of all natural rhythms and structures. Together with climate, time collapses. The moon, tides, and seasons are no longer. In this timeless state of cold and darkness, both humanity and all of nature are wiped from the earth:

> The world was void,
> The populous and the powerful—was a lump,
> Seasonless, herbless, treeless, manless, lifeless—
> A lump of death—a chaos of hard clay.
> The rivers, lakes, and ocean all stood still,
> And nothing stirred within their silent depths.[22]

If nature is extinguished, all that will remain of the earth is a bleak lump without living processes, without plants, without seasons, without tides. The end of climate is a morbid standstill, the end of nature's temporality. Byron's catastrophe vision is not just a brutal crisis experiment on humanity but also a thought experiment on the ultimate destruction of nature. What will remain of an earth deprived of light and warmth? The absence of seasons, vegetation, and the water cycle is an image for the destruction of an ever-moving network of natural flows and energies whose interdependence had constituted the very vitality of nature. This constant motion is now literally frozen and dead:

> The waves were dead; the tides were in their grave,
> The moon their mistress had expired before;
> The winds were withered in the stagnant air,

And the clouds perish'd; Darkness had no need
Of aid from them—She was the Universe.[23]

Climate and weather—the latter synonymous with "time" in some European languages—are cast as the pacesetters of life on planet Earth. Byron's vision of catastrophe erases the very temporality of nature, a temporality of life that would have also contained the future.

Byron's hopeless catastrophe—the destruction of mankind, nature, and time—responds to a new knowledge: geology. Modern geology is the study of climate history with attention to some of the slowest cycles and transformations of nature. Inspecting the archive laid down in the crust of the earth, scientists started to understand these layers as the deposits and vestiges of bygone life and bygone states of climate. Examining this archive of nature thus meant looking into the "abyss of time," as one geologist put it.[24] Over the course of the eighteenth century, the natural-historical studies by James Hutton, Buffon, and other geologists demonstrated that the earth had to be far older than the six thousand years suggested by the biblical account of things.[25] Buffon argued for an age of 75,000 years and thus spearheaded a debate about the history of the earth that would ultimately undermine the validity of the biblical creation myth. He based his estimation on an experiment. Assuming that the earth was once an incandescent globe, he tried to estimate the time a globe of this size would need to cool to today's temperatures. Cooling, Buffon speculated, is the process that made life on earth possible. But at some point, the planet would become too cool to allow for organic life. In his *Epochs of Nature* (1778), Buffon casts the role of humans in this irreversible cooling process. By altering the climate through agriculture and canalization, he argued, humans might be able to slow the cooling of the planet's climate.[26] Nevertheless, Buffon opens up a catastrophist perspective on the history of the earth. In a letter written in the Year Without a Summer, 1816, which he spent with Byron in Geneva, Percy Bysshe Shelley remarked: "Buffon's sublime but gloomy theory is that this earth which we inhabit will at some future point be changed into a mass of frost."[27]

In Buffon's footsteps, Georges Cuvier, the founder of paleontology, developed an entirely novel theory about the history of life on earth, a theory in which recurring climate catastrophes play a crucial role. While studying fossils, Cuvier discovered that there had obviously once been species that no longer exist. This raised the question about the historical reasons for this extinction. Cuvier concluded that there must have been gigantic cataclysms wiping out entire species of animals. Cuvier conceived of the biological history of nature as a history of death and extinction.[28] This, of course, led to questions about the events that might have caused such large-scale disappearances to occur.

In his *Essay on the Theory of the Earth* (1825), Cuvier radicalized the idea of changing climate conditions into a natural history of catastrophes. Huge cataclysms, he concluded, must have suddenly occurred and destroyed all life in given regions of the planet:

> Life, therefore, has often been disturbed on this earth by terrible events. Numberless living beings have been the victims of these catastrophes; some, which inhabited the dry land, have been swallowed up by inundations; others, which peopled the waters, have been laid dry, from the bottom of the sea having been suddenly raised; their very races have been extinguished forever.[29]

Cuvier's theory about the "revolutions" of the earth (the original title of his book is *Discours sur les révolutions de la surface du globe*) is a theory of rapid and destructive climate change, extinction, and spontaneous reemergence, and it places disasters and annihilation at the center of natural history. For Cuvier, these cataclysms had already taken place several times, though on a local basis and on a smaller scale, before the advent of human beings, and they would continue to occur again and again. The most widespread image of such a catastrophe was that of an ice age. Cuvier's assumption that mankind had only appeared after the last of these catastrophes and had thus never witnessed an ice age would later be refuted by Charles Lyell.[30] In the course of the nineteenth century, Cuvier's catastrophism was superseded by Lyell's gradualism, which presupposed a gradual and localized change of species and landscapes. Nevertheless, the idea of an impending cooling catastrophe pervaded the entire nineteenth century.

In his novel *Underground Man* (1896), for instance, the sociologist Gabriel Tarde imagined the earth freezing over and the subsequent formation of a utopian society deep under the ground. The overwhelming majority of humans and all animals freeze to death, and the few remaining survivors retreat beneath the earth to be warmed by its glowing core. Underground, they build a high-tech society and foster a harmonious way of life entirely independent from nature. Tarde's intention in this book, the only novel he ever wrote, however, was not to formulate a sociology of catastrophes. The novel rather serves as a thought experiment to work through the consequences of his own sociological theory of imitation, which he would more fully lay out in his book *The Laws of Imitation* (1903). The cooling catastrophe, the end of nature, as it were, for Tarde leads to a triumph of humaneness: a cultivated and peaceful society of mutually imitative individuals.[31]

Other late-nineteenth-century depictions of the end of the world are less utopian than Tarde's sociological speculations. All of them revolve around the idea of a gradually extinguishing sun. Camille Flammarion, a French astronomer, spiritualist, and one of the great popularizers of astronomical knowledge in the nineteenth century, portrayed just such a scenario in his apocalyptic novel *Omega: The Last Days of the World* (1894). Above all, the story was meant to convey an up-to-date understanding of astronomy. First, in the near future, the earth barely escapes being struck by a meteor; ten million years later, however, the planet enters a state of dryness and coldness because the earth's core has cooled and its surface water dissipated. Here, too, the end of the world comes in the form of a climate change:

> Then the surface water gradually diminished; it united with the rocks, in the form of hydrates, and thus disappeared from circulation.... This vapor of water in the atmosphere had made warmth and life possible; with its disappearance came cold and death.... From all the rest of the globe the human race had slowly but inexorably disappeared—dried up, exhausted, degenerated, from century to century, through the lack of an assimilable atmosphere and sufficient food. Its last remnants seem to have lapsed back into barbarism.[32]

While the earth's climate changes, the surviving people degenerate into pitiful half-starved hordes huddling under furs to ward off the cold. For Flammarion, climate change brings forth a change in the human species. In a reverse process of evolution, humanity, deprived of the energy and resources that allow for civilization, devolves to a prehuman past.

The close connection between climate and the constitution of man, a core tenet of the ancient theory of climate and culture, was still a central issue in the late nineteenth century. But now this connection is projected into a fictional future. In the coldness and scarcity that will visit the expiring planet, mankind, too, will only exist in a degenerate form. Human evolution will begin to reverse. This idea is expressed even more radically in H. G. Wells's most famous science-fiction novel, *The Time Machine* (1895), which appeared a year after Flammarion's novel. The first part of this novel takes place in the year 802,701, by which point humanity has degenerated into two separate species, the Morlocks and the Eloi, with the former hunting down the latter. In the novel's final chapters, however, Wells gives an even more radical account of the degeneration of the species when his narrator travels to an even-more-faraway future. The sun is now a murky red ball that no longer rises or sets and no longer casts warming rays on the planet. The air has become thin and cold, a perpetual bleak twilight:

> The sky was no longer blue. North-eastward it was inky black, and out of the blackness shone brightly and steadily the pale white stars. Overhead it was a deep Indian red and starless, and south-eastward it grew brighter to a glowing scarlet where, cut by the horizon, lay the huge hull of the sun, red and motionless.[33]

As in Byron's poem, almost all the movements of the air and water have come to a halt. The changed climate, however, has also altered the life forms on earth. The last living beings encountered by the time traveler do not have any human characteristics. There is a screaming white butterfly, a gigantic red crab, and finally a black tentacled creature hardly recognizable as an animal. While it is unclear whether these last creatures are late successors of human beings, it is clear that, on the expiring earth, nothing is still alive that even remotely resembles us. With the end of times, the end of humanity is sealed.

The cooling brings about the cessation of all life processes. This form of catastrophe is not conceived of as an event but rather as a gradual process, spanning not only generations but eons in the vast scales of geological time. It knows no event, location, or precise moment; it is a ubiquitous global process affecting the entire earth. The cooling fantasy is a fantasy about the slow cessation of life, a fading extinction to which there can no longer be any witness. In the cooling fantasies of the nineteenth century, the notion of climate morphed from a geographical and cultural concept into an immemorial temporality. It became the medium of a geological "deep time" that, in its immense time scales, could also represent a distant and menacing future.[34]

NUCLEAR WINTER

If the nineteenth century's cooling was conceived of as a gradual creep over the earth, the twentieth century's Great Freeze was imagined to arrive onstage with a bang. Its depictions of a global winter are images of a sudden and abrupt cooling of the earth, a catastrophic flash-freezing of the entire planet.

> One minute after the final explosion, more than half the human race will have died, the dust and smoke from the continents in flames will vanquish the sunlight, and absolute darkness will once again rule the world. A winter of orange rains and icy hurricanes will reverse the weather of the oceans and change the course of the rivers, whose fish will have died of thirst in the burning waters and whose birds will not find the sky. Perpetual snows will cover the Sahara Desert, vast Amazonia will disappear from the face of the planet, destroyed by hail, and the age of rock music and transplanted hearts will return to its glacial infancy. The few humans who may survive their terror, and those who had the privilege of safe refuge at three in the afternoon on the fateful Monday of the extreme catastrophe, will have saved their lives only to die afterwards because of the horror of their memories. Creation will have ended. In the final chaos of rains and eternal night, the only vestige of what life once was will be the cockroach.[35]

This bleak scenario derives from a speech delivered on August 6, 1986, by Gabriel García Márquez to commemorate the anniversary of the atomic bombing of Hiroshima. Nothing here of gradual paralysis and degeneration. Márquez's speech is instead a reaction to a novel understanding of nuclear warfare that emerged late in the Cold War. In the early 1980s, scientists had begun to focus not on the immediate consequences of a nuclear attack but on its potential side effects, the so-called nuclear winter. Besides its effect in showcasing the dangers of nuclear warfare, it was this new kind of climate modeling—a climate catastrophically altered by human intervention—that laid the foundation for current climate research.

Nevertheless, the fear of a nuclear attack's effect on global climate was not entirely new. The first speculations about the possible effects of a nuclear explosion on weather patterns had been made as early as 1957 by Samuel Glasstone and Philip J. Dolan, but their guess was that such an explosion would increase the amount of particles in the air as little as 1 percent more than did the eruption of Krakatoa in 1883, which had caused the global climate to cool quite notably for two consecutive years.[36] Yet it was only at the end of the 1970s that a group of researchers commissioned by the Swedish Academy of Sciences began a systematic investigation into the climatic effects of atomic bombs. Their results were presented in 1982 and were a cause of immediate concern. The Nobel Prize–winning atmospheric chemist Paul Crutzen and the climatologist John Birks had drawn up a sinister scenario: Large-scale fires produced by nuclear explosions—but also by any other massive fire, such as a volcanic eruption—would stir immense amounts of ash into the atmosphere, and this would drastically reduce sunlight and stunt the growth of plant life. They projected that the amount of sunlight to reach the earth would be reduced by at least 50 percent, at worst by up to 99 percent. Additional repercussions would include the destruction of the ozone layer by nitrogen oxide and extreme increases in carbon dioxide and airborne toxins from the incineration of cities and underground fields of natural gas and oil. According to their analysis, even those who managed to survive the immediate nuclear strike would have little prospect of survival:

> In this study we have shown that the atmosphere would most likely be highly perturbed by a nuclear war. We especially draw attention to the effects of the large quantities of highly sunlight-absorbing, dark particulate matter which would be produced and spread in the troposphere by the many fires that would start burning in urban and industrial areas, oil and gas producing fields, agricultural lands, and forests. For extended periods of time, maybe months, such fires would strongly

restrict the penetration of sunlight to the earth's surface and change the physical properties of the earth's atmosphere. The marine ecosystems are probably particularly sensitive to prolonged periods of darkness. Under such conditions it is likely that agricultural production in the Northern Hemisphere would be almost totally eliminated, so that no food would be available for the survivors of the initial effects of the war. It is also quite possible that severe, worldwide photochemical smog conditions would develop with high levels of tropospheric ozone that would likewise interfere severely with plant productivity. Survival becomes even more difficult if stratospheric ozone depletions also take place. It is, therefore, difficult to see how much more than a small fraction of the initial survivors of a nuclear war ... could escape famine and disease during the following year.[37]

Crutzen and Birks's scenario was thought through in greater detail over the course of the 1980s. Scientists associated with the climatologist Richard Turco and the astrophysicist Carl Sagan began to analyze the various factors of such a nuclear winter with computer simulations.[38] Their calculations yielded an even bleaker picture than that of Crutzen and Birks: sinking temperatures of up to twenty degrees Celsius, a complete disruption of the biological balance of the oceans, darkness comparable to that at the poles in winter, and increased exposure to radioactivity and ultraviolet radiation for at least ten to twelve years. A worldwide ecological catastrophe in the form of a nuclear winter, they argued, would bring about several hundred million deaths. Carl Sagan also presented this scenario in a popular book published in 1983, the title of which was the first to introduce the concept of "climate catastrophe."[39]

The scenario of nuclear winter combined the old fears associated with climatic cooling—darkness, cold, and famine—with the new fears of the atomic age: radiation, poisoning, epidemics. In spite of its resonance with older fears, the nuclear-winter scenario involved a decisive shift in terms of the political and strategic understanding of nuclear warfare. While traditionally the use of nuclear weapons was cast within the framework of mutually assured destruction (MAD), nuclear winter is a scenario not conceived in strategic and geopolitical but in ecological and global terms. It presumed the possibility that a single nuclear attack would not just destroy the bombed area but disrupt global climate in a way that could possibly cause, in Sagan's dramatic words, "the extinction of the human race."[40] This argument annulled the logic of MAD. It was therefore no coincidence that American and Soviet research groups were in surprising agreement about the validity of this hypothetical scenario.[41] The nuclear-winter scenario shifted matters from the level of strategy and political calculus to the fundamental level of humanity's long-term biological survival.

The nuclear-winter scenario also offered more concrete modes of representation. It lent itself to images that were both different from and far more tangible than the tables of casualty rates or the euphemistic "duck and cover" stories long derided since the 1960s.[42] The apocalyptic imagination of the 1950s and 1960s as analyzed in chapter 1 had treated the possibility of nuclear war as an abstract metaphor for the collective finitude of mankind. In the catastrophe scenario of the 1980s, lurid images of nuclear death suddenly emerged.

Tellingly, this becomes particularly clear in the weather scenes that the respective eras associated with the nuclear catastrophe. Nevil Shute's novel *On the Beach*, published in 1957, relates the tale of a world depopulated by radioactivity as a summer story in which the last survivors in Australia await their end while enjoying picnics and parties on the beach.[43] In contrast, the film *The Day After*, released in 1983, presents the consequences of an atomic attack on a small town in Kansas in faithful and ghastly detail. An exploding fireball is followed by ashen darkness, fallout resembling snow, and then a pale winter light on empty fields. A prewar summer suddenly changes into a postattack winter. What was new about the highly successful TV production was that it presented the physical effects of an atomic attack with clinical naturalism—from victims burnt by the explosion's heat to those dying slowly of radiation sickness. Collective death following a nuclear strike could no longer merely be a metaphor for our collective finitude; it was now definitively a total massacre. The abstraction of nuclear-death imaginations—from Kahn's tables to the "bare rooms" of Beckett's postapocalyptic survivors in *Endgame*—gave way to concrete images, catalyzing waves of protesters against nuclear arsenals. No one wanted to die this way. No one wanted to survive this way, either.

The nuclear-winter scenario tapped precisely into this new catastrophic naturalism. After all, "winter" is something tangible and familiar—and nothing is worse than the idea of a year-long winter. Yet in fact, the scenario was not something *familiar* at all. It was neither based on empirical observations nor on experiments but rather on a novel combination of diverse data about volcanic eruptions and the subsequent clouding of the atmosphere, hypotheses about the behavior of ozone in the stratosphere and the atmosphere's warming or cooling, all processed in computer simulations of climate behavior. The nuclear-winter scenario was made out of simulations; it was a model, not a phenomenon, as the historian of science Thomas Brandstetter remarks: "The clouds of dust and soot that had been billowing since the mid-1980s in the computer simulations conducted by meteorological institutes were not real. They were rather the result of hypothetical explosions and a handful of parameters that scientists and programmers had put in place more or less arbitrarily."[44] Consequently, the scenario was highly contentious. The conflict concerned not only its political implications but above all its epistemic status: "Where there is smoke these days, there is no fire, just a computer model," as one skeptic remarked.[45] The debate was no longer just about scientists meddling in politics (there was much talk about a conspiracy in favor of disarmament) but rather about the status of scientific knowledge derived from hypothetical figures.[46] Yet, as Herman Kahn had already made clear, knowledge about nuclear war could not be gained by way of experimenting. To the calls for empirical evidence Richard Turco offered the caustic response: "This is not a subject amenable to experimental verification—at least not more than once."[47]

This new knowledge on atmospheric behavior gave rise to a "hybrid" scientific object that "could be clearly assigned neither to the side of culture nor to that of nature."[48] It underscored not only the intricate connection between human behavior and the processes of nature but also the system-shaped nature of life. The nuclear-winter scenario is based on the convergence of an immense number of interdependent factors: the effects of dust on sunlight, the effects of sunlight on photosynthesis, the effects of photosynthesis on the lifecycle of plants, the role of plants in the nutrition of animals and humans, and so on. "Climate" thus came under scrutiny as a hypercomplex web of organic and inorganic factors that could not be examined independently, and this interdependence made it nearly impossible to calculate. Brandstetter again: "The concern here was not with 'life' but with the multiplicity of relations among different objects of knowledge. If something like life ever appeared in this process, it was only as a nodal point in a network of interrelated conditions composed of various scientific disciplines, including planetary research, meteorology, chemistry, biology, medicine, agronomy, and ecology."[49]

The nuclear-winter scenario is thus the most compelling image of a new sort of catastrophic knowledge that takes into account human interactions with the earth's life system. The study of environmental damage and ecological catastrophe had, since the 1960s, largely focused on local disasters—a good example being Rachel Carson's ecological classic *Silent Spring* (1962). The nuclear-winter scenario was the first to envision a potentially global phenomenon of manmade ecological disruption. Simulations of nuclear winter were, in fact, the first models of global anthropogenic climate change. The ironic twist is that today's climate research, which derives from those earlier models, is concerned with warming rather than cooling.

Although the environmental movement and early climate research had discovered the interconnectedness of the earth's life system and its vulnerability to human intervention, they remained relatively uninterested in its specific consequences for humankind. Hundreds of millions of deaths, the collapse of medical care, psychological disorders, water shortages, and famine—such was the dry list of horrors that scientists had to offer. Not scientific scenarios but fiction set out to provide an internal perspective from the darkness of the winter in the aftermath of a nuclear attack, be it as a survival community in *The Day After*, as a pack of motorcycle rockers fighting a Hobbesian war in the Mad Max trilogy (1980, 1981, 1985), as a struggle for survival in a crumbling wintery city in Paul Auster's *The Country of Last Things* (1987), or—more recently—as hopeless survivors of unnamed disasters in Michael Haneke's film *Time of the Wolf* (2003) and Cormac McCarthy's novel *The Road* (2006).[50] Auster's and McCarthy's novels take place in wintery cold weather; Haneke's film contains long stretches of darkness, rain, or pale light. Here, climate is cast as the very expression of dire social and material conditions. Winter implies vulnerability and resource scarcity; it is a situation in which everything depends on securing a space of warmth, security, and provision—either with others or against them.

The nuclear-winter scenario, too, is a catastrophe without event. Even though it is triggered at a particular place and time, the impact pales in comparison with its global consequences. It is a side effect of destruction;

it unfolds belatedly, and its consequences are indirect. In this regard, the failure of photosynthesis and the extinction of insects are more important than the question of how many people have died in the nuclear blast itself. A catastrophe without event is also one without a specific location. As a global disaster, there is nowhere to take refuge. Nuclear winter is thus an ironic commentary on the fantasy of control and rationality that pervaded the other Cold War scenarios. Humanity will annihilate itself, though unintentionally and indirectly, and with it, life as we know it.

THE FRAILTY OF EVERYTHING: CLIMATE IN McCARTHY'S *THE ROAD*

McCarthy's drastic novel *The Road* is a radical analysis of what will remain of humanity in this catastrophic scenario. In a strangely monotone style, the novel tells the story of a journey: A man wanders with his young son through a barren landscape in the middle of a winter that does not ever seem to end. All the plants have died, the snow is as gray as ash, it is grim and cold, and the never-ending winter is one of hunger and permanent danger. Traveling south toward the coast in the hope that it might be warmer there, they transport their few but vital possessions in a shopping cart. Other survivors live in groups that hunt, capture, and eat other humans—a biopolitical worst-case scenario, dealt with in detail in the next chapter. The father's one and only concern is to ensure his son's survival. Again and again, they have to defend themselves from cannibals, hide, and flee; again and again, the father must refuse to help other people, despite his son's pleas to do so. The father and son reassure each other that they will never stoop to cannibalism. At the end of the novel, the father dies of exhaustion. The child is taken in by another family, and it remains open what will happen to him. The climate remains cold.

The success of this dark novel even baffled its author. It won several prizes, was selected for Oprah's Book Club, and was made into a movie starring Viggo Mortensen and Charlize Theron.[51] Celebrated as an eco-parable, the novel actually depicts the end of mankind as the end of nature. It is an anthropological experiment stripping away everything that makes humans human: the world, nature, elementary cultural taboos, the most basic rules of coexistence, and the meaning of things. Winter here is the climatic setting for this experiment in the destruction of civilization. As an image of a final climate, the winter proves that there can be no human civilization without nature being intact.

The surprising success of the novel, however, is not because of the precise rendering of the catastrophe but rather of the fact that this initial catastrophe remains entirely vague. Although the narrative dwells at length on its harrowing aftermath, the cause of the initial disaster is never explicitly mentioned. It could have been anything from a natural catastrophe to a nuclear attack. All the information we get is: "The clocks stopped at 1:17. A long shear of light and then a series of low concussions. He got up and went to the window."[52] The consequences, in contrast, are portrayed far more clearly: icy cold weather, gray snow, and pale, dim sunlight: "the noon sky black as the cellars of hell."[53] Nothing is alive; the plants are withered and charred. Ash continues to fall from the sky years after the catastrophe: "The land was gullied and eroded and barren. The bones of dead creatures sprawled in the washes. Middens of anonymous trash. Farmhouses in the fields scoured of their paint and the clapboards spooned and sprung from the wallstuds. All of it shadowless and without feature."[54] There must have been intense fires, for the asphalt of the streets has melted. Nearly all humans and animals who survived the firestorm have starved to death. There are no longer any fish in the rivers or seas, as the water has been polluted or poisoned. A gray wintery landscape under a gray wintery sky.

Although the initial catastrophe is only hinted at, the consequences betray its character. The world depicted in *The Road* is the world of the nuclear-winter scenario as devised by Crutzen/Birks and the TTAPS group: a world overshadowed by ash particles and toxic aerosol floating in the upper atmosphere and filtering sunlight to the point of making photosynthesis impossible. "Virtually all crops and farm animals, at least in the Northern Hemisphere, would be destroyed. . . . Most of the human survivors would starve," as the TTAPS group points out.[55] While there could be causes other than a nuclear strike—a comet strike, a volcanic eruption, or a chemical accident—the ubiquitous fires mentioned in the novel hint at atomic weapons as the cause of the disaster: "They sat at the window . . . and watched distant cities burn."[56] The melted streets, the raining ash, the scorched land are indicators of an atomic attack.

While staying clear of having the novel labeled as "nuclear apocalypse fiction," McCarthy nevertheless gives the reader enough hints to reconstruct the type of disaster in question. The novel's winter is manmade, sudden, and global, yet it consists in nature's reaction to human intervention. The most uncanny aspect of McCarthy's scenario—but also its radical topicality—lies in the fact that manmade disasters and natural disasters can no longer be separated.

By making their way south, the protagonists nevertheless attempt to escape from the cold around them: "There's no surviving another winter here."[57] However, as this wintery climate is global, there is no "outside," no "elsewhere." At the end of their journey, they stand on the shore of a lifeless sea, and though they have walked hundreds of miles farther south, climate and landscape have not become any more hospitable. Nothing is growing; there is nothing to eat, nothing alive. The winter is everywhere.

Everybody who is still alive is a survivor. Yet what does it mean to "survive" in a global winter? As Crutzen and Birks made clear, in a nuclear-winter scenario survivors are simply those who will die later: "It is . . . difficult to see how much more than a small fraction of the initial survivors of a nuclear war . . . could escape famine and disease during the following year."[58] It may be possible to survive an impact and the subsequent radiation (the manmade part of the disaster), but it will be impossible to survive the ensuing winter (the natural disaster). So the question is what "survival" can mean other than "dying a little later." The annihilation of nature leaves humans behind as the last living beings, and they have to serve as their own resource, leading up to a Malthusian disaster scenario, as I will analyze in the next chapter.

Postapocalyptic fiction—ranging from Mary Shelley's *The Last Man* (1826) to George A. Stewart's early Cold War novel *Earth Abides* (1949) or Alan Weisman's nonfiction work *The World Without Us* (2007)—usually opposes a pristine, if deserted, nature to the plight of humankind on the verge of extinction. Nature remains either untouched or revives once relieved of the presence of humans. If McCarthy's novel still shares some features with the tradition of the postapocalyptic novel, he nevertheless makes sure to present not only a very different picture of the Last Men but also a very different picture of nature. In *The Road*, nature does not return to creep quaintly over the ruins of human civilization—nature too is annihilated. Now that nature has ceased to exist, humans have become the last animal. The environment remaining after the end of nature consists of nothing more than its decaying remnants. So the cannibals roaming the landscape for prey represent an ultimate truth about mankind: as humanity has devoured the world, it has unveiled its intrinsic fragility, as the novel says: "The frailty of everything revealed at last."[59]

Looking at the remnants of humankind as the "last species," McCarthy's novel gauges what a world without humans would be—or could have been. The enigmatic ending of the novel, as I suggest we read it, hovers between the image of an intact nature *without people*, a wild and thriving nature outlasting the end of man, and a *world after people* forever bearing the marks of this species' presence. In the puzzling last paragraph of the book, the narrator turns away from the protagonists and addresses the reader, evoking the world before the disaster—just as the father spoke to his son, who never saw the world intact.[60] The paragraph recalls a token of the world that is now eradicated:

> Once there were brook trout in the streams in the mountains. You could see them standing in the amber current where the white edges of their fins wimpled softly in the flow. They smelled of moss in your hand. Polished and muscular and torsional. On their backs were vermiculate patterns that were maps of the world in its becoming. Maps and mazes. Of a thing which could not be put back. Not be made right again. In the deep glens where they lived all things were older than man and they hummed of mystery.[61]

The image of the trout is as mysterious as the paragraph itself. With its unreadable patterns, it is an image of the delicate puzzle that nature really was—a puzzle that has vanished along with the trout, which had once borne its "maps and mazes." What the picture expresses is humanity's relation to this bewildering nature, a relation suspended between two extremes: On the one hand, there is the instrumental rationality involved with catching a fish and holding it in one's hand; on the other, there is the contemplative astonishment about its mysterious patterns and the mossy strangeness of its smell. Beheld by a human gaze, grasped by a human hand, the trout is taken out of the mountain stream that is its element. The relation to nature symbolized by the grasping hand is one of exploitation, for we catch the trout to eat it. But humans are also capable of close observation and contemplation of natural signs. The patterns on the fish's back signify a logic of nature that exceeds anything human. The maps and mazes do not refer *to* humanity and are not *for* humanity; they are not decipherable in any technical or semiotic sense. Rather, they point beyond the physical body that bears them to the world at large in which the animal moves, mapping and symbolizing this world. They indicate the depths of time in which the world existed long before humankind. To hold a trout in one's hand is a relationship of "possession" and "mastery," a relationship described by Serres as the legacy of the Cartesian approach to the world: "Mastery and possession: these are the master words launched by Descartes at the dawn of the scientific and technological age, when our Western reason went off to conquer the universe.... Our fundamental relationship with objects comes down to war and property."[62]

Serres's critique opposes Cartesian knowledge with the "incredible knowledge of *meteora*"—an understanding of the "hovering," the atmospheric, the unpredictable within the system of life: "the place of disorder and the unforeseeable, of local danger, of the formless."[63] The maps and mazes on the trout's back belong to this realm, as do its sensuous qualities, the soft white edges of its fins, the mossy smell. They are tokens of a different approach to the world, the earthy, experience-led approach of "farmers" and "sailors," experts in the uncertainties of weather and climate.[64]

Yet there is even more to the trout than the allegory of both our instrumental grip on the world and our potential to contemplate a world beyond mankind. It is no coincidence that this trout happens to be a *brook* trout (*salvellinus fontinalis*). Its name refers to the source (Latin *fons*) in which it lives. Its place of origin is one in which, as the novel concludes, "all things were older than man and they hummed of mystery." The brook trout is one of the most sensitive varieties of its species; it cannot tolerate water pollution or variations of pH levels, oxygen content, or temperature. Its skin is especially delicate; to hold it in one's hand is to risk wiping off the layer of mucus that protects the animal from infection. The mysterious bearer of a prehuman world is thus also a symbol of absolute delicacy and frailty that, once damaged, "could not be put back."[65] Once touched by our coarse hands, the trout can no longer be returned to the water, as it will die. In a dual sense, it is something that cannot be put back, neither into the water nor restored. With its specific physique, sensitivity, and strangeness, it is a precise embodiment of the "frailty of everything" presented in McCarthy's catastrophic scenario. This frailty includes human beings and their social bonds as well as nature and its infinite, labyrinthine web of animals, plants, light, water, materials, and energy. The disintegration of this web, which is both delicate and potent, is that which cannot be "made right again."

GLOBAL WARMING AND THE POLITICS OF EVIDENCE

No spring will follow this long winter of catastrophe. It is a *final climate*. Yet, unlike Romantic darkness that befalls mankind from the outside, it is also a demonstration of the power possessed by human beings. The irony is that this winter, while manmade, is not an intentional aspect of nuclear warfare but an uncontrolled side effect. With the notion of a global nuclear winter, climate is no longer a thing of nature but an object, a result of human history. Nature and human technology can no longer be separated. Yet unlike the autumnal scenario of natural and gradual extinction on a slowly cooling planet, it is caused by a single decision. In this act of will, humankind of the Anthropocene can make itself lord over nature one final time.

The atomic scenario remains based on the idea that the catastrophe would be the result of a *decision*. The scenario of global warming, on the contrary, lacks this dimension of an identifiable agency and a moment of contingent decision making. Global warming does not come with a flash of lightning or the keying in of the launch codes. It does not have a single origin but an endless number of factors and agents contributing to it. It is manmade, like nuclear winter, but it is made by *anonymous* and *countless* human beings. It cannot be tested by means of experimentation but only anticipated in simulation models or extrapolated from heterogeneous data. Climate change is therefore not a catastrophe in the traditional sense of the Greek word *katastrophē*; it is not an abrupt "downward turn." Rather, it is the most uncanny version of a catastrophe without event. Its slow gradual warming shows how, in Paul Crutzen's words, "mankind is capable of creating a catastrophe both unwittingly and unintentionally."[66]

This is the insight contained in the concept of the Anthropocene, first suggested by Crutzen. The world is now in the hands of multiple, uncoordinated agents who have no idea what they are doing.[67]

Like the scenario of climatic cooling, global warming, too, is a *longue durée* process consisting of inconspicuous, incremental changes. These slow changes are hard to represent—and thus equally hard to set on the stage of political negotiations. How to "show" an abstract, slow, and incremental process? One option is to represent climate through weather events: a flood, a giant tornado, hail storms, and a deep freeze (as in *The Day After Tomorrow*); a glistening heat wave and drought (as in the German film *Hell* from 2011, a hot and bright version of McCarthy's dark and cold *The Road*); or a monstrous hurricane (as in Bruce Sterling's novel *Heavy Weather* from 1994). In a different vein, the change in climate can be made palpable through the eyes of a particularly qualified protagonist, a narrative pattern adopted by many of the more recent novels. Ilija Trojanow's novel *The Lamentations of Zeno* (2011), for instance, adopts the angry perspective of a glaciologist whose object of research, a glacier in the Alps, has melted away. Zeno therefore has to work as a tour guide on an Antarctic cruise ship. The ruined life of the scientist and the sullying of the pristine landscape of Antarctica by tourism provide a perspective for a process that is simply *not* evident. Barbara Kingsolver's *Flight Behavior* (2012) works in a similar way, by illustrating the growing awareness of climate change from the perspective of a young, uneducated housewife named Dellarobia Turnbow, who notices that the migratory patterns of monarch butterflies have changed drastically. Numerous examples of generic climate fiction ("cli-fi") have treated extreme climates as tokens of an imminent and sinister future. Novels such as Octavia Butler's *The Parable of the Sower* (1993), Will Self's *The Book of Dave* (2006), T. C. Boyle's *A Friend of the Earth* (2000), Jean-Christophe Rufin's *Globalia* (2004), and Paolo Bacigalupi's *The Water Knife* (2015) use the potential effects of global warming—from an oven-hot California to a flooded London—as the backdrop for their dystopian plots.

Climate change may be a catastrophe without event, but this does not mean that nothing happens. It involves a variety of local scenarios and symptoms but is hard to represent "as such." Gradual warming lacks the perceptibility of an ice age or the brutal suddenness of a flood or nuclear winter. Even if certain tipping points can theoretically be predicted, the consequences of a shift of the entire system often cannot. And the tipping point itself is hard to anticipate—before it is reached, everything seems to be following its normal course. Some texts and films dealing with climate change have taken this very problem of representability as their point of departure. Their challenge is to find images to illustrate a process that does not consist of situations or events.

In the early 2000s, amid the heated debate between climatologists and self-proclaimed skeptics about the scientific evidence for climate change, it is a question of creating visual evidence. Emmerich's *The Day After Tomorrow* (2004) simply resorts to weather disasters, assisted by a choice of protagonists from climate science, providing handy explanations about the climatic background of the strange weather. In spite of its brilliant images, even climate scientists were quick to debunk Emmerich's scenario as being far from realistic.

A different approach to representing climate change is to abandon the idea of a global perspective. The climatologist James Powell's fictitious "oral history" of the future offers an array of local scenarios, from the flooded Netherlands to huge droughts and famines.[68] Even though the book is meant to underscore the ubiquity of the disaster brought about by climate change, it also demonstrates how various and unjust the local consequences of global warming might be. Minor floods are imagined beside harrowing droughts, falling property prices alongside the deaths of millions of refugees.

Coming out in the early 2000s, during a contentious debate about the accuracy of climate-change predictions and the reality of climate change, Al Gore's award-winning "slide show" *An Inconvenient Truth* tackles the problem of a general representation of climate change in a more didactic manner.[69] Gore kicks off his slide show with an old symbol of the environmental discourse, the famous photograph *Earthrise* (fig. 2.2). It presents Earth from outer space, rising over the horizon of the moon, as a delicate and unique miracle in the universe. In Carl Sagan's words: "From Earth's orbit you are struck by the tender blue arc of the horizon—Earth's atmosphere seen tangentially. You can understand why there is no longer such a thing as a local environmental problem."[70] The external view of the planet not only evokes the fragility of its thin protective layer but also illustrates the meaning of the word "global." There is no place on earth that would *not* be affected by any changes in the atmosphere.

FIGURE 2.2 According to Al Gore, the environmental movement began with this photograph, *Earthrise*, which opens his documentary *An Inconvenient Truth* (2006). The image of Earth from outer space demonstrates the totality of the globe but also its fragility.

Source: Still from *An Inconvenient Truth* (2006).

Gore follows *Earthrise* with a cascade of images, from photographs to graphs and even comic strips, all aiming to provide evidence, that is, visual proof, for the fact of climate change: glaciers that have all but disappeared over the course of just thirty years, graphs illustrating the recent spike in rising temperatures, computer animations that simulate the flooding of large coastal cities, and an animated film that mockingly explains the greenhouse effect "for children." The idea behind this flood of images is to visualize the slow process of global warming, fast-forwarding natural processes via time-lapse recordings, simulations, before-and-after photos, or graphs. The images are supposed to transform the latency and unrepresentable nature of gradual climate change into bodies of evidence that could then be the basis of sound environmental politics.

Gore, however, doesn't rely solely on the power of visual evidence. He adds a narrative that fuses isolated data—such as local temperatures, CO_2 levels, and their fluctuations—into a general scenario. A bright red and sharply rising line on a graph (displayed without a scale) is explained as follows: "This is the image that started me in my interest in this issue, and

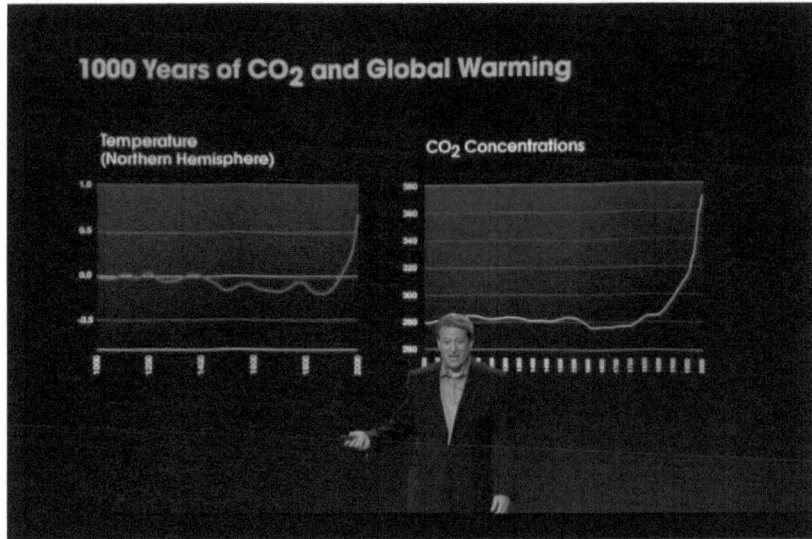

FIGURE 2.3 One thousand years of rising CO_2 levels (right) and global temperatures (left) in Al Gore's *An Inconvenient Truth*. The film aims at creating simple visual evidence by presenting the two parallel graphs in the form of the famous "hockey stick."

Source: Still from *An Inconvenient Truth* (2006).

I saw it when I was a college student" (fig. 2.3). The graph was first shown to Gore by his professor Roger Revelle, one of the first geochemists to study the rise of CO_2 levels in the atmosphere: "He saw where the story was going after the first few chapters.... He drew the connections between the larger changes in our civilization and this pattern that was now visible in the atmosphere of the entire planet. And then he projected into the future where this was heading unless we made some adjustments. *It was just as clear as that.*" Gore's technique of creating evidence both by displaying visual proof and adding a narrative that offers a clear-cut trajectory of past and future events has both an educational and a political intent. In the first decade of the 2000s, it was more than necessary to inform the audience at large about the widespread scientific consensus about climate change as a reality, in the face of self-proclaimed "climate skeptics," who contested both the scientific evidence and the extent of the consensus.[71] Gore clearly has this goal in mind with his documentary. However, climate research is not as clear as Gore portrays it.

In his study on the history of climate research, Paul Edwards has pointed to some of the deeper epistemological complications of climate research. From the outset, the transition from local and nonstandardized meteorological data to a universal model has been riddled with innumerable problems. To give a global and long-term picture of climatic dynamics, data were needed that relied upon common standards, standards that had to be painstakingly established and implemented throughout the nineteenth and twentieth century. Nonstandardized or incomplete data, Edward explains, lead to "data friction."[72] Incompatible data thus undermined the creation of a global set of knowledge: "It's like trying to make a movie out of still photographs shot by millions of different photographers using thousands of different cameras."[73]

Beyond this, climatology depends on large-scale simulation models. Each model, however, "reads" the data in a different way, in order to integrate them into an overall picture—a picture, however, that the isolated data might contradict. That there is a cooling trend in certain areas of the world doesn't, however, mean that there is no global warming. The hypothetical nature of simulation models has nevertheless been used by climate skeptics as evidence of their unreliability and thus for the lack of trustworthiness in any scientific research pointing to a global warming trend. What cannot be tested empirically, the "skeptic" argument goes, must necessarily be "false" or "unreliable."

This confusion is, in fact, created by an outdated, fallacious conception of science as only reliable if based on replicable experiments, finite and homogeneous datasets, and physically secure evidence. In contrast, as Edward's history of climatology reveals, scientific knowledge about climate consists of what he calls "shimmering data":

> The climate knowledge infrastructure is constantly opening itself up, reexamining every datum and data set, reanalyzing its data, adding to its metadata. Over time, countless iterations of that process have brought us shimmering data, an ever-expanding collection of global data images that will keep on growing, but never resolve into a single definitive record.[74]

The use of models, the medium of computer simulation, and "shimmering," ever-reassessed data are not evidence for the invalidity of climate research but of the uniqueness of its hypercomplex object. Like molecular biology or physics, climate research relies on simulations and models that cannot simply be dismissed as "pure constructions" and consequently untrue.[75] The uncertain knowledge about long-term global climate will always rely on models and hypotheses—and thus a certain degree of "fiction." Whereas the inevitable fictions of such disciplines as safety engineering or technological impact assessment are accepted heuristic principles (as we will see in chapter 4), this aspect of climatology is used by deniers of anthropogenic climate change as a sweeping argument against an entire discipline and its findings.

The scenario of rising temperatures is undoubtedly the most uncanny of all catastrophes. It is, however, not a recent example of cli-fi but a book written long before the unsettling findings of the IPCC that succinctly elaborates this uncanniness. J. G. Ballard's novel *The Drowned World* (1962) begins with a seemingly harmless sentence: "Soon it would be too hot."[76] The novel is set in a world where intensified solar radiation and atmospheric depletion have caused worldwide temperatures to rise sharply. The polar ice caps and glaciers have mostly melted, submerging the big European cities in silt and water. London, where the novel is set, has become a tropical lagoon, its flora and fauna metamorphosing into that of the Triassic period. There are giant ferns, huge insects, and reptiles, while humans, reduced to a mere five million gathering around the poles, are almost the last mammals alive. A biologist by the name of Kerans stays in the submerged, swampy London while most of the small group of military and research personnel retreat to the cooler zones up north.

Kerans gets more and more drawn into the atmosphere of a transforming nature. Species devolve back into Paleozoic life forms adapted to the temperatures of the Triassic, clocks start running backward, and humans have intense dreams set in the deep time of paleohistory. As nature evolves (or devolves) in response to the heat and the high mutation rate caused by intensified radiation, the novel develops a theory of time as climate— and *climate as time*. The changes in the physical world go hand in hand with profound changes in the psychical world. One character tries to make sense of it:

> As we move back through geophysical time so we re-enter the amnionic corridor and move back through spinal and archaeopsychic time, recollecting in our unconscious minds the landscapes of each epoch, each with

a distinct geological terrain, its own unique flora and fauna, as recognisable to anyone else as they would be to a traveller in a Wellsian time machine.[77]

Observing the metamorphosis of life forms around him, Kerans longs "to descend through archaeopsychic time to reach its conclusion," a state before civilization, individuality, and even man.[78] He eventually heads farther south, traveling in the time machine of heat, while trying to escape the erratic violence of another character, Strangman, who tries to bring back a crude form of human civilization by draining the swamp in which London has drowned.

In Ballard's logic, heat is a reversal of time, an opening into an abyss of planetary past and a species memory that relates the modern individual back to a deep time of the becoming of life. Heat sets the human in relation to a prehistory that transcends civilization and consciousness. It is a posthuman force that ultimately will make the species disappear—just like the novel's protagonist, Kerans, who in the end vanishes into the jungle. Like the cooling in Flammarion's novel, heat triggers a reverse evolution. It not only brings about the return of primeval species; it also causes a reversion to mankind's primal psyche.

Long before the discovery of actual global warming, Ballard picks up the insights of the old theory of climate, which conceived of human beings as products of their climatic environment. His humans are imbued and transcended by the forces of climate. Kerans literally melts into the world around him:

> Kerans felt, beating within him like his own pulse, the powerful mesmeric pull of the baying reptiles, and stepped out into the lake, whose waters now seemed an extension of his own bloodstream. As the dull pounding rose, he felt the barriers which divided his own cells from the surrounding medium dissolving, and he swam forwards, spreading outwards across the black thudding water.[79]

Tapping into the old tradition of climate as a formative influence on bodies, minds, and civilization, Ballard flips climate, which used to be a local concept, onto a temporal axis: climate is *time*. In returning to the high temperatures of former planetary epochs, humans revert to the mindset of those epochs. Within the logic of the novel, humans become the medium of a planetary deep time expressed in their innermost reflections, desires, dreams, social behavior. If climate is the shorthand for environmental influences, Ballard takes this idea to its most radical conclusion.

Ballard's novel lacks the political rhetoric of today's climate fictions. It is neither a lament nor a depiction of a dystopian future but rather a narrative experiment that addresses humanity's deep relation to climate. It formulates an aesthetics of heat that demonstrates how an altered climate might affect human culture and psyche.[80] Here, climate appears as a medium of history that both encompasses and goes beyond the mere history of mankind. The phantasmagoric forest into which Ballard's protagonist disappears is an environment that is both his inner world and its external manifestation. Imagining global warming as an anthropological process, Ballard presents an insight about climate change that goes deeper than the overtly political catastrophe rhetoric of Gore, Emmerich, Kingsolver, Trojanov, and many others. Ballard depicts climate as a cultural and psychical force, a historical reservoir of all the species' forms of existence and also of our individual dreams, agonies, and memories.

Climate imagination, as we have seen, does not just revolve around a change of environment. With the climate, humankind also changes, be it by devolving into a prehistoric state, as in the cooling scenarios of the nineteenth century or Ballard's fantasy of heat, or by losing any trace of humaneness, as in the abrupt death of nature in the nuclear-winter scenario as imagined in *The Road*. Climate is both within us and outside of us; it is both our environment and our innermost essence. As the old concept of climate (from Aristotle to Montesquieu and Herder) implied, climate is the *place* in which humans interact with their environment, but, as modern climatology and climate history (from Cuvier to the experts on the IPCC) claim, climate is also the *time* that contains human history and evolution. It is internal and external time, time shaped by human beings but also large-scale planetary time. Climate being the medium that contains and preserves humanity, its disruption cannot fully be grasped and represented by the stark imagery of disaster. Climate change is a catastrophe without event. Nonetheless, even to begin to understand the scope of this disruption, all we have are narratives and images.

3

SURVIVAL

The Biopolitics of Catastrophe

ON HIGH ALERT: SURVIVAL MOVEMENTS

> *Anyone ... can unexpectedly find himself in a dangerous situation and should thus be familiar with basic survival techniques.... Even our everyday experience is full of dangers that threaten us and can, in the most extreme cases, take our lives. We are not even safe in our apartments or in our own homes.... The struggle for survival begins at our front door.*
>
> —HARALD KRUSE, *ÜBERLEBENSTECHNIK*

The moment you leave your front door, it's about survival. The survival manual quoted in this chapter's epigraph, however, is not concerned with the 925 million people who are currently living below the poverty line or in war zones and whose everyday experience is, in fact, a constant struggle to stay alive. Here, the survival writer Harald Kruse is addressing the broad movement of well-off citizens in Europe and the United States who are preparing for the worst by learning survival techniques. They read survival handbooks. They stock up on food and water, keep a large supply of gasoline on hand, and make sure that their field packs are ready at any moment. They live on properties a safe distance from the city, convert their backyards into vegetable farms, and learn how to catch and skin a rabbit. These so-called survivalists or preppers live in a constant state of alert.

They are preparing for an imminent catastrophe—for power, food, and water shortages; for ubiquitous violence; and for hunger, epidemics, and looting. In doing so, they have created and disseminated a highly specific type of knowledge: techniques for surviving outside of civilization. Originally developed by travelers, the military, and youth organizations such as the Boy Scouts for long journeys through inaccessible or treacherous terrain, the survival movement has, since the 1980s, been transformed into a permanent exercise in preparing for catastrophe.[1]

Whereas Kruse, for whom the struggle for survival begins "at our front door," still had in mind the dangers posed by traveling or wilderness sports, today's survival gurus are concerned with nothing less than outliving TEOTWAWKI ("the end of the world as we know it"). This acronym is the common denominator of the many different shades of the survivalist mindset. It nails down their conviction that "the catastrophe" is likely to happen and is imminent. Yet no one knows exactly what form it will take. The present attitude toward catastrophe is no longer focused on a specific scenario but rather on an unpredictable breakdown of existing conditions. No one knows for sure what this transition will look like, beyond that it will involve the utter collapse of infrastructure and the disintegration of social order. When faced with a threat so diffuse, there can be only one imperative: Be prepared![2]

The Cold War had been preoccupied with the singular and overwhelming disaster scenario of a nuclear strike: a local (though large-scale) attack with shock waves, conflagrations, deaths, and radiation sickness followed by long-term consequences such as increased mortality rates and physical deformities. Herman Kahn's infamous book *On Thermonuclear War* filled hundreds of pages with statistics and scenarios depicting the potential destruction.[3] During the 1980s, nuclear attack, which experts like Kahn had played out in countless variations, was expanded into a global scenario—nuclear winter. In the wake of the environmental movement and the 1986 disaster at Chernobyl, nuclear disaster expanded to include additional scenarios of widespread radiation poisoning: radioactivity in food and water, supply shortages, consequences detrimental for generations to come, and so on. But compared with this relatively manageable catalogue of disasters of the nuclear age, today's survival guides and websites are concerned with a nearly unfathomable portfolio of catastrophes. Under the header "How to Survive (Almost) Anything," the homepage of *National Geographic Adventure,* for instance, has links to articles about how to survive the following "unthinkable" scenarios: a tsunami, a drought, a megafire, a power-grid failure, a pandemic, a failed state, and a GPS meltdown.[4] Today, the range of possible scenarios has become entirely heterogeneous: The failure of infrastructure and information networks or the breakdown of state institutions are given the same weight as natural or manmade disasters such as environmental catastrophes, major technical accidents, or nuclear attacks. Local disasters of the type discussed by *National Geographic* are supplemented with globally devastating events such as meteor strikes or the eruption of a supervolcano. People have also been advised to arm themselves against "economic collapse" and "the coming apocalypse," among other things.[5] While disaster is just around the corner, its concrete form is entirely uncertain. Therefore, the art of survival can only consist of being ready for anything.

Today's lack of clarity about what form disaster will take changes the type of advice about how to survive after doomsday. The relation between survival techniques and the anticipated disaster has today not only become more dramatic but also more confusing than in the late 1950s and 1960s. British and American campaigns to prepare society for a nuclear attack during the Cold War are notorious for their comically infantile tone and for trivializing the threat: "Alert Today—Alive Tomorrow." In educational films of the 1950s, a cartoon character named Bert the Turtle urged people to "duck and cover" under a table or against a wall to protect themselves from falling debris (fig. 3.1). To counteract fallout, housewives were advised to keep the house as dust free as possible, while fathers were given instructions for building a private underground shelter for their family (fig. 3.2). According to Guy Oakes, civil defense against a nuclear attack was presented as a "do-it-yourself enterprise" that ultimately depended on "the traditional American virtues of self-determination, personal responsibility, and voluntary cooperation."[6]

The threat scenario began to change as early as the 1970s. With a growing awareness for the environment and the precariousness of the Western lifestyle brought about by inflation and the oil crisis, survivalism came into fashion as a retreat from urban civilization and into "nature." Don and Barbie Stephen's *The Survivor's Primer and Up-Dated Retreater's Bibliography* from 1976, for instance, provides advice about how to build a safe refuge in the country because, in the event of a catastrophe, it was

FIGURE 3.1 Bert the Turtle was the main character of the American civil-defense film *Duck and Cover* (1951). It explains to children how to protect themselves against a nuclear attack by crawling under a table and covering their heads. The film is noteworthy for implying that an attack has to be expected at any time and for understating the nature of the threat.

Source: Cover of the comic book *Duck and Cover* (1951).

understood that one would need to flee the city as quickly as possible. Actually, shortly after the publication of their book, the authors moved from California to the mountains in the northwestern United States, in order to be in safety even before any potential crisis. As the nature of impending danger became increasingly diffuse, simple survival guidance provided by cartoon turtles was no longer enough. Instead, preparing for catastrophe became a way of life.

Already here we can identify the core idea of later survival movements. It is a matter of going entirely "off the grid," eliminating one's dependency on state-run infrastructure and luxuries such as grocery stores. It is about providing for oneself. In the event of a catastrophe, not only will it no longer be possible to trust modern technologies, but the government and

FIGURE 3.2 The cover of Chuck West's *Fallout Shelter Handbook* (1962). The manual contains nutritional tips, recipes, bunker-building instructions, and advice about how to administer first aid, disinfect drinking water, etc. The first chapter explains "How You Can Survive a Nuclear War."

Source: Copyright: Penguin Random House/Reproduction: Ward Jenkins.

the economy will also be useless. They will neither be able to maintain "public order" nor ensure the availability of basic provisions. Thus, in the eyes of "retreaters," survival entails fleeing to the deep countryside—and then coping with life there.

It is the diffuse nature of today's catastrophe scenarios that have made the ways of preparing for them so much more complex. Many recent survival websites have thus stopped talking about "preparedness" and instead emphasize "resilience," among them the website waldenlabs.com, operated by the military and business consultant John Robb. Robb makes a point of mocking preppers who hoard a few groceries and always keep a full tank of gas but are not ready for a long-term collapse of all infrastructure: "A prepper may be concerned with short-term survival following a catastrophe, resiliency dictates that we plan for long-term success; now and in an increasingly uncertain future."[7] The movement's slogan is "Don't just survive, thrive!" Whereas traditional survivalists plan for brief breakdowns of the system, members of the resilience movement organize their entire lives in such a way as to rely as little as possible on official infrastructure. They produce their own electricity with solar panels and their own protein by keeping rabbits and chickens (which is easier than raising cattle but more difficult than growing beans). They have their own water cisterns, their own vegetable gardens, and so on. Here, self-sufficiency is meant to solve two problems at the same time: On the one hand, the resilient lifestyle is supposed to lead to ecological sustainability; on the other, it enables people to be ready for the potential collapse of state infrastructure. The focus is no longer on the mere preparation for catastrophes but rather on the ability to be affected minimally by them, to limit their impact, or to remove oneself from harm's way as quickly as possible.

What is noteworthy about both the government-sponsored civil-defense programs as well as the private survival/prepper programs is that they are exclusively concerned with the individual and his or her nuclear family. *Duck and Cover* had addressed the population of the United States as a conglomeration of individual households that should hole up at home and protect themselves. According to such educational campaigns, traditional family values could be counted on as effective measures against shock waves, fallout, and radiation. For the more recent retreater and survivalist movements, the idea is to abandon (urban) society in order to survive as individuals. The basic conviction is that survival strategies only work for individuals or individual families, that larger groups of people themselves represent a threat, not something to fall back on. "In anticipation of imminent mass destruction," according to Uta Kornmeier, "the survival movement concentrates above all on the manageable and controllable survival of the individual, who is generally preparing for the breakdown of civil order and a possible retreat away from cities and into the forest."[8] It is possible to understand this, as does Kornmeier, as an example of the "individualization" that sociologists, in the wake of Ulrich Beck, have identified as a key feature of modern industrial society and the so-called risk society. Whereas the risks involved with nuclear power, pollution, and climate change were once democratized, risk prevention has since increasingly become, according to Beck, a matter of self-reliance and personal responsibility. Survivalists have responded to this loss of security and growing instability by emphasizing the autarky of the individual.[9]

Yet this is not just a matter of individualization; it is also a matter of creating *different* forms of community, ones characterized by a deep mistrust of the state's capacity to deal with catastrophe. On survivalist forums and blogs, there is constant discussion about how to build social networks and communities that will, when the time comes, prove to be "catastrophe proof." The resilience movement differs from the preppers in its desire to develop sustainable social networks in which, among other things, knowledge and goods can be exchanged. Other survivalist platforms have likewise recommended forming reliable small groups in preparation for the catastrophe to come.[10] And no introduction to the art of survival fails to mention the lack of solidarity in society, occasionally with strongly xenophobic undertones, as in the case of the German website ernstfall.org.[11] The catastrophic imaginary, the impetus behind the survival movement, does not just revolve around the dream of an entirely autonomous individual. It also dreams up a new and different kind of community that will arise and endure in the face of impending disaster. It is concerned with the possibilities of creating a *community as a survival community*. In this regard, survivalists are unanimous in their belief that, in the case of emergency, state institutions and public infrastructure cannot be relied upon. It is this anti-institutional attitude that makes them retreat from government authority or develop alternative social networks. They regard institutions and infrastructures not only as oppressive but above all as fundamentally weak. The ultimate survivalist goal of self-sufficiency is thus an expression of deep insecurity, of a strong sense of society's fragility. Be it by retreating to the wilderness, changing one's lifestyle, or forming informal networks, the resilience movement believes that the only way an individual can be saved in the event of a catastrophe is by him- or herself. In this sense, the catastrophe in question is also a revelation, an apocalypse. It brings to light the fragility and unreliability of government authority and existing social bonds. The events in the wake of Hurricane Katrina in 2005, for instance, were seen as a glaring example of this. It is for such cases that the survival and resilience movements are preparing: Social order, they believe, can be brought down by a single storm, stockmarket crash, flood, or epidemic.

THE PATHOS OF EMERGENCY

The survival movement's profound skepticism toward institutions is only one way that the popular imagination contemplates communities facing a catastrophe. Just as widespread as this isolationist take on disaster is its opposite: the idea of the community rising up to face adversity. The conviction that the next disaster—of whatever sort—is imminent, that self-reliance is the only way to overcome it, and that radical autonomy thus represents the only chance for survival is countered by the pathos of communities who, activated by crises, come together in acts of spontaneous solidarity. In the event of an emergency, it is hoped that unexpected forms of practical assistance will appear out of the blue and that heroes will occasionally emerge. Individuals will sacrifice themselves for the group, strangers will help strangers, resources will be shared, and the tasks at hand will be tackled communally. Such, at least, is the hope. Nothing else can explain the bubbly enthusiasm with which news stories celebrate, in lengthy reports, any act of neighborly goodwill and solidarity whenever a natural disaster occurs. Minor disasters—such as the floods in 1997, 2002, 2006, and 2013 in Germany or Hurricane Sandy on the American East Coast in 2012—are always discussed in terms of the astounding civil order and practical humanity that they occasioned.

Nevertheless, it may be doubted whether emergencies really bring out the best and noblest in us—or whether some other impulses might not be at play. Byron's early thought experiment in "Darkness" about mankind's readiness for disaster reaches a devastating conclusion, and McCarthy's catastrophic vision in *The Road*, which I will revisit here, is hardly more optimistic. Yet it is clear that catastrophe brings something to light that is difficult to perceive as long as civilization is intact, when provisions are readily available, and infrastructure is functioning. No one trusts the solidarity of his neighbors in an acute emergency. Yet it may be a thrill to play it out in a thought experiment. Herein lies the very appeal of catastrophe fictions. They enable the analysis of a society's fragility while outsourcing it to a distant future, to the imagination, or to science fiction. This space allows people to develop and play through ideas that in fact lurk as realities beneath the surface of our civilization and our social bonds.

The catastrophe fictions of modernity carry out crisis experiments in a grand style. Disaster is depicted as an irruption of the Real—or, more precisely, as a *fantasy* of such an irruption.[12] This fantasy of a reality that only manifests itself during states of emergency motivates the preparations of survivalists as much as it fuels the emotional reaction to citizens piling up sandbags during a flood. It is a fantasy based on the belief that catastrophe will bring out the true face of society—be it a smile of unexpected solidarity or a grimace of chaos, lawlessness, and brutality. Forcing us out of civilization's cocoon, the emergency will supposedly reveal our true nature as social beings. The imagined crisis, after all, will expose certain aspects of society under heightened conditions, from mutual assistance or heroic self-sacrifice to radical self-defense and the simple and brutal striving for survival. Catastrophe thus enables a particular form of experimental knowledge: It demonstrates whether certain bonds are sustainable and whether certain forms of solidarity are possible, while also revealing which all-too-human impulses—weakness, egoism, or even cruelty—must also be considered. It shows which values and assets really matter, which communities can stick together, and which decisions might need to be made: decisions between friends and enemies but also decisions about who should survive and who should be left behind.

As opposed to real catastrophes, of course, fictitious catastrophes enjoy the advantage of narrative hindsight. For however bloody they might be, they never suffer from the chaos and unpredictability that make genuine disasters so traumatic. Fictitious depictions of catastrophe (usually) concentrate on those individuals fortunate enough to survive. Their events focus on characters who will make it in the end and have acted in a heroic, decent, or at least helpful manner. The narrative perspective is that of the survivors and the virtuous. Thus they allow us to identify with their protagonists while, as spectators, maintaining a reflective position, a gaze from the outside. In this way, such fictions impose narrative order on disaster. They tell their stories from a perspective that is "right" in hindsight because it is the perspective of those who have survived and thus made the "right" decisions during the moments of chaos. At the same time, this perspective also shares the viewpoint of the victims, for it is positioned within the disaster. This is how the double perspective—from both inside and outside the disaster—can convey a reality effect: "This is the reality. This is the view of those who were affected. This is how things 'really' were."

BLOOD TIES: THE BIOPOLITICS OF CATASTROPHE

The twentieth century produced thousands of such fictitious catastrophe scenarios, devised in response to the collective anxieties of its major epochs. Whereas such depictions involved degeneration and a "war of the worlds" at the turn of the century, total enmity over the course of the two World Wars, and, during the Cold War, an invisible enemy (either foreign or native) that had infiltrated society, more recent scenarios have increasingly featured natural catastrophes, resource shortages, epidemics, or the utter destruction of the environment. Despite the differences between these scenarios and their respective protagonists, their common theme is always the path of a community forced to become a community of survivalists. A group or a society is put to the test: What has to be done for that community to survive? The disaster scenarios play out on various scales. Sometimes it is just the population of a village or a city that is hit by a disaster—be it killer bees, earthquakes, fires, or even a local nuclear strike (which a small American town had to endure, for instance, in the 1983 movie *The Day After*). Sometimes, and especially during the Cold

War, an entire nation (usually the United States) is attacked by Soviet stand-ins such as aliens, zombies, or monsters. Most often, however, catastrophe fictions are concerned with nothing less than the community of *humankind as a whole*. Cold War disaster fictions, in particular, involve either humankind awaiting its imminent demise (for instance, in Shute's *On the Beach*, Kubrick's *Dr. Strangelove*, or Lumet's *Fail-Safe*) or Last Men struggling to survive the invasion of an evil nonhuman species (*The Invasion of the Body Snatchers* [1956, 1978, 2007 as *The Invasion*], *The Day the Earth Stood Still* [1951]). Humanity, this is the general message, comes together to fight against a nonhuman form of life, such as Martians, intelligent machines, mutants, animals, or zombies.

The first example of this scenario is H. G. Wells's *War of the Worlds*, first published in 1898. Its core idea was that humanity must defend the earth from alien attackers. Through this common endeavor, humankind discovers its species solidarity *as humanity*. The vulnerability of the entire species—the possibility of humanity's collective death, stylized during the Cold War into an oddly appealing fantasy—calls for a new solidarity of humankind that transcends cultural and political differences. In all of the later adaptations of the *War of the Worlds*—Orson Welles's radio play (1938) and the films by Byron Haskin (1953), Piotr Szulkin (1983), and Steven Spielberg (2005)—as well as in movies such as Roland Emmerich's *Independence Day* (1996), M. Night Shyamalan's *Signs* (2004), or Marc Forster's *World War Z* (2013)—the primary lesson is that only a united humanity will ever be able to muster the forces to overcome such an enemy.[13] With striking regularity, fictions about the end of the world are apotheoses of a global community that can only come into being under the condition of impending annihilation.

Juxtaposed to this worldwide community of humankind formed under the pressure of maximal threat is always a highly familiar microcommunity: the nuclear family. Its salvation or restoration provides the basic plot to most catastrophe narratives. If, as Georg Seeßlen and Markus Metz have remarked, "the wicked die, the virtuous are sacrificed, and the valuable are spared," then the family represents the "valuable" entity that deserves to be saved.[14] The family is saved in a dual sense: its members have to survive, but the family must also remain together or be reunited as such in order to start a new life. There is no place for a divorcee or a patchwork family in the classical popular disaster plot. In this regard, the nuclear family serves as a simple and obvious model for a "proper" form of community: an unbreakable and biologically established union beyond all optionality. When it comes down to survival, most disaster fictions suggest that neither friendships nor human solidarity will matter, only tight knots of kinship. Singles are usually killed off or give themselves up voluntarily. Patchwork families—as in Emmerich's *2012*, for instance—are "cleansed" of invaders such as the wife's second husband so that the original family can be restored. Most of Hollywood's conventional disaster films are thus little more than either romances to bring a couple together or tales of family reunion. A few individuals are saved in the foreground while the masses die in the background. The German author Kathrin Röggla remarks on this generally conservative undertone of current disaster movies:

> Recent productions have mainly focused on the restoration of *one family*, which is trying to reunite and usually succeeds in doing so, even while *the rest of the world* is falling apart. It's as if there is a desire to repeat Margaret Thatcher's legendary claim: "There is no such thing as society. There are only individuals and families."[15]

The communities that survive are either communities that fight or nuclear families—communities, in any case, whose bonds are based on blood, the blood shared by kin or the blood shed by the enemy. Beyond an ideological fixation on "individuals and families," I believe that there is something more at work here, namely, an underlying *biopolitical program* of catastrophe narratives. They showcase, as Nitzan Lebovic has observed, "a society that sees itself *mediated* through an historical model of a catastrophe (of 'all against all') and of the regulation and regeneration following it."[16] The fantasy of catastrophe as an irruption of the Real (Žižek) hinges precisely on the feedback between biological life and politics that led Michel Foucault to coin the term "biopolitics" in the first place: "For millennia, man remained what he was for Aristotle: a living animal with the additional capacity for a political existence; modern man is an animal whose politics places his existence as a living being in question."[17] Modernity has turned life into the true object of the political: population politics, social security, health care, and policies of risk prevention being its main components. Both protective and highly disciplinary, these elements of modern biopolitics are part of the state's genuinely modern concern for the biological life and survival of its population. In biopolitics, the primary instruments are not laws, rights, and punishments, that is, the judicial dimension of power, but rather the control and regulation of life through a specific form of governmentality concerned with the body of a population (its health, its reproduction, its demographic structure, its consumption styles, etc.). Biopolitics is thus not an expression of legal sovereignty but rather the administration of life's processes at the Malthusian level of populations. In the words of Thomas Lemke, "it deals with legal subjects that are at the same time living beings."[18] This modern manifestation of politics has, as Roberto Esposito has pointed out, an intrinsic catastrophic dimension:

> The object of politics is no longer a "life form" . . . but rather life itself—all life and only life, in its mere biological reality. Whether an individual life or the life of the species involved, life itself is what politics is called upon to make safe, *precisely by immunizing it from the dangers of extinction threatening it*.[19]

This task of immunization, however, is one that constantly requires politics to intervene in life; it is a task of segregating populations, letting people die, killing, or exposing people to death. While biopolitics is (according to its own logic) concerned with inhibiting, repelling, and preventing the imminent threat of life's extinction, it deploys death as one of the instruments to preserve and enhance life. It is an ongoing attempt to ward off catastrophe—even as this endeavor is itself heading toward catastrophe.

As Giorgio Agamben has recently argued, biopower is not only the ability to produce and support life. It has always also been the power to kill in the name of life. It suspends rights and laws in order to generate "bare life" that is essentially exposed to death, as Agamben has shown in the figure of *homo sacer*.[20] "Unhealthy" forms of life have to be prevented, "worthless" or infested life has to be eradicated, "anormal" bodies have to be kept from reproducing, and competing or inimical life forms have to be eliminated. According to Foucault, twentieth-century racism, ethnic cleansing, segregation, mass sterilizations, and wars have to be seen as part and parcel of a politics of life whose flip side has always been a politics of death. Biopolitics "is primarily a way of introducing a break into the domain of life that is under power's control: a break between what must live and what must die."[21] Biopolitics is thus always "thanatopolitics"—the paradox of killing to prevent death, that is, exterminating certain individuals or groups to prevent the extinction of the whole. The fundamental biopolitical decision is thus precisely this act of segregation: the separation of those who deserve to live from those who, in the name of life, have to die (or be prevented from being born). According to this inexorable biopolitical economy of life and death, the survival of one side has to be purchased with the death of the other.

WAR OF THE WORLDS

It is precisely this coupling of survival and death so central to modernity that has been exalted in scenarios of global catastrophe. People do not survive on account of their competence, virtue, or bravery, and neither are they spared because they have certain rights. Rather, they survive *because others die*. Depending on who has to die in a given catastrophic moment, however, there are two types of narratives—two types of political caesura. I would like to suggest that there is a modern and a postmodern narrative: a modern War of the Worlds and a postmodern Lifeboat Earth. The matrix for the former model, which is of a classically modern sort, was designed by H. G. Wells in *War of the Worlds*, which conveys a simple yet effective message: a common enemy must die in order for humanity to survive.

Wells's genre-defining work depicts an invasion of Martians who arrive on Earth in a cylinder, landing before the bewildered and curious population of southern England. As soon as their space capsule has cooled, they arm themselves with gigantic, three-legged fighting machines and immediately begin to eradicate people with heat rays and poison gas. An anonymous first-person narrator reports, in a journalistic tone, on the futile efforts of the British artillery to defeat the alien weapons. What he observes is the intentional slaughter of every person the Martians encounter, the destruction of houses and landscapes, and the depopulation of the entire region. Beyond the total annihilation of humanity, however, the Martians' goal remains entirely unclear. The destruction is harrowing, and mankind is utterly defenseless against it. Toward the end of the book, the narrator wanders through a corpse-strewn London in despair, hoping to be put out of his misery by the invaders, but they have suddenly vanished without a trace. He discovers that, miraculously, the Martians have all died. They were killed by an infection from terrestrial bacteria to which—unlike humans—they were not immune. Radically Darwinian in its outlook, Wells's novel is not about apocalyptic justice but rather about a biological confrontation between two species. In fact, any allusion to a religious interpretation of the event as apocalypse or divine judgment is treated with outright irony in the novel. At issue is rather a biological process: two species fighting over the same habitat. The Martians invaded Earth because their own planet had become too cold to support life. The surprising end of the invasion provides a textbook illustration of Darwin's theory that only those organisms will survive that are best suited to their environmental conditions. Unlike humans, the invaders are not equipped for life on earth, because they are not immune to its pathogens. Yet our fitness for our environment, as Wells reminds us, was not acquired without a price. The life-saving immunity of human beings to earthly bacteria came at the cost of millions of lives, or so the narrator explains: "By the toll of a billion deaths man has bought his birthright of the earth, and it is his against all comers. It would still be his were the Martians ten times as mighty as they are. For neither do men live nor die in vain."[22] Even the somewhat happy ending of the Martians' sudden death strengthens the biopolitical metanarrative of death for the sake of life. It is only by sacrificing millions that humanity was able to develop its immunities and thus its "fitness" to the earthly environment. At the heart of Wells's story is thus the basic motif of a Darwinian understanding of life: the struggle between two species over a limited habitat.

This sounds more imaginative than it really is. For at its core, the ineluctable life-and-death confrontation imagined by Wells is just an outline of the model of total enmity that would characterize the political rhetoric of the twentieth century. Already in Wells's novel, the enemy is defined by its radical otherness: different bodies, different sensory organs, different forms of communication, and scarcely ascertainable intentions that boil down to nothing but annihilation. The Martians do not consider the humans as an equal form of life, and vice versa. The attack against the humans is compared to a shoe stomping on an anthill. Wells's narrative of a war between two competing species thus elucidates an ontology of enmity that, starting with the rhetoric of the First World War, would pervade the political discourse of modernity throughout the Cold War and into the so-called War on Terror. Its core is the idea of an enemy that is not fighting for any particular reason and is not different in certain aspects but is rather radically and essentially different. On the basis of the enemy's radical otherness, a sense of community—vague and abstract but absolutely hostile—can be formed. This community is essentially one of aggression and defense; it is a community held together by the basic operations of surviving, killing, or dying. The enemy is simply the other who threatens my existence and therefore has to be resisted by all possible means (economic, intellectual, religious, military-technological, strategic, and so on). The German political philosopher Carl Schmitt placed this ontology of the total enemy at the center of his definition of the political. With the emergence of total enmity, Schmitt argues, a total war must ensue, erasing all limits that had restrained traditional warfare up to the end of the nineteenth century. In total war, there is no longer a sharp separation between combatants and civilians; now the hostility in question encompasses entire *populations*.[23] According to the theory of total enmity, conflicts no longer revolve around specific resources, territories, or liberties but rather around the mere *existence* of the adversary. The enemy is, in Schmitt's words, "the other, the stranger; and it is sufficient for his nature that he is ... existentially something different and alien." His strangeness, Schmitt continues, "negate[s] his opponent's way of life."[24] The total enemy is an enemy with whom there is no common basis of humanity; it is vermin at once super- and subhuman. For this reason, extraterrestrials have been the most prominent and popular representations of the total enemy.

It is well known how this ontology of the enemy became historically effective: The First World War was stylized, at least from a Continental European perspective, as a war between cultures in which, as Werner Sombart or Georg Simmel would have it, "merchants" went to battle against "heroes," "culture" against "civilization." War was cast as a confrontation in which incompatible cultural forms were fighting for their very existence.[25] Later, National Socialism's racist modeling of the enemy radicalized this version of existential, annihilatory hostility, which sees its own demise in the mere existence of the other. The Cold War would fall back on this model to cast the East-West conflict as a war of systems and worldviews. It is therefore no surprise that the most prominent catastrophe fictions from this period involve alien invasions. The primary point of these works is to imagine the enemy as invisible and omnipresent—especially in the various film adaptations of *The Invasion of the Body Snatchers*. A community whose cohesion is defined by hostility must constantly worry about the enemy infiltrating its ranks, "sleeping" unrecognized within it, like the "reds under the beds" or the 9/11 terrorists referred to as "sleepers." Here, the disaster lies in society's infiltration by an invisible enemy that, in the course of the plot, needs to be unveiled and eliminated.[26]

Later variants of the "war of the worlds" narrative, such as Roland Emmerich's congenial revival of the motif in his *Independence Day* (1996), would bring the modern ontology of enmity into the postmodern era.[27] With impressive imagery, *Independence Day* stages a threat scenario that resembles a technically updated version of Romantic darkness: The alien spaceships—depicted as colossal metal discs—darken the skies and cast their shadow upon a nearly defenseless humankind. By covering the sky like an evil cloud, the spaceships close off the openness of the human horizon (fig. 3.3). In step with Wells's Darwinism in *War of the Worlds*, Emmerich likewise presents the confrontation between humans and aliens in terms of a war of annihilation. At first glance, the humans are once again the underdogs, not least because some of them fail to grasp the nature of the threat and cheerfully welcome the invaders. Asked by the American president about what the aliens expect the humans to do, they respond with a single word: "Die!" Mutual extermination is the central theme of the movie. This annihilatory desire also gives rise to all of the forms of individual heroism typical of this type of disaster narrative. The male heroes are depicted as feisty fighters against the aliens, convincingly portrayed by Will Smith as a cocky African American bomber pilot and Jeff Goldblum as his Jewish intellectual sidekick, a team reflecting the multicultural message of the nineties. The female heroes display a hands-on readiness to take care of their children and communities and defend their families, a theme embodied by the male leads' respective wives. And in an ironic twist of Wells's microbial deus ex machina, team Smith and Goldblum infect the aliens with a computer virus that disables their defense system, rendering them vulnerable to terrestrial artillery.

FIGURE 3.3 The alien invasion in *Independence Day* (1996) alludes to the darkened sky of the Romantic end of the world. The alien spaceships cover the sky over human cities like tombstones. Yet instead of the melancholic contemplation of Romanticism, modernity's battle call is to fight against the looming end.

Source: Still from *Independence Day* (1996).

Yet this black-and-white stroke of genius is just the individual side of the struggle for survival. The threat of annihilation engenders a global community of fighters that Emmerich portrays with ample folkloric clichés. Before the decisive battle, the film displays a montage celebrating the worldwide brotherhood of man: Israelis cooperating with Arabs against the aliens, jubilant Africans dressed in traditional tribal garb and shaking spears at the sky, Asian people with looks of awe and astonishment, and finally Europeans speaking with British accents. Humankind comes together as one in the struggle against the invaders (figs. 3.4a, b).

Of course, all of this takes place under the leadership of the United States, which in classic Hollywood fashion can be counted on to save mankind. As a community, humanity is only able to conceive of itself as a whole when faced with an existential threat, and what ultimately unites it is nothing more or less than the biopolitical argument of blood ties: its existence as a species in a struggle against another species. The ending of *Independence Day* expresses this by unironically stating that, following the defeat of the invaders, all of humankind can now celebrate its new "Independence Day," which happens to coincide with the American Fourth of July. Aside from the patently chauvinist act of elevating

FIGURE 3.4 (a) In the end, humans are able to successfully resist the alien attempt to exterminate them in *Independence Day*. Around the world, alien spaceships come crashing down around famous landmarks such as the pyramids. (b) Emmerich depicts the human community as one of warriors, drawing heavily on national stereotypes and folkloristic imagery. In the global war between species, Africans, for instance, are depicted in traditional garb, shaking their spears.

Source: Stills from *Independence Day* (1996).

American symbols to those of all humankind, this trope illustrates quite precisely the workings of biopolitics in the twentieth century. The biopolitical agenda of a war of annihilation between species erases all internal political differences. Local conflicts disappear before the radical otherness of the enemy. Humanity is *one* community that is fighting for its biological survival. The biopolitical program elevates any political conflict to a matter of life and death, annihilation or survival. The *War of the Worlds* narrative—from Wells to Emmerich—casts the biopolitical program of total enmity in the most compelling imagery, evoking both the cohesion of humankind as a community and the need to fight and kill for its survival.

LIFEBOAT EARTH

The association between surviving and killing presented by this ontology of enmity has the survival of one species depend on the extinction of the other. The ideological effectiveness of this type of catastrophe scenario is obvious. In the absence of aliens, communities can come together by stylizing a total enemy. What may in fact just be a limited conflict can then freely be cast as a catastrophe of existential scope. Yet this is only one possible variety of modern biopolitics that existentially links survival to killing. It seems as though the modern ontology of enmity has recently been superseded by another type of catastrophe narrative. Since the 1990s, that is, since the end of the Cold War, an increasingly popular catastrophe scenario has emerged, a model that I call the Lifeboat Earth model of catastrophe narrative. Instead of the crude biologism (or racism) of the War of the Worlds model of catastrophe, the latter's logic seems much more egalitarian: Everyone is equal, and everyone has the same right to live—yet some people nevertheless have to die to enable the survival of others. In the Lifeboat Earth model, catastrophe does not involve a struggle between two life forms but rather a crisis that requires "tragic" choices to be made, choices that separate those who will be spared from those who will be left to die.

For this scenario to occur, there is no need for alien invaders or their variants in the form of zombies, intelligent machines, evil swarms, etc. Stories of this kind typically revolve around natural catastrophes— that is, fateful but morally neutral calamities. On account of their global repercussions, favorite topics include meteor impacts, worldwide pandemics, catastrophic weather events, environmental destruction, or climate changes such as nuclear winter. In these cases, there is no "other" to fend off; instead, humankind is alone in the midst of some sort of global chaos. Films such as *Deep Impact, Armageddon, The Day After Tomorrow, Outbreak, Contagion, Blindness,* or *2012* are concerned with catastrophes that cannot be circumvented by mere fighting. All that matters in them is the seemingly apolitical struggle for survival. Of course, the salvation of the nuclear family also plays a prominent role. No climate disaster can take place without a man rescuing his son from the cold (*The Day After Tomorrow*), there is no epidemic without a father desperately trying to bring the rest of his family to safety (*Contagion*), a quarantine would not be the same unless a wife follows her sick husband into it (*Blindness*), and it goes without saying that geological disasters necessitate the restoration of a patchwork family to its original form (*2012*). Yet this trope of saving the nuclear family conveniently conceals another problem that regularly confronts such disaster communities: not everyone can be saved. For some to survive, others have to die. Not everyone can have a space in the bunker or on the ark; not everyone can be released from quarantine. In *Contagion*, an entire American town is sacrificed to prevent a virus from spreading any further. In this type of disaster plot, decisions have to be made about who should be saved and who should be left to die. The survival of the brave and valuable foregrounded in such catastrophe stories is set against the dark background of a huge death toll of those who—for whatever reason—couldn't be saved.

One of the most explicit illustrations of this background is Mimi Leder's film *Deep Impact* (1998). An asteroid is discovered whose path, within a year, will intersect with Earth's orbit. Its impact is expected to cause devastating floods, earthquakes, and a year-long darkening of the planet by the ash and dust that will be released into the atmosphere—much like the aftermath of Mount Tambora's eruption in 1815. During the year remaining before the anticipated collision, the world has time to attempt to prevent the impending disaster (on the one hand) and prepare for the worst (on the other). A space shuttle is launched with the objective of exploding and diverting the asteroid, but the mission fails, after which the American government then presents an emergency plan for the country: In the limestone caves of Missouri, bunkers have been built that can accommodate a million people in the event that the earth will remain entirely uninhabitable for two years after the strike. Now, well, some decisions have to be made, or at least this is how the American president puts it in his address to the people: "Now we have to make some decisions together. What do we do? You have a choice. We have a choice. Right now. Ever since the comet was discovered, we've been hoping and working for the best, but we've also been planning for the worst." The noteworthy thing about it is that it is *not* an emergency plan for everyone. The president presents this backup plan as though it concerns everyone. While the bunkers will house no more than a million people, the president aptly avoids mentioning the fact that the remaining 99.7 percent of Americans will inevitably be left to perish in the unforgiving darkness in the wake of the impact. The government faces the problem of how to decide who should be allowed into the bunker and thus be granted a chance to survive: "On August 10," the president goes on, "a computer will randomly select Americans to join the scientists, doctors, engineers, teachers, soldiers, and artists who have already been chosen. Other countries are preparing similar ways along those lines, ways they consider best to preserve their way of life. This is ours."[28]

One million out of roughly three hundred million American citizens is not very many: only 0.3 percent will be allowed to survive. Although there is talk here about saving humanity and preserving certain ways of life, what is truly at stake is letting 299 million people die. In Roland Emmerich's *2012*, the survival rate is even worse. Whereas the vast majority of humanity perishes in earthquakes and colossal tidal waves, four hundred thousand business leaders and members of the super-rich have secured for themselves, at the cost of one billion euros per head, a seat on one of six "arks" designed to outlast a catastrophic process of continental drift.

What these plots highlight is that measures to ensure the survival of the population are rarely ever meant for the *entire* population. They display another type of biopolitical decision—the decision about who should be allowed to live and who may, under specific circumstances, be left to die. This takes an act of segregation that no longer deals with distinguishing friends and enemies, as Carl Schmitt analyzed it. Rather, the decision has to be made about one's own people, and thus the decision-making process itself gains an entirely different degree of tragic urgency. If the criteria for survival no longer depend on specific qualities, everything hinges on the *process* of choice. Catastrophe is an experimental field for such processes.

In *Deep Impact*, two kinds of processes are implemented, both of which deserve a closer look. On the one hand, two hundred thousand "scientists, doctors, engineers, teachers, soldiers, and artists" are welcome in the bunker, that is, people considered extraordinary or useful for the project of preserving "the American way of life" after the disaster. There is thus a qualitative criterion, a particular qualification, authority, or prominence, making a person valuable enough to be allowed to survive. The second process, on the other hand, is not at all based on particular qualities but operates on the assumption that, in fact, everyone is of equal value. A lottery is carried out to select the remaining eight hundred thousand American citizens who will get a place in the bunkers. This is an indiscriminate selection process based solely on statistical probability, though the chances of winning are extremely slim. Yet, even in this case, certain criteria are introduced in the form of two restrictions: people over the age of fifty are not allowed to participate, and immigrants are not even mentioned. Here, the biopolitical scalpel is wielded to excise a fairly large group of people who will be left behind to face certain death.

While preserving the same essential intention, selection processes may vary with different movie scenarios. In *The Day After Tomorrow*, extreme cold encroaches on the North American continent. Asked for a potential evacuation scenario, a climate scientist simply draws a line at the fortieth line of latitude: only those south of this should be evacuated (fig. 3.5). As for the rest, there is nothing that can be done. In *2012*, the issue of survival is determined on a monetary basis, and the film, which otherwise makes a great deal of pathos around the notion of human solidarity, seems to have no qualms about the justness of this criterion.

Unlike Emmerich's various disaster blockbusters, however, *Deep Impact* is intelligent enough to underscore the tragedy of this process. The film emphasizes how this separation will affect groups and families. The protagonist is a famous journalist who first broadcasts the story about the approaching meteor. As such, she has a place in the bunker. Yet her father and mother are excluded from the survival lottery on account of their age; her father is abandoned by his young second wife, and her mother commits suicide. In front of her colleagues, who are doomed to remain behind, the television reporter is supposed to be flown out to take her place as a VIP in the bunker, but following the family-loving logic of Hollywood, as a single woman she ultimately decides to give up her seat to a colleague with a small child and ultimately dies alongside her father. In *Deep Impact*, families are not saved but rather torn apart because only certain members happen to be valuable enough to be spared. Here, the

FIGURE 3.5 A thin red line: In *The Day After Tomorrow* (2004), the climatologist Jack Hall (Dennis Quaid) draws a line between those inhabitants of the United States who can still be evacuated from the impending deep freeze and those in the north, for whom nothing more can be done. The line drawn between those saved and those left to die is emblematic of the biopolitics of scarcity.

Source: Still from *The Day After Tomorrow* (2004).

politics of survival is a politics that cuts sharply into the flesh of society, even into its biopolitical sanctum, the family.

TRAGIC CHOICES

What these scenarios intend to make plausible is the idea of Earth as a lifeboat: as a place with drastically limited resources. The catastrophe here brings about a situation of scarcity that makes it necessary to kill or leave behind some of one's *own* people. Whereas the War of the Worlds scenario implies the imperative to kill the "other," the Lifeboat Earth scenario entails an inevitable selection from within one's own community. The survivors on the lifeboat are the result of a laceration within the community. While the War of the Worlds scenario amounts to an ideology of blunt enmity, the Lifeboat Earth scenario raises fundamental ethical and political questions. What is the value of a life? Do numbers count? Under which circumstances can certain individuals be denied the chance to survive?

The common denominator to these questions is a scenario of radical scarcity, be it of space in a bunker, seats in a lifeboat, food, shelter, medical care, or other goods. What the Lifeboat Earth scenario addresses is thus a biopolitics of scarcity. This biopolitical program presents itself as inevitable necessity: a case of emergency where tragic choices must be made. Even though the basis of the scenario is one of blunt physical needs, the problems raised by the scenario have often been cast in legal terms and discussed as a question of individual rights and distributive justice.

In 1975, the philosopher Onora O'Neil (writing under the pen name Onora Nell) published a pioneering article entitled "Lifeboat Earth." In it, she ponders the questions of distributive justice and of allowing people to die, and the basis of her reflections is the scenario of a lifeboat that lacks sufficient resources for everyone on board, a disaster example that has been discussed since antiquity.[29] After a few general considerations about the difference between "killing" and "allowing to die," she begins to imagine emergency scenarios in order to develop criteria to determine when an act qualifies as killing and is thus unjustifiable. This situation leads to a number of grave conundrums: May one out of six passengers be allowed to die of thirst if there is only enough water for five? May a seventh and eighth passenger be refused admittance on board? From whom, moreover, should water be withheld: the healthiest passenger or the one who is closest to death? Just like Hollywood's blockbusters, O'Neill's thought experiments rely on fictions. To illuminate the complicated implications of such drastic ethical decisions, stories are needed.

O'Neill's fundamental distinction between killing and allowing to die defines as "killing" all situations in which people die by means of the actions or neglect of other people when, had other choices been made, this death could have been avoided. Presupposing a fundamental "right not to be killed," she claims that unavoidable killings—for instance, if one of the passengers on a lifeboat is denied water—must be justified. Such decisions require, among other things, a fair selection procedure and transparent criteria regarding the distribution of resources. The president who announces the emergency plan in *Deep Impact* has clearly taken to heart O'Neill's argument: The lottery used to select survivors is an example of such a "fair" process, since everyone has the same chance of being selected.

More problematic, however, is the principle that no one over fifty years old is eligible (presumably because their utility for perpetuating the human species is no longer given) and that certain "especially important" (that is, prominent, powerful, deserving, wealthy, etc.) people should be saved in any case. Yet it is precisely these cases that reveal that biopolitics is not about rights but about bodies. Reproductive functions, health status, abilities useful to the community, or even just the means to purchase a seat in an ark encroach on the legal or ethical rules of fair chances for everyone.

The two selection processes featured in *Deep Impact* fit into the four basic procedures for allocating scarce resources outlined by Guido Calabresi and Philip Bobbitt in their classic study *Tragic Choices*.[30] The book is one of the first contributions to the debate over the equitable distribution of scarce resources, and it discusses the possible procedures for doing so. As such, it is a foundational text for the ethics of resource allocation, that is, the question of the ethical principles behind the distribution of limited resources, such as basic medical and nutritional provisions during a famine. In their introductory chapter, Calabresi and Bobbitt outline four possible processes of distribution: first, "the pure market" (everyone decides on his or her own how valuable it is to have access to a given resource); second, "the accountable political approach" (the idea that resources should be distributed according to the usefulness for the community, for example, by giving them to particularly "useful" individuals); third, "the lottery" (any random selection process, including a "first come, first served" principle); and fourth, "the customary or evolutionary approach" (essentially, the avoidance of any systematic process). By focusing on these approaches, the authors acknowledge that there can be "tragic" choices in the sense that there might not be any desirable options, yet situations can arise in which such decisions are unavoidable. Calabresi and Bobbitt therefore propose rational processes of distribution that take into account the moral and social costs—"the costs of costing," as they put it.[31]

Thus, when the president makes his announcement in *Deep Impact*—"Now we have to make some decisions together"—what is meant by this is that some tragic choices must be made. We have to make a choice that will be wrong no matter what—a choice that poses two equally important values against each other (in this case, the equality of all individual lives and the necessity of selecting just a few *productive* lives). The position is one of having to choose between two options, the better of which is only slightly less terrible than the other: Everybody or "only" 99.7 percent of people die. Should such quantities even matter? Is it ever acceptable to treat lives as mere numbers on a balance sheet?[32]

THE BIOPOLITICS OF SCARCITY: MALTHUS

Catastrophe scenarios of the Lifeboat Earth type address the problems of a politics of scarcity—a type of politics concerned with survival under conditions of scarce resources. What may, during times of plenty, seem to be a debate about distributive rights and justice will suddenly become a question of life and death during an emergency. According to the logic of biopolitics, this legal and political problem contains a solution that no longer is based on legal predicaments but rather on vital necessities. From being heroic or comforting, the disaster community in this scenario turns out to be tragic, making impossible choices. The survival of one person entails the killing of another (in O'Neill's sense). As the philosopher Weyma Lübbe has remarked, a *political* theory of biopolitics calls for a sound justification and rational process when it comes to this killing or letting die, instead of shamefully leaving such matters to the "darkness of destiny."[33] The decision over life and death should at least be one that is rationalized and justified. However, as Agamben has argued, this type of *bio*political decision ultimately eludes a purely juridical sphere, as it opens up a "zone of undecidability" between the realm of the law and the realm of mere physical necessity.[34] Tragic choices invoke a brutal factuality that does not seem to allow for any third way or nontragic solution. This factuality, however, is created by the very *narratives* of lifeboats, arks, and scarce resources.

This shift from a logic of enmity to one of tragic choices in a catastrophe can be traced back to a precise moment in history. The first publications devoted to the ethics of resource allocation and distributional justice began to appear in the 1970s, shortly after the Club of Rome released its drastic inaugural report. Titled *The Limits to Growth* (1972), it prognosticated superexponential population growth accompanied by an extreme scarcity of resources, especially of water, food, and fossil fuel.[35] Its key concepts, "scarcity," "overpopulation," and "environmental destruction," have characterized predictions of the future ever since. Depending on the growth rates used in their respective models, some of the report's scenarios depicted situations in which depleted resources and poisoned landscapes would bring about catastrophic struggles and a potential end to mankind by the end of the twenty-first century.[36] In her essay from 1975, it is clear that O'Neill shared this outlook. She was unequivocal about the topicality of her lifeboat metaphor:

> Lifeboat situations do not occur very frequently. We are not often confronted starkly with the choice between killing or being killed by the application of a decision to distribute scarce rations in a certain way. Yet this is becoming the situation of the human species on this globe. The current metaphor "spaceship Earth" suggests more drama and less danger; if we are feeling sober about the situation, "lifeboat Earth" may be more suggestive.[37]

The historical background of O'Neill's prognosis was undoubtedly the acute famines of the early 1970s in Biafra, Sahel, Ethiopia, and Bangladesh. Since the 1960s, large-scale catastrophic famines in the global South have regularly featured in predictions of the future. For instance, in their bestselling nonfiction book *Famine 1975!*, which appeared in 1967, the brothers William and Paul Paddock predicted that a global famine would break out as early as the year exclaimed in the title of the book.[38] From this point on, the question of whether letting die is equivalent to killing took on an acute historical urgency.

By the 1970s, Malthus's pessimistic view of the future, which, as we have seen, had already informed the catastrophic imagination behind Romantic darkness, had clearly experienced a revival. Malthus's statistical examination of the European population in relation to its resources was unexpectedly readopted as a global model. Besides *Limits to Growth*, the most trenchant publication in this regard was Paul and Anne Ehrlich's 1968 study *The Population Bomb*.[39] Their prognosis is hardly less alarmist than that of Malthus, as is evident in the book's apodictic opening lines: "The battle to feed all of humanity is over. In the 1970s and 1980s hundreds of millions of people will starve to death in spite of any crash programs embarked upon now. At this late date nothing can prevent a substantial increase in the world death rate."⁴⁰ The Ehrlichs claimed that a massive famine would strike the developing world as early as the 1970s and that even the West was heading toward an unsustainable population density. They also discussed factors such as environmental pollution and housing deficiencies in urban areas. Both *Limits to Growth* and *The Population Bomb* thus provided an update to the Malthusian model of catastrophe that casts growth itself as potential disaster. Now, the Malthusian model is expanded to include environmental issues and the problems caused by the lack of available space. The Ehrlichs also raised the possibility of actively intervening in human reproduction. In this regard, their proposals were rather brutal, among them compulsory sterilization or the withdrawal of developmental aid from countries with high population-growth rates. Even though the book's immediate predictions never came to pass, and even though the world's population increased after 1968 more dramatically than anticipated without causing a global crisis over resources, the rediscovery of scarcity in the 1970s nevertheless led to a new biopolitical way of thinking. It situated human reproduction as one factor in a systemic view on life on earth, pitting human reproduction and consumption against the availability of vital resources.

This perspective on human lives as an intrinsic threat to human well-being also came to be reflected in fictional catastrophes and dystopias, for instance in the thriller *Soylent Green* (1973). Directed by Richard Fleischer, the film offers a detailed illustration of the Ehrlichs's arguments. Even its opening credits show a sequence of terrifying political visions from the late 1960s and 1970s: poisoned landscapes, droughts, masses of people, air pollution, mountains of garbage (fig. 3.6). This sequence of images persuasively demonstrates how overpopulation has become a catastrophe that directly links the present of the 1970s to the dystopia in which the film is set. The Ehrlichs began their book in a similar fashion by describing a "stinking hot night in Delhi" that made the problem of the "population explosion" strikingly clear:

> As we crawled through the city, we entered a crowded slum area. The temperature was well over 100, and the air was a haze of dust and smoke. The streets seemed alive with people. People eating, people washing, people sleeping. People visiting, arguing, and screaming. People thrusting their

FIGURE 3.6 The opening credits of *Soylent Green* (1973) illustrate the catastrophic mood of the 1970s: overpopulation, environmental destruction, air pollution, mounds of garbage. Today, they look uncannily topical.

Source: Still from *Soylent Green* (1973).

hands through the taxi window, begging. People defecating and urinating. People clinging to buses. People herding animals. People, people, people.⁴¹

This scenario of feeling anxious in an overpopulated "Third World" city, which the American Ehrlichs experienced in New Delhi, is precisely the condition of New York City in *Soylent Green*, which takes place in the imagined year of 2022.⁴² By that time, the city has swollen to forty million inhabitants (to date, New York's metropolitan area has seventeen million). What the film depicts is a "Third World" megacity situation with crammed streets, people sleeping in entryways and stairwells, and long lines outside soup kitchens. In the biting heat, water is rationed to poor people while it flows freely from the faucets of the rich. The message of the movie is clear: With an outsized population, even New York will become the Third World. Its plot, in which a police detective (Charlton Heston) has to solve a murder that took place at a board meeting of the Soylent Corporation (a food-production company), is rather hazy. It becomes clear that the victim had known an important company secret and that he was killed for fear that he might share it. What the film is really about, however, is its vision of a hopelessly overpopulated city. It is a situation in which traditional foods such as strawberry jam, vegetables, or meat are only available at horrendous prices; where only the privileged have their own apartments; where even stairwells are inhabited by throngs of people; and where running water has become a luxury. Hunger riots are a constant threat. One of these revolts is quelled by means of a garbage truck, as though the people were trash that must be removed from the street. In the dystopian world of the population bomb, humans are garbage and are accordingly cleared away.

The actual secret of the film, which the detective discovers toward the end, concerns the nutritional replacement known as "soylent" distributed in place of traditional food. Despite its name, the green variety of "soylent," rich in proteins, consists neither of soybeans nor of lentils, as its name suggests. At the end, the police detective learns that it is in fact made of human beings, recycled to feed the ever-expanding population. In the last moments of his life, he dramatically yells out the secret: "Soylent green is people!" In this film, resource scarcity is depicted as a normal, if horrifying, condition. People have to die in order for others to have something to eat.

It is precisely here that the neo-Malthusian turn of biopolitical thinking comes full circle. The biopolitics of scarcity, as first pointed out by Malthus, argues that human life can be overabundant—an idea that is entirely foreign to the "war of the worlds" scenarios, where strength in numbers just serves as a signum of biological success. Seen from the vantage point of a biopolitics of scarcity, the biopolitical enhancement of life now suddenly becomes a self-endangering tautology. Life is stifled by its own prosperity—it eats itself up, as it were. This may be the secret core of the recurring image of cannibalism that has pervaded catastrophic thinking from Byron's "Darkness" to the present day. In the figure of the population bomb, human life becomes a threat to itself. Cannibalism may thus be a feverish dream of biopolitical thought, a politics of life being threatened by its own success, which eventually turns against life itself.

During the 1970s, therefore, drastic programs to reduce birthrates were proposed and enacted, such as the one-child policy in China, in effect between 1979 and 2015; the ongoing *dua anak cukup* (two kids are enough) campaign in Indonesia; and many more or less efficient programs for birth-control in African countries. In the industrialized world, the 1970s saw the slow rise of energy-efficient and environmentally friendly technologies, working on a model of a more economic use of resources than directly on population control. During the 1980s and 1990s, however, the Malthusian model lost its convincing force, as a fundamentally flexible upper limit to the earth's "carrying capacity" was established as a guideline for social change and technological development.[43] Since the late 1960s (and thus not yet on the radar for authors writing in 1968), the introduction of the birth-control pill in the industrialized world brought about a sudden decline in birth rates, and this too has since been regarded as a problem. For nearly three decades, the theme of overpopulation was thus banished from sight in the First World, having been outsourced to the Third World and developing nations.

Yet the long-prevailing optimism about the earth's infinitely expandable "carrying capacity," enabled by improved agricultural technology and the better exploitation of resources, has recently and vehemently been called into question. Among its detractors, for instance, is Alan Weisman, who has written works with revealing titles such as *The World Without Us*. His most recent book, *Countdown*, which is about the imminent destabilization of the earth's ecosystems through overpopulation (and overconsumption), reads like an alarmist preface to his previous book about a world uninhabited by people. While in *The World Without Us* Weisman's vision of an earth purified of *Homo sapiens* described a sort of healing, the lurid images of *Countdown* are concerned with what he perceives to be the planet's sickness: an ever-growing human population that is becoming catastrophic to itself and its basis for life, the earth.[44] Recently, this line of thought has been taken up by trying to establish a "safe operating space for humanity" without disrupting basic parameters of the earth's life system, as proposed by a group of resilience researchers.[45]

The biopolitics of scarcity is thus not a purely historical phenomenon spanning from Malthus to *Limits to Growth*. Neither is it limited to the issues of overpopulation and the earth's carrying capacity. With the recognition of the fundamental scarcity of certain goods (from the allocation of resources to health care), we are constantly left to make tragic choices. Even in entirely uncatastrophic contexts, these types of decisions are intensively discussed today under the general term of "resource allocation." Questions of this sort include, for example, acceptable costs for expensive therapies for elderly people or the terminally ill. Tragic choices are faced when there is not enough for everyone yet when everyone has a legitimate claim on a particular resource. However, even these uncatastrophic fields have their initial source in situations of emergency. Beyond lifeboat scenarios, an early historical response to such tragic choices was so-called triage on battlefields. A decision had to be made about which wounded soldiers should be the first to receive medical attention: the severely wounded, who need the most urgent care but are unlikely to survive; the moderately wounded, whose lives still hang in the balance; or the minimally wounded, who, if given the proper attention, have the best chances of coming out alive. Other questions related to soldiers having priority over civilians.[46] Today, triage has become common practice with victims of accidents or natural disasters. Whether present, anticipated, or imaginary, it is the intensity and dramatic nature of catastrophes that justifies the need for tragic choices. Disasters are situations with limited options, intense time pressures, and great danger, yet it is in precisely such emergencies that people are forced to act and make grave decisions.

This is why fictional disaster narratives are so politically effective. They bring order into the complicated, tragic, or just obscure situations that social life has to confront. The fiction of an ongoing catastrophe enables the suspension of certain rules of justification and due process in favor of the swift and brutal decisions solicited by states of emergency. Promoting a biopolitics of blood relations, the "war of the worlds" scenario presents familial or species solidarity as the main figure to unify society against an enemy yet to be defined. This scenario taps deep into an ideology of enmity at work throughout the twentieth century, and will, most likely, continue to inform the ongoing "War on Terror."

The more recent Lifeboat Earth scenario that is an element of many catastrophe fictions in the past few years is harder to brush aside as ideology. Films such as *Deep Impact* involve a narrative that makes certain decision-making situations conceivable while at the same time justifying the decisions at hand by presenting them as the only, if tragic, option. This narrative underscores that the community facing an emergency is not simply a locus of individual heroism and interpersonal solidarity. Rather, it shows that any community wishing to survive such a situation will face impossible decisions. It will have to kill as well as justify this killing. In a catastrophe, such decisions can be justified with regard to the exceptional circumstances. As states of emergency, they justify the suspension of otherwise inviolable rights and values. Catastrophe narratives therefore function not only as a fantasy about the irruption of the Real but also as a training exercise in the politics of emergency. Garnished with the pathos of survival or salvation they make the (ethically) unthinkable thinkable. Disaster suspends the ethical bonds we usually endorse. However, disaster scenarios can also become a space for reflection. A film like *Deep Impact* is an ethical and political thought experiment that does not just "sell" the tragic choices it presents but also opens up space for analysis and discussion. Thereby it may also shine a light on the conflicts and impossible choices that take place in everyday life—even without a catastrophe to justify them.

AFTER THE END: BECKETT'S *ENDGAME*, McCARTHY'S *THE ROAD*

Survival, especially within the modern scenario of a war of the worlds can also be seen as a form of triumph. According to Elias Canetti, survival is always a victory, an affirmation of power: "The moment of *survival* is the moment of power. Horror at the sight of death turns into satisfaction that it is someone else who is dead. . . . In survival, each man is the enemy of every other."[47] Yet to survive during and after a catastrophe does not necessarily entail salvation or triumph—quite the contrary. Imagining disaster does not necessarily involve a victory, that is, the narcissistic satisfaction of having outlived everybody else, as Canetti has it. Most often narratives of survival envision a solitary and bleak afterlife, a life without the world. The Last Man is a deeply melancholic figure. The world has been destroyed, social bonds have been ripped apart, yet the individual is still in this world that no longer exists. Survival is a form of life after life.

No author has grasped this empty core of mere survival better than Samuel Beckett. Beckett's characters, as the philosopher Günther Anders aptly observed, "are simply still alive; they are no longer part of the world."[48] He who survives is "simply still alive"; he is reduced to his purely biological existence. The survivor has saved his bare life, while the world and time have perished along with the community that had given him his *bios*—his identity, connections, norms, meaning, and aspirations.

The classical distinction between *bios* (political life, life in a community) and *zoē* (bare, biological life) is nowhere more blatantly evident than in the case of mere survival: *bios* is a communal life, a life in the world, a life within systems of references, a life as a person; *zoē* is what remains after all of that has gone away. Nothing illuminates this existential mode of bare life (*zoē*) more clearly than scenarios of survival—scenarios of living on after the end of the world.

Beckett's protagonists, and especially those of *Waiting for Godot* and *Endgame*, are just such survivors. They are captives in a "being without time."[49] It is no coincidence that Beckett's early works were created during the coldest phase of the Cold War, the era that, under the spell of the atom bomb, kept describing itself as humanity's last generation. According to Anders, the apocalypse has "always already" happened because the possibility of our nuclear extinction can no longer be revoked. Survival, the condition of being-still-alive, is the appropriate image for this catastrophe that has always already happened.[50] Beckett refrained from making any references to the historical contexts of his works, and scholars have usually followed suit.[51] Yet *Endgame* in particular, which was written in 1954 and first performed in 1957 (as *Fin de partie*), almost too easily lends itself to be read as a postapocalyptic scenario of the atomic age.[52] The setting of the play is a bunker-like, almost entirely unfurnished room that is referred to as a "refuge"; the landscape outside is "gray" or "light black" (31–32); there is no horizon and no sun. "The light is sunk" (30). The characters are sitting in a sort of hell, but beyond the wall lies "the other hell" (26): "Outside of here it's death" (9). All four of the characters—Hamm; his servant, Clov; and Hamm's parents, Nagg and Nell—are physically debilitated in various ways and are unable to leave the room. Hamm is in a wheelchair; his parents are legless and live in dustbins; and Clov, for his part, is unable to sit. At regular intervals, Clov looks out of the window and reports on the nothingness that he sees there. Hamm longs for the woods, knowing all the while that not only are they unreachable for him but also, and above all, that they are no longer there. Seeds no longer sprout (13), which is a sign that they have been poisoned or, more likely, irradiated. The players of *Endgame* are the survivors of a nuclear attack.

Endgame plays out in a space and time after the end. To survive is to wait for the end—and in the meantime, they talk about the end, the waiting, and the talking itself. The play begins with an ending: "Finished, it's finished, nearly finished, it must be nearly finished" (1), and soon thereafter Hamm remarks: "Enough, it's time it ended, in the shelter, too. (*Pause.*) And yet I hesitate, I hesitate to . . . to end" (3). Survival in the age of atomic destruction is a life after the end of life, something that exists to end and consists precisely of the "hesitation" that Hamm expresses at the beginning of the play. It quickly becomes clear that the outside world is in a state in which nothing more exists. "There are no more bicycle wheels" (8). "There's no more pap" (9). "There's no more nature" (11). The world outside is a landscape of ruins, and the waves of the sea are "lead" (31), frozen as in the final image of Byron's "Darkness." All that remains are eating, speaking, waiting, and agonizing bodies that exist in a static choreography of mutual dependency: the master and servant Hamm and Clov, the mother and father Nell and Nagg. As Christoph Menke has recently observed, Hamm and Clov are engaged in a game, competition, or struggle between dominance and servitude.[53] It is on this game of speaking, moving, and waiting that the countless analyses and interpretations of Beckett's text normally focus.

Far less attention, however, has been devoted to examining the framework in which this game takes place or the conditions under which it is even possible—in the sense that none of the characters even has the possibility of leaving the scene and thus the struggle. The framework of *Endgame* is a postcatastrophic setting, an existence in a bunker. It is a scenario of surviving in a place that has obviously been desolated by an atomic explosion, as depicted in so many contemporary visions of the nuclear apocalypse.[54] Beckett, however, is eager to erase any specific reference to a historically identifiable situation in order to maintain an existential vagueness. Yet time and again, the play cannot avoid alluding to the atomic apocalypse that weighed so heavily on his era. "He keeps it nebulous," in the words of Adorno, who was keenly aware of the postapocalyptic references in the play: "The end of the world is discounted, as though it were a matter of course."[55] Beckett's survivors are bodies that have nothing to await in terms of salvation—they are already "saved," as survivors, as decaying and damaged bodies. "But we breathe, we change! We lose our hair, our teeth! Our bloom! Our ideals!" (11). This can be taken as a general reflection on aging, but it is more convincing as a reference to mild radiation damage. It is a life witnessing its own disintegration, a life marked by its own foreseeable end.

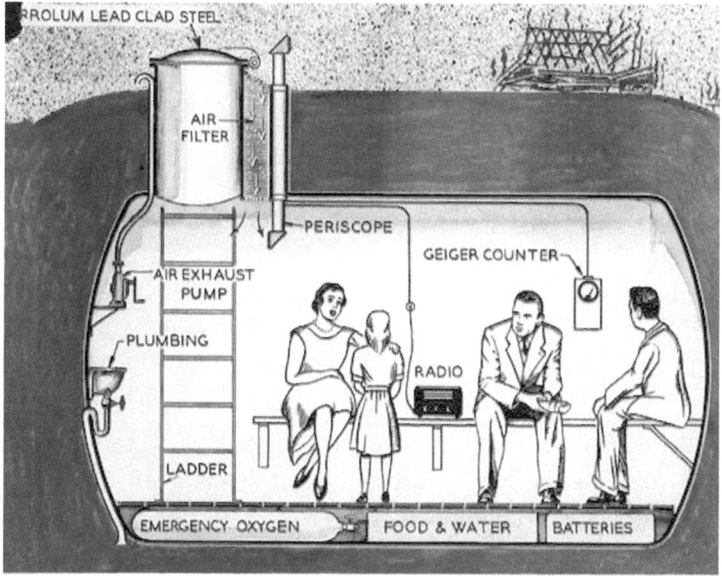

FIGURE 3.7 Beckett's "bare interior" reminds us of the bunker designed to harbor the nuclear family. A model of a private fallout shelter from the early 1960s.
Source: Getty Images.

This reading is supported by the desolate landscape, the leaden waves, the gray light, the vanished sun, the rubble, but also by the fact that even Clov, who is still able to walk, no longer leaves the room despite his repeated gestures to do so. The room is obviously a fallout shelter, as designed by the civil-defense programs of the 1950s and equipped with everything that a family might need for their survival (fig. 3.7). As the inhabitant of such a shelter, Hamm has provisions that others lack. People in need had repeatedly sought out Hamm for bread and lamp oil. Although he always refused to assist anyone, he remembers it with lachrymosity:

> All those I might have helped. (*Pause.*) Helped! (*Pause.*) Saved. (*Pause.*) Saved! (*Pause.*) The place was crawling with them. (*Pause. Violently.*) Use your head, can't you, use your head, you're on earth, there's no cure for that! (*Pause.*) Get out of here and love one another! Lick your neighbor

as yourself! (*Pause. Calmer.*) When it wasn't bread they wanted it was crumpets. (*Pause. Violently.*) Out of my sight and back to your petting parties!

(68–69)

As becomes evident from Hamm's stories and reminiscences, survival is also a question of others' survival—the others whom one "might have helped" but failed or neglected to save. At the end of the piece, a small boy (perhaps) appears outside; Clov, at least, claims (or feigns) to have seen one. "If he exists," Hamm remarks, "he'll die there or he'll come here" (78). The difference here is not so much that of life or death but rather of "here" or "there." One will either die *in* the bunker or *outside*, in the "other hell." Hamm indulges in stories about how he refused to save anyone—such as the long and fragmented story about the man who requested bread for his child and in Clov's recollection of Mother Pegg dying "of darkness" because Hamm refused to give her oil (75). Read in this sense, *Endgame* is not only a play about a language game and a power struggle between people inhabiting a closed space; it is also about the ethical and political "costs" of survival, about "all those I might have helped."

Even if this line of interpretation of Beckett's play might reduce matters to a highly selective historical reference, it rightly gets to the political core of survival tacitly underpinning *Endgame*.[56] With its stories of not saving, not sharing, and not helping, sentimentally recalled by Hamm, the play reflects a logic of catastrophe much akin to the Lifeboat Earth scenario. Survival always implies—and occasionally justifies—the death of others. Hamm is clearly a passenger aboard Lifeboat Earth. Those who have survived have allowed others to die. Yet the logic of Beckett's work does away with the tragedy of "tragic choices," which insists that impossible decisions have to be made yet also justified. For Hamm has never made any *tragic* choices. Tragic decisions need to be considered in the light of their justifiability; they are concerned with both physical and moral survival. They are choices consciously made in a moment of crisis, in deciding between two unwelcome alternatives. According to Bonnie Honig, this distinction between mere survival and moral survival, a survival in which tragic choices can still be justified, can be understood in terms of the difference between what she calls "mere life" and "more life."[57] More life is life that, despite whatever tragic decisions need to be made, remains morally justifiable, whereas mere life means acting based on nothing but one's own preservation. Beckett's characters desire and exemplify nothing but mere life—an existence beyond moral decisions, reasoning, and justification, an existence that strives for nothing but its own perpetuation. Hamm does not rationalize his decisions but rather underscores their contingency and arbitrariness and his renunciation of ethical criteria. His sighing remark—"All those I might have helped"—indicates that he very well could have made a different decision, and that he knew as much. Hamm thus embodies the brutal, bare, and untragic side of the biopolitics of survival, that is, the possibility that the decision over life and death is not even a tragic choice but is made arbitrarily and without justification. Underneath the urgency of the catastrophic situation, according to Beckett, there is, in truth, nothing but decision without any ethical basis.

With his figure Hamm, Beckett demonizes the idea of tragic choices as the caprice of a half-dead, paralyzed tyrant. But his text also lashes out at the holiest of the survival community: the family. The four characters of the play represent the traditional nuclear family at the heart of Cold War civil-defense films and educational campaigns: father, mother, son, and Clov in the role of one of Hamm's "sons." In its misfortune, however, this is not simply an admittedly bizarre but otherwise "entirely normal" family, as Stanley Cavell believed.[58] It is rather a family in a state of emergency, a family that has survived whatever has made the outside world so "light black" and sunless. I would propose that *Endgame* is thus not about an odd but otherwise normal world in which the rules of normal language games apply. It is about a world in a state of catastrophe where everything is anormal, and in this anomaly it casts a light on the hidden presuppositions of everyday reality. The text explicitly trashes the catastrophic imagination of the 1950s and its family-fixated rhetoric of "duck and cover." Furthermore, *Endgame* does not celebrate blood ties but openly condemns them. Hamm refers to his own father as an "Accursed progenitor!" (9): "Scoundrel! Why did you engender me?" (49). The parents, who are, almost too explicitly, placed in garbage bins, signify a blatant rejection of the family as the biopolitical unit of salvation. In Beckett's work, the family is no longer a heroic or tragic survival community but rather just a lamentable reminder of the purely biological fact that one has been born. Having been "engendered" is the state of mere life. And this is what is saved in survival, as Beckett presents it. His survivors carry this bare life like a burden that they can neither bear nor shed. They exemplify the fact that, as Adorno noted, "even the survivors cannot really survive, on a pile of ruins that even renders futile [the] self-reflection of one's own battered state."[59] Beckett's analysis of survival hinges on exactly that: on the question of what it means to go on existing in a world that is not a world anymore.

In Beckett's hands, survival becomes an experiment in reduction. His characters are reduced to eating, speaking, and waiting for an end that has in fact already arrived. An outside world to talk about, or (for Clov at least) to escape to no longer exists. Not only does *Endgame* strip speech of its meaning; it also deprives the characters of a social context that could give their behavior any significance. In a certain sense, Beckett repeats—at a different time, with a different scenario, and with different epistemological interests—Byron's experiment in "Darkness" with an anthropology of catastrophe by taking away the frameworks of civilization and society. Whereas Byron was concerned with eradicating the idea of the rational and noble-minded man, Beckett reveals the sheer arbitrariness and contingency of the norms and bonds that, during an emergency, serve to implement and justify a biopolitics of survival. The "real" that manifests itself during a catastrophe becomes a hollow space of speech and activity. In Beckett's work, survival is the final stage of reduction, waiting for an end that has already come.

The most recent and bold revival of the literary experiment to strip things bare is—to return to this text for the last time—Cormac McCarthy's *The Road* (2006). It tells the survival story of a man and his young son after a disaster that, according to my reading in chapter 2, represents a nuclear winter.[60] Through this cold and desolate world, where nature can no longer regenerate and hordes of survivors hunt down others, a father and son wander toward the coast in search of food and shelter. McCarthy has transplanted Beckett's locked-in survivors into a world outside of the bunker—a world that no longer offers any nature, resources, or safe places. It is the same world in which Byron's despondent Last Men live in terror of one another. McCarthy transfers this modern anthropology of catastrophe into an uncanny setting, both strange and familiar, as it is not a scenario in the distant future nor an abstract and timeless "bare interior" (1) but the remains of our present-day world, post destruction.

McCarthy's bleak scenario is so intriguing because it draws an unambiguous connection between ecological and social disaster and thus lends itself to an explicitly political and ethical reading, something that Beckett sought to avoid. What is there to eat if nothing grows anymore? What sorts of behavior and rules of caution are needed to survive? What forms of violence arise from this situation? With its touching scenes of the father caring for his son, McCarthy's book, as many critics observed with a certain relief, depicts a vestige of humanity within a dehumanized world. Oprah Winfrey naively called the novel a "love story."[61] The novel's commercial success however, is also thanks to a calculated ambiguity: McCarthy refrains from describing the precise nature of the event that has destroyed the world. On account of this vagueness, *The Road* was quickly interpreted as an ecological parable, as "the most important environmental book ever written," according to George Monbiot's gushing review.[62]

Yet the point of the novel is neither the "love story" between father and son nor its plea for environmentalism. McCarthy depicts survival in a disaster that viscerally speaks to us because the ruins presented here are the ruins of *our* world: the soda cans, shopping carts, the homes that we live in today, and the banal objects of everyday life. It is the fragility of this world—the world in which we live—that McCarthy showcases by imagining its decay. Faced with the destruction of nature and human society, survival is not really survival any more—at least not in Beckett's sense of a bare and purely biological perpetuation of life decoupled from any political or ethical dimension. McCarthy is in fact concerned with precisely this dimension of an ethics of survival, with questions of inviolable bonds, solidarity (whether offered or denied), and moral depravity. Admittedly, the affinities between Beckett's postapocalyptic bunker community and McCarthy's scenario have been underscored just as often as those between Beckett's pared-down language games and McCarthy's formally simple style.[63] Yet the differences between them are instructive. For, in *The Road*, survival is not a matter of waiting for death but rather of postponing it. In a final exchange between the man and his wife, who commits suicide shortly thereafter, it becomes clear that surviving the catastrophe is not really surviving at all—it is just delaying the inevitability of being killed:

> We're survivors he told her across the flame of the lamp.
> Survivors? She said.
> Yes.
> What in God's name are you talking about? We're not survivors. We're the walking dead in a horror film.

> I'm begging you.
> I don't care. I don't care if you cry. It doesn't mean anything to me.
> Please.
> Stop it.
> I'm begging you. I'll do anything.
> Such as what?
>
> (47)

McCarthy makes it unmistakably clear that his survivors are zombies, that they are in fact already dead. Their continued existence is a cruel afterlife in the wake of a catastrophe that cannot be overcome. The wife's suicide merely seals what had already happened some time ago. The man and his son, on the contrary, endeavor with infinite resolve and caution to push their final death just a little further into the future. To survive is to delay, "borrowed time and borrowed world and borrowed eyes with which to sorrow it" (110). There is no life, no world in which to seek refuge; there is no "south" to take refuge in from the winter of the disaster. There is also no conceivable future: "Old and troubling issues resolved into nothingness and night. The last instance of a thing takes the class with it" (24). All of life—all issues—are at an end. The Romantic figure of the Last Man appears yet again, father and son being the last instances of a humanity that has already perished.

In their tenacious daily struggle, McCarthy's Last Men are put to the same test as that posed by Lord Byron, and in similar weather conditions. As it says in "Darkness," "The meagre by the meagre were devour'd."[64] Just like Byron, McCarthy also evokes a bleak Malthusian image of men as famished cannibals. His protagonists are little more than "two hunted animals" (110) or "farm animals" standing in the rain (17). They are constantly in search of food and on guard against the cannibals from whose rotten teeth hang human flesh: "The reptilian calculations in those cold and shifting eyes. . . . Who has made of the world a lie every word" (64). In McCarthy's work, humanity is divided into the cannibals and the virtuous, as the father never tires of explaining to his son.

Thus, in contrast to Byron's and Beckett's, McCarthy's test of man's resilience delivers results that are less bleak. His anthropology of disaster is as devastating as it is comforting—a typically American combination. Unlike Byron or Beckett, McCarthy effectively falls back on the good old family bond that, as the last bastion of love, solidarity, and humanity, features so often in the biopolitics of survival. What remains after the end, his novel teaches us, is the unassailable community of father and son, and it does so in a form of resilient perseverance that has no goal beyond living through another day: "This is what the good guys do. They keep trying" (116).

Undoubtedly, this mixture of heroism and family ties is the secret to the novel's success. It is thanks to its humanism, which seeks the essence of humanity—as though *ex negativo*—at the point of its utmost depravation. When there is nothing more to eat, when there are no more plants, and when no animals have survived, human beings become the only available prey. One of the most gruesome scenes that ever made its way into literature describes the discovery of a basement in which people have been locked up. Half rotten, hardly still alive, and with amputated limbs, these captives are being kept as cattle, food for the cannibals who locked them up (93–95). The father and son, catching a brief traumatic glance into the cellar, barely escape the same fate. In a dry, overly simple exchange, they promise to each other that they would never do this:

> We wouldn't ever eat anybody, would we?
> No. Of course not.
> Even if we were starving?
> We're starving now.
> You said we weren't.
> I said we weren't dying. I didn't say we weren't starving.
> But we wouldn't.
> No. We wouldn't.
> No matter what.
> No. No matter what.
> Because we're the good guys.
> Yes.
> And we're carrying the fire.
> And we're carrying the fire. Yes.
> Okay.

(108)

The question of cannibalism is used to draw a line between being or no longer being human. It marks the ethical difference between mere life and more life, which Beckett expressly avoids. The dialogue is presented in an extremely pared-down style that avoids all the wordplay with which Beckett's protagonists spend their time. McCarthy's language is not about hollowing out the everyday meanings of language, as in Beckett. On the contrary, it charges the simplest formulas—especially the repeated use of "okay" and "yes"—with an aura of fundamental affirmation: an affirmation of being human after the end of humanity.[65] McCarthy's dialogues celebrate the mutual confirmation of a father and son with a constant repetition of short, almost corny expressions that seem to come right out of a Boy Scout's dictionary. The author deliberately relies on a number of fairly hackneyed phrases ("We're the good guys," "We're carrying the fire"), but he only does so by charging these well-worn phrases with a new pathos. "To be the good guys" and "to carry the fire" is to preserve a final vestige of civilization in a situation that has no room for humane behavior. Starvation is at hand. Whereas the cannibalism among Byron's Last Men is just another detail in the bleak scenario of mankind's demise, in McCarthy's work it becomes the central criterion for the last stage of mankind's utmost reduction in this crisis experiment. Regarding the biopolitics of scarcity, McCarthy's novel taps into the state outlined in my previous section: the point at which human beings become their own resource. What remains at this stage of radical social anomie is far beyond any "tragic choices." For, as the novel repeatedly illustrates, "to be the good guys" does not entail helping or saving others. It has nothing to do with abiding by an enlightened ethos of sympathy or solidarity—the father always brushes aside such impulses, despite the protests of his son. It does not require them to help the people in the basement.[66] What the father and son mean by "carrying the fire" is the preservation of a vestigial form of ethics that is reduced to two basic taboos: Do not kill, and do not eat people. In the catastrophe depicted by *The Road*, the political and ethical dilemmas posed by the biopolitics of survival are reduced to a final stage, the last remnants of both nature and human civilization.

This concern with remnants is focused not only on mankind but also on things. The father and son rummage through the ruins and remains of destroyed civilization in search of things that might still be useful for survival: dregs of gasoline, expired canned goods, desiccated apples, rags, tarps, old pieces of clothing. They use a shopping cart to carry their measly belongings. In the world after the end of civilization, such things acquire new meanings and new forms of use.[67] Everyday objects that used to be readily available are now either entirely worthless or become vital. What is the survival value of a pen, a blanket, a shopping cart? In the light of catastrophe, McCarthy stages a reevaluation of use value. One of the happiest scenes in the novel is a moment when father and son discover a private fallout shelter built during the Cold War—or maybe by more recent survivalists. For a brief moment, they find a meticulous choice of things needed for survival: food, clean water, bandages, and shelter.

McCarthy's approach to things is no different from that of today's survival manuals: What will be of use when there is no more electricity and the internet no longer exists? Which are the objects that can be used to make a fire? The fetishes of our times, electronic devices, have become completely worthless, as have summer clothes, baking powder, or books. Yet what we today would see as garbage, such as expired groceries or worn-out clothing, have become so valuable that they might be worth killing for. Blankets are stripped off corpses, and their shoes are stolen. The hopelessness with which the father and son scrabble for anything edible casts a pale, apocalyptic light on the everyday objects that surround us in our current forms of life. What McCarthy has made clear is that the value of things in the present depends on a viable future. When this future is no longer there, everything loses its function: "He'd not have thought the value of the smallest thing predicated on a world to come. It surprised him. That the space which these things occupied was itself an expectation" (158).

McCarthy's novel is about the future as catastrophe inscribed in our very present. Yet unlike the zealous preppers, who turn "the frailty of everything" into a program of constant preparedness and resilience, McCarthy's novel analyzes the present through the melancholic lens of its potential destruction. McCarthy seems to know how much there is to lose. The future is not only the horizon for human designs but also the horizon of values and actions. The true catastrophe in *The Road* lies in this loss of the future, a loss that renders any prospect of survival entirely meaningless. With his "borrowed eyes" the Last Man gazes upon a world whose end has preceded him. A world that consists of nothing more than the scrap value of a world once made by humans.

4

THE FUTURE OF THINGS

Accidents and Technical Safety

Everything created by the hands of man can be subject to an accident. By a kind of compensation . . . the more these works are perfected the greater the accidents to which they give rise.

—FÉLIX TOURNEUX, "ACCIDENS"

MELTDOWN

It came down to a single safety test that should have been carried out before activation. Conducted hastily and during normal operations—and thus already too late—the experiment was meant to gauge the reactor's emergency power supply. By testing the reactor in an event of malfunction, it was intended to make the nuclear technology safer. On the night of April 26, 1986, the plan was to test whether the rotational energy of the turbines could supply enough electricity for a power outage lasting one minute. In addition, a revision of the reactor running at 20 percent of its capacity was planned. What followed was the catastrophic nuclear accident at Chernobyl, which took more than thirty lives, heavily contaminated 150 people with radioactivity, caused increased cancer rates and deformities in the region, covered Europe with radioactive fallout, and left behind an irradiated "restricted zone" still uninhabitable today.

The prologue to the disaster began the night before. On April 25 at 1 a.m., engineers began gradually to reduce the capacity of Reactor 4, which was to be tested. Because of high power demand in Kiev, however, its output was left at around 50 percent throughout the day, instead of being brought down to the planned 20 percent. Unbeknownst to the personnel on duty, this caused the reactor core to accumulate xenon, which, over the next few hours, led to an uncontrollable drop in power output. At two o'clock in the afternoon, the emergency cooling system was switched off for the test. Late in the evening, approval was granted for the test, and the reactor was reduced to 25 percent of its capacity. The night shift took over at midnight. Twenty-eight minutes later, the test was begun under the direction of the engineer Anatoly Dyatlov. On account of an operating error or a technical defect, the output level began to plummet to just 1 percent of capacity, far below the level at which the reactor could remain stable. This reduction accelerated the xenon poisoning of the reactor core, which in turn prevented the power from being raised back to the necessary level. Dyatlov thus ordered all of the control rods to be extracted from the reactor, for which the automatic control system had to be overridden. This caused the reactor to become even more unstable. Despite the protests of the other engineers, Dyatlov insisted that the test be continued. He increased the water supply to the reactor in order to deactivate the emergency warning signals. At 1:23 a.m., the actual test started by closing the turbine valves. The coolant began to heat up, and the steam pressure became so high that the 750-pound covers on top of the fuel rods began to lift. The automatic control system inserted the fuel rods into the reactor, which caused the power output to increase even more. Losing his nerve, the shift supervisor Alexander Akimov manually initiated an emergency shutdown. This, as it turns out, unleashed the true catastrophe. The reactor's control rods, which were equipped with graphite tips, were designed in such a way that they would initiate a brief but intensive power boost upon being inserted. The emergency shutdown procedure involved all of these rods being inserted at once, and all of a sudden the reactor's output climbed to a hundred times its nominal capacity. The ensuing heat caused the rods to get stuck in the reactor. The pressure lines burst, and the coating of the rods and the graphite reacted with the intruding steam. Multiple explosions followed, and the reactor caught fire. Although weighing one thousand tons, the roof of the reactor was blown

FIGURE 4.1 (a) The ruins of Reactor 4 at the Chernobyl nuclear plant, April 1986. Images of the destroyed reactor were made public several days after the event but were only published in this form in the Western media. In the USSR, only retouched versions were published in order to downplay the extent of the catastrophe. (b) A cross section of Reactor 4 after the accident.

Source: (a) AP Images. (b) Reproduced by permission of UNSCEAR.

off by the explosions, and the burning facility was now exposed to the open air (figs. 4.1a, b).

Via the burning graphite, radioactive iodine and cesium were released high into the sky, where they spread as a giant cloud toward Scandinavia and later southern and western Europe. Two hundred and thirty-seven people, who came immediately after the disaster to put out the fire or were simply in the vicinity, were exposed to massive amounts of radiation, and thirty-one of them died within the next few weeks. Two days later, 135,000 people were evacuated from the nearby city of Pripyat and the surrounding area. The Soviet government did not allow the state media to report on the accident until the event had already been widely covered in the West. To date, the rates of cancer and deformities in people and animals

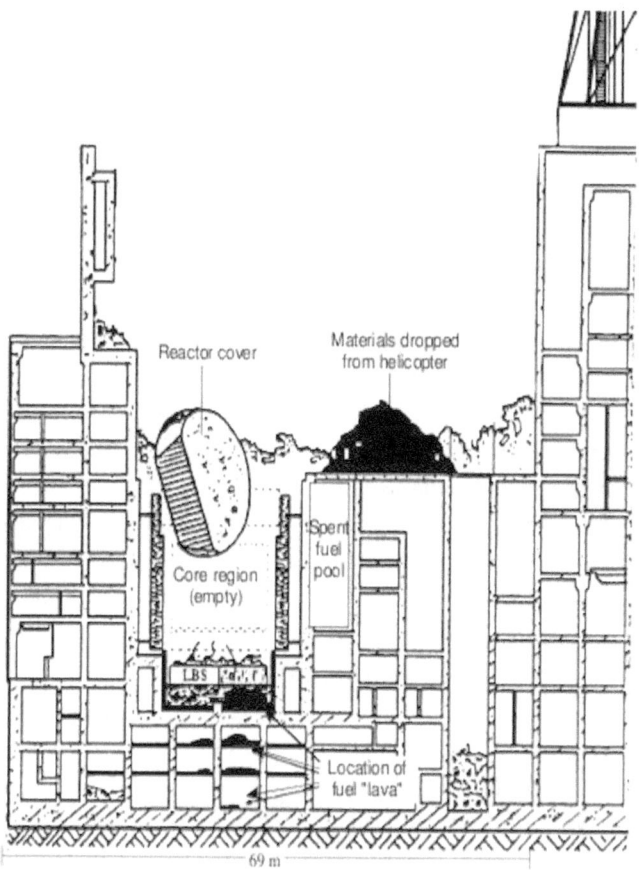

FIGURE 4.1 (*continued*)

remain high in the region. The zone around the reactor is still restricted, though a few residents have returned to the general area. The abandoned city of Pripyat has become a ghostly piece of scenery that has long attracted photographers and more recently tourists. There are overgrown streets between deserted apartment blocks, vacant spaces that still contain the forsaken belongings of former inhabitants, and a defunct Ferris wheel that had been built for the May Day celebration of 1986, which of course never took place. This setting was the inspiration behind the 2012 horror movie *Chernobyl Diaries*, which feeds off of the uncanny scenery of the abandoned city and incorporates spectral images from the contaminated zone and the inside of the reactor.[1] Pripyat is a mummified city, a monument to a catastrophe that has yet to subside.

Chernobyl is the prototype of the *accident* as a technological catastrophe. Its cause was neither the violence of nature nor any human intention but instead an interaction between humans and highly advanced technology. This kind of major accident is thus a specifically modern type of catastrophe because it depends on an advanced state of technology. Accidents reveal technology's secret essence: its tendency to *break down*. The Chernobyl catastrophe has been referred to as a "beyond maximum credible accident" or "beyond MCA." An MCA is a foreseeable, "design-basis accident" (DBA). Anything *beyond* that, however, denotes the sort of malfunction that can technically neither be anticipated nor prevented. The idea of the "design-basis accident" derives from a concept of safety according to which complex technical systems have to be designed to withstand certain malfunctions (and prevent whatever damage might be caused by them). A nuclear power plant must be able to sustain a design-basis accident without allowing radioactive material to leak into the environment. But accidents do not follow the rules put in place by those who design technical systems. Chernobyl was thus neither an MCA nor a DBA but, as it were, a "super-MCA," an accident that exceeded the safety parameters built into its design.

Within any piece of technology, there is a potential accident that the initial design cannot account for. "The shipwreck," writes Paul Virilio, "is consequently the 'futurist' invention of the ship, and the air crash the invention of the supersonic airliner, just as the Chernobyl meltdown is the invention of the nuclear power station."[2] Technical disasters expose an essence of technology: the breakdown, the derailment, the malfunction inherent to its functionality. Such things, as Stephen Graham and Nigel Thrift have noted, "are not aberrant but are part of the thing itself."[3] Chernobyl is a good case in point, as it brought together various dimensions of "the accident" in general.

First, Chernobyl exemplifies a large-scale accident with highly complex technology. On April 25 and 26, 1986, a variety of factors converged: a faultily designed reactor that lacked essential safety mechanisms (such as a safety container beneath the reactor core) and whose output, instead of being reduced, *increased* uncontrollably when the emergency shutdown was initiated; the delay of the test by half a day, which led to xenon accumulation; mistakes made by the staff during the preparation and execution of the test, above all Dyatlov's decision to go through with the test given the reactor's condition. Additional factors included inexperience and incompetence, violations of safety procedures, and possibly a technical defect that might have caused the target value for regulating total capacity to be set at the wrong level. Like the more recent case in Fukushima, Chernobyl was a highly complex accident that resulted from an improbable convergence of various individual factors: a so-called chain of unfortunate events. The complexity of such accidents is the negative side of the complex technology that produces them, as the epigraph to this chapter points out. They are improbable; they do not have a single but rather several causes; and they exceed, in their complexity, the safety technology meant to keep them under control.

Second, Chernobyl illustrates the intricate connection between technological risk and safety. Ironically, the disaster was the result of a safety measure intended to simulate an emergency. The ultimate cause of the accident was the very safety and control regime meant to regulate the reactor. It was not just the test and its sloppy execution but rather the control technology itself that led to a type of accident for which no reactor is designed. The "beyond maximum credible accident" is the blind spot of safety technology. In the case of Chernobyl, this blind spot was literally in the middle of the reactor, in the graphite tips of the control rods.

Third, the ineluctable bond between the past and the future of a catastrophe is epitomized by the mummified city of Pripyat. The city is not only the ghostly afterimage of the catastrophe; it is also the place of its continuing effects. As Guillaume Grandazzi has remarked, it has become a laboratory for a long-term experiment.[4] The contaminated residents who were evacuated, the "liquidators" who helped construct a concrete sarcophagus around Reactor 4, the people in Kiev who unwittingly bought radioactive household goods—all of these people became the guinea pigs in an ongoing experiment about the consequences of radiation exposure.[5] Even the plants and animals in the zone around Pripyat have been made part of this experiment. Affected, too, were the Europeans who, in the immediate wake of the accident, found out that suddenly ordinary activities such as drinking milk or taking a walk were now "dangerous"—as pointed out in Christa Wolf's 1987 novel *Accident: A Day's News*. "The victims of Chernobyl," as Ulrich Beck noted, "are today, years after the catastrophe, not even all born yet."⁶ Chernobyl was not just a momentary disaster but is an example of the prolonged latency period in which the long-term consequences or side effects of an accident unfold. Technical catastrophes may not always consist of a big bang but may continue to have invisible and unpredictable effects decades after the event. They thereby create a very specific catastrophic future—a future of fear.

THE ILLUMINATING ACCIDENT

Accidents become intelligible only in hindsight. Only by reconstructing the course of events—by dissecting the factors and steps leading up to an accident—can we begin to understand something that, in the fleeting instant of its occurrence, defies observation. "Just a moment earlier something there had broken ranks; falling sideways with a crash," or so begins Robert Musil's account of a car accident in the first chapter of *The Man Without Qualities*.⁷ Accidents have always already happened "a moment earlier." This epistemological belatedness is the crux of their understandability and preventability. Therefore, they solicit the application of innumerable forms and practices of knowledge in an effort to understand the remains, rubble, corpses, wreckage, and ruins they leave in their wake. Yet this delayed reconstruction is just one side of an accident.

The other is its futurity. Catastrophe, as we have seen, is a mode of revelation, an emergence of the latent and hidden, a manifestation of that which threatens us. Every actual accident hints at yet another possible accident in the future of a specific technology. Accidents are the most powerful demonstration of everything that can go wrong with a piece of technology or with a practice. It is thus their "future form." Virilio therefore sees the accident as the "accidental," that which (according to Aristotle) is added to a substance for it to take form. An accident is a feature or condition anything can assume, its latent characteristic or potential: "Every technology produces, provokes, and programs a specific accident."⁸ Virilio's acute technophobia aside, he has a point in assuming this "futuristic" perspective on things or technologies. It requires us to examine things and technology in the light of their flaws, their uncontrollability, their dysfunctionality, or their misuse. Accidents explore a technology's realm of possibility. The accident is therefore not just that which has always already happened but also what is *always already about to happen*. All measures and mechanisms of technical safety are such "futuristic" considerations of their object, attempts to discover what can or will go wrong under certain conditions. In this sense, the potential accident illuminates the future of things.

The attempt to investigate this uncanny future of things has created an immense and diverse range of practices, institutions, types of knowledge, disciplines, legal regulations, and administrative measures. They constitute the vast field of what is known as technical safety. Certain types of knowledge associated with it, such as occupational safety, fire prevention, environmental protection, and disaster control are subfields within the general discipline of safety science, each with its own curricula, research programs, and multidisciplinary publication venues.[9] Other aspects of this discipline, such as reactor safety or airline safety, are special areas of research focused on the type of technology in question. Yet another area of safety science concerns the development of norms and safety standards. Last, among the most important instruments of accident prevention are the institutions responsible for monitoring technical maintenance and conducting inspections. In Europe, technical inspection associations such as HM Railway Inspectorate in England, founded in 1840, or the Technische Überwachungsvereine (TÜV) in Germany, were created in the nineteenth century. In Germany, safety inspections were initially designed to monitor the safety of steam engines. Today, the successors of these technical-inspection associations test the technical safety of virtually all technical devices, from motor vehicles to refrigerators to hair dryers. To date, the two largest German safety associations (TÜV Nord and TÜV Süd), which grew out of regional associations, have become international service providers that conduct inspections of technical facilities, authorize new products, and monitor automobile safety standards (by conducting crash tests, for instance).

The sciences, norms, and classifications concerned with the prevention of accidents model dangers in order to convert them into calculable risks. To comprehend the moment of, say, a crash, it has to be broken down into small optical segments—as in the stop-motion photographs of crash tests (figs. 4.2a, b, c). By means of slowing down and fragmenting time by the

FIGURES 4.2A-C The stages of a collision from a crash test.

Source: Copyright Euro NCAP—European New Car Assessment Programme.

medium of film, the brief and unintelligible moment of collision can be analyzed in its individual phases. To analyze a more complex potential accident, however, a *narrative* is needed that not only establishes a chronological sequence of the accident but also elucidates the causal connections between multiple yet interdependent factors. Thinking about safety thus yields its own imaginations and processes of representation, from the accident protocols of crash tests to the tables of "failure modes and effects analysis" (FMEA). This requires very specific *epistemic aesthetics* in order to generate and structure knowledge concerning the future of things. This epistemic aesthetics of the accident is what safety sciences and the accidents in action and horror films have in common. Spectacular Hollywood crashes and the crash-test films share a common interest in the minute details and steps toward a disastrous accident, exploring not so much a specific technology as the infinite possibilities of its malfunctions. It is thus not a coincidence that, parallel to the rise of modern safety science, the accident became a literary and cinematic object of fascination. Accidents express modernity's profound ambivalence toward technical innovation and its social repercussions. The accident is "futuristic," the emblem of a concern about potential, future, probable, or improbable disasters at the heart of technological progress.

The accident is a peculiar form of event without agency, a causal puzzle. It simply happens. Its actual agent is not a human but rather a particular technology or practice. Just as the accident lacks a perpetrator, it also has no duration—only an unpredictably long aftermath. As early studies of "railway spine" and postcollision trauma made clear, the accident's brevity obscures what is actually happening. Instead, its long-term consequences are studied all the more intensively.[10] It only exists in belated and laborious reconstruction or in the traumatic memories it has left behind. Beyond that, the security measures undertaken to prevent its recurrence trace a strange, overblown afterimage of the actual accident.

Not surprisingly, imagined accidents, in literature as well as in films, try to fill the gap created by the inability to observe the accident. Slow motion, an endless sequence of shots from different angles, countless witness narratives, and so on try to grasp the accident as an event that eludes representation. Thus, fictional accidents provide their own analysis of the accident. In literary accounts or meticulous film shots, not only is it possible to perceive, neatly and in detail, the occurrence, development, and consequences of an accident; it is also possible to let the victim narrate his or her experience. In this way, an "internal" perspective of the accident can be developed. In the imagined accident, regularities can be projected onto the singular and inaccessible event: whether it be by statistics, which assigns a certain frequency to any type of accident; by a "theological" perspective, interpreting the accident as punishment for technological "hubris"; or by analyzing the causal sequence leading up to such a complex and improbable event.[11]

Imagined accidents are representations of the unrepresentable. They also make this type of event accessible to affects and emotions. From D'Annunzio's crashing pilot, the tragic hero of modern technology,[12] to the endless crashes and explosions in action movies, imagined accidents have always been, as the German philosopher Hans Blumenberg put it, "shipwrecks with spectators"—catastrophes, seen from the observer's point of view, accessible to emotions and insights that are traumatically excluded in real accidents.[13] Imagined accidents therefore can never be "realistic" representations. Rather, they have to be understood as models that explore specific aspects of an accident; it may be an individual's ability to experience something that typically eludes experience. It may be about the dangers of certain technologies. Or it may be about the social conditions responsible for the accident, as in insurance coverage or accident prevention. Given these different perspectives on accidents in fiction, it makes no sense to discuss *the* accident and *its* poetics. In the attempt to investigate and understand the billions of different ways in which things can go wrong, it is necessary to analyze accidents in their plurality, by differentiating between specific types of accidents and the specific forms of knowledge and modes of representation to which they give rise.

CRASH: THE PROBABLE ACCIDENT

The prototypical accident in the modern imagination is not the highly complex technological accident, such as the Chernobyl reactor meltdown, but rather the everyday and all-too-familiar collision: the car crash. The early twentieth century was fascinated by the car crash as a disaster resulting from the acceleration of modern life, which was seen as both a boon and a bane.[14] Still today, the spectacular car crash—complete with rollovers and explosion—is the most prevalent special effect in movies.

Cars crash. Thus the advent of the automobile was unavoidably accompanied by a new kind of accident: the crash. The argument against cars in general would repeatedly be made in the name of the pedestrians, children, and animals that were (and continue to be) put in harm's way by the new mode of transportation. While the earliest collisions tended to be car against obstacle or pedestrian, with growing amounts of traffic cars increasingly tended to collide with one another. Having conquered public space, the new transportation technology was quickly understood as a threat to this space, not just because of reckless drivers but because of the speed of the cars themselves.[15]

The car is thus among the most powerful collective symbols of a highly ambivalent futurity. On the one hand, it symbolizes ever-increasing acceleration and the unlimited spatial usurpation of the world, an epitome of modernization. On the other hand, with the ever-present possibility of the crash, the car embodies, as the cultural theorist Matthias Bickenbach writes, "the pure violence of speed. The accident invented by the car is the crash or collision in all of its variations."[16] Ever since, these variations have been repeated and reimagined in literature, films, and works of visual art, occasionally as an explosive endpoint to which everything has been leading, sometimes as a tragic turning point, and sometimes as the mere expression of chance and coincidence. Yet in every case the crash is a matter of an individual destiny, which distinguishes this type of accident from others. The car crash is the individualized accident. Unlike any other type of accident, the car crash is highly dependent on the individual as the "human factor" in its cause and development. More than 90 percent of accidents are caused by a driver's lack of attentiveness or ability behind the wheel, reckless driving, fatigue, or alcohol consumption. This individualizing perspective adopted by statisticians of accidents characterized even the earliest studies. From the fact that certain people seem to experience more accidents in their daily lives than others, the statistician Karl Marbe derived the notion of individual "accident proneness" (*Unfallneigung*) in the 1920s.[17] His view on the regularities within large crowds leads to an individualization of accident causes: it's always the individual's fault.

One of the most famous literary examples of an accident scene, the first chapter of Robert Musil's *The Man Without Qualities*, presents exactly this link between a statistical and an individualizing view on accidents. On a "fine day in August 1913," as the scene begins, "automobiles shot out of deep, narrow streets into the shadows of bright squares." Musil provides a bird's-eye view of a city pulsing with traffic, a city as the site of innumerable "collisions of objects and interests."[18] Suddenly, a crash: "Just a moment earlier something there had broken ranks; falling sideways with a crash, something had spun around and come to a skidding halt—a heavy truck, as it turned out, which had braked so sharply that it was now stranded with one wheel on the curb." What is left is a traumatized driver and a pedestrian who, having clearly been hit by the truck, is lying on the ground "as if dead." A man and a woman, coincidental witnesses of the event, start talking about the situation and its causes. The man mentions that the brakes on heavy trucks "take too long to come to a full stop" and cites (hugely exaggerated) "American statistics" about accidents: "'According to American statistics,' the gentleman said, 'one hundred ninety thousand people are killed there every year by cars and four hundred fifty thousand are injured.'"[19]

While the woman believes she has experienced an exceptional, if not tragic, event, the man emphasizes its normality, statistically speaking. The individual affected by the accident is nothing but an occurrence with a particular degree of probability. Thus, early on, the car crash is the prototype of an event that came to be viewed not in terms of its singularity but according to its statistical frequency. The all-encompassing glance Musil casts over the large city at the very beginning of his novel replicates the epistemological structure of this statistical overview. With an expected degree of regularity, a certain percentage of cars in the city will suffer an accident. "The spread of statistics . . . is thus associated with a type of event that leaves behind the dichotomy between the fictitious and the factual and dissolves events into varying degrees of probability. . . . That which has not even happened is thus treated as a fact."[20] In other words: What has yet to occur—that which is not yet a fact but rather a possibility, a probability—is the future. The "fact" of the accident is a fact of and in the future.

The car accident is thus associated with a number of safety practices that have one thing in common: Although they attempt to reduce the severity and frequency of accidents, they nevertheless fundamentally accept their possibility and probability. The very practice of driving a car is never called into question. Instead, accidents are insured. This does not prevent any accidents, but it at least provides compensation for the financial burden a crash might cause. In addition, there are also safety regulations and preventive measures that are meant to reduce the frequency of accidents, from traffic rules to the constant improvement of automobile safety. These are based on insights gained from accident statistics (such as the effects of seatbelts or speed limits). Or they are based on test crashes, which provide information about how future accidents can be avoided or how damage can be minimized. It is clear, however, that the crash is an acceptable accident, an instance that may be quantitatively reduced but not entirely prevented. The crash is a type of accident that, as Bickenbach puts it, "always already will have happened," an individualized and finely distributed disruption.[21] Just like cancer, heart attacks, and other human infirmities, car accidents are not seen as a "catastrophe" but rather as isolated mishaps. This is why the crash is a paradigmatic type of accident for a safety mechanism of modernity based on statistics. Its aim is not to prevent accidents outright but rather to soften and reduce their effects *statistically* by technical safety measures and insurance. Seatbelts, for instance, do not save the lives of drivers in every accident (when they were introduced, it was argued that they might be harmful, for example, in the case of a burning car). Statistically, however, they lower the frequency of severe injuries and deaths suffered in car accidents. Traffic safety measures mainly revolve around the accident's *social* consequences (such as healthcare costs, material damages, loss of earnings, etc.), which is why insurance is so vital. To the extent that these social costs are relatively minimal and, thanks to the distribution of risk through insurance, socially tolerable, the crash, however horrible it might be for its individual victims—is an acceptable accident and not a catastrophe. Traffic accidents will continue to take place as long as there are cars on the road. And we will allow them to do so. As a probable future awaiting everyone who dares to venture onto the street, with or without a car, car accidents teach us a lesson about risk and its management in modern societies. What we learn from it is a statistical reflection on our very finitude: this can happen to anyone, this is a possible future waiting for any of us.

A CHAIN OF UNFORTUNATE EVENTS: THE IMPROBABLE ACCIDENT

There are, however, different types of accidents, inspiring entirely different images, narratives, and forms of knowledge. Whereas the crash is an individualized and singular event, a fleeting moment, there are accidents such as Chernobyl that do not occur in a single instant. This type of accident takes its course. The human being is not its main factor but one among other, mostly technical factors. This kind of accident has often been called a "chain of unfortunate events," a formula evoked to explain disasters with complex etiologies. Yet this chain is itself a puzzle, not a valid explanation. It refers to an accident as a highly improbable concatenation of multiple entities, a chain reaction, a domino effect, an escalation. If, as is often remarked, a vehicle crashing is something that defies experience in its suddenness, the chain of unfortunate events always has to be narrated, reconstructed, and staged in order to be understood in hindsight as a sequence of events leading up to the final catastrophe. This catastrophe, however, will erase the delicate and insidious process that brought it about, and it may even leave behind utterly misleading traces. The chain is a secret asking to be deciphered in hindsight: What really happened? What factors contributed to this course of events? Yet this deciphering of the accident's traces is always future oriented: Trying to understand the dynamic behind the catastrophic concatenation of factors is the basis of preventing accidents of this type. Reconstructing the history of a complicated accident is constructing a safer future.

What is striking about complex accidents is their statistical improbability. Chains of unfortunate events cannot be ascertained with statistics. Often they look like a malicious plan carried out suddenly by the things themselves—a conspiracy of things against humans. An early theory about this phenomenon can be found in the works of the German author and philosopher Friedrich Theodor Vischer, who became famous for his ideas about the "malice of the object" (*Tücke des Objekts*), which has since become a common expression in German. His 1879 novel *Auch Einer* (*Someone Too*) contains a scene at a wedding banquet, narrated by the unlucky protagonist. It brilliantly captures the malice of things:

Who, for example, would ever care to attribute any wickedness to a simple button? Yet just such a rascal recently tormented me in the following way. Against all my fundamental beliefs, I allowed myself to be tempted to attend a wedding feast; a large silver platter covered with a variety of appetizers came to be placed before me; I failed to notice that it was protruding somewhat over the edge of the table against my breast; a woman, my neighbor, dropped her fork, I wanted to pick it up, a button on my shirt caught on the edge of the platter with devilish cunning, lifted it up as I quickly stand, truly up in the air, all of the rubbish that it was holding, sauces, preserves of all sorts, a partially dark red fluid, spills, flows, shoots across the table. I, still wishing to save the situation, knock over a bottle of wine, its contents stream out onto the bride's white wedding gown, I step down hard on my neighbor's toes; another man, who hoped to intervene in a helpful manner, flips over a serving spoon, a third knocks over a glass—oh, it was a fuss, a full-fledged blowout, in short a truly tragic case: The fragile world of all that is finite seemed to want to shatter into pieces.[22]

Vischer's hero then goes on to explain the "wickedness" of the button, which started everything, with a theory that assigns agency and intentions to inanimate things themselves:

From daybreak to late at night . . . the object thinks about mischief and malice. One has to deal with it like an animal tamer dealing with a beast when it stirs in its cage; he never takes his eye off the beast, and the beast never takes its eye off him. . . . Thus does every object lie in wait, every pencil, pen, inkwell, paper, cigar, glass, lamp—everything, everything is waiting for the moment when one is not paying attention. But who in God's name can be so vigilant? Who has the time?[23]

Objects, according to Vischer's protagonist, behave with intention and a plan. They lead lives of their own that are antagonistic toward the everyday lives of human beings. Objects are not simply at hand but lurking and ready to pounce, as in the case of the wedding feast, in order to have their own party. Vischer's novel thus unfolds a grotesque poetology of things going awry: from an unruly pocket watch and a moderate domestic accident to the accidental death of the protagonist's beloved.

The demonic nature of things expounded by Vischer is not just a comical observation about everyday life but rather a philosophical attitude attuned to the late nineteenth century. It hovers, as Jörg Kreienbrock has shown, between a tragic and a comic dimension of the object's resistance against the subject and between an aesthetics of the grotesque and the sublime.[24] Yet it is also the symptom of a new way of thinking about technology that fundamentally conceptualizes the latter as anthropomorphic. The grotesque domino-effect accident at the wedding is the exact counterpart of Ernst Kapp's *Philosophie der Technik* (*Philosophy of Technology*), which appeared two years before Vischer's novel. Kapp's theory of technology regards human tools as "projections" of the human body.[25] This anthropomorphism of technology shared by Kapp and Vischer not only derives the form of technological tools from human organs (cameras or microscopes from the eyes, manual tools from the hands, etc.). It also endows devices with their own humanoid agency and imagines them as active and cunning counterparts to human beings. While today this may sound rather absurd, it had far-reaching consequences for early approaches to technical safety. The malice of things calls for an attitude of absolute attention and constant distrust. The demonic nature of things requires precise knowledge about their possibilities and flaws. Vischer's and Kapp's idea about the anthropomorphic malice of things can be seen as the basis for an early regime of technical safety calling for permanent watchfulness and distrust toward machines. For the Hegelian Vischer, coincidence was an immediate quality of the object, an act of opposition against the ends that the subject has assigned to the object. Vischer thinks of the relation between people and things, subjects and objects, on the model of the master-slave relationship. According to Hegel, this relationship is always more precarious for the master than it is for the slave.[26] Vischer's theory of the malicious object is, in fact, a theory about things/objects taking their revenge on the subject.

The coincidental nature of the concatenation of events is the epitome of what humans can neither control nor stop. It seems so demonic and malicious because of its improbability. The wedding accident in Vischer's novel exceeds any kind of statistical conceptualization. However, it calls for a description that discloses some kind of regularity, a "law" that governs the complexity of the accident's development. This kind of "law" is known by the ironic name of Murphy's Law, according to which anything that can go wrong will go wrong. Of course, this law is not a law, as its principle is not one of regularity but is instead entirely contingent. Whatever goes wrong confirms the law—and if nothing goes wrong, this lack of an accident is simply not a case that would fall under the law in question. Tellingly, Murphy's Law is an offspring of the modern safety sciences. It is named after the American aerospace engineer Edward A. Murphy, who conducted an experiment for the US Air Force in 1949 to test how much deceleration a person could withstand in a crash. This risky experiment had a surprisingly good safety record. When asked how this was achieved, one of the engineers claimed that the team worked according to a series of highly pessimistic rules, according to which only the worst of all technically possible outcomes should be expected to occur.[27] Clearly, Murphy's Law is not a law at all but a rule of preventive safety behavior. One of Murphy's colleagues even reformulated it as follows: "Avoid any action with an unacceptable outcome."

Besides the narratives, models, and "laws" revolving around safety measures, there is yet another dimension to the demonic nature of things and coincidences: its psychological and aesthetic side. Sigmund Freud referred to the peculiar psychic effect of things coming alive and coincidences betraying an underlying, hidden intention as "the uncanny." Uncanniness is the psychic reaction to the highly improbable. The uncanny, according to Freud, derives from an intricate coincidence, one that seems to be guided by intention, as in the recurrence of the same motif over and over again: "It is easy to see that ... it is only this factor of involuntary repetition which surrounds what would otherwise be innocent enough with an uncanny atmosphere, and forces upon us the idea of something fateful and inescapable when otherwise we should have spoken only of 'chance.'"[28] The demonic nature of things—their apparently intentional behavior—evoked for Freud certain archaic and long-repressed impulses: the belief in the omnipotence of thoughts and the animation of things. These are the effects of the unconscious belief that a secretly scheming and punitive power lies behind everything. Improbable coincidences or complex chains of chance events are processed by the psyche with primitive emotions such as fear or feelings of guilt. For Freud, humans are emotionally unable to process coincidences for what they really are.

Today, the effect caused by the uncanniness of things has found its genre and aesthetic style in horror movies and their burlesque counterpart, slapstick comedy.[29] In both genres, objects become alive and join forces either to butcher their screaming victims or to conspire against them in practical jokes. Informed by the characteristics of the genre, the audience always already knows that the seemingly inanimate world is maliciously lying in wait for its next victim. In horror and slapstick, there is no such thing as coincidence but only the vicissitudes of Murphy's Law. While in slapstick movies people are the overwhelmed but ultimately victorious tamers of things, horror movies depict people as the helpless victims of things. Denying that anything can be a "mere accident" or pure coincidence, horror movies are a demonstration of "destiny," a fate that will mercilessly and inevitably catch its victims.

The film *Final Destination* (2000), whose lasting success has since spawned five sequels, makes the improbable accident, aka "destiny," its very topic. It features cascades of unfortunate coincidences that all end in death. It all starts with the explosion of an airplane full of high-school students on their way to Paris. While buckled into his seat on the plane, one of the students (Devon Sawa) has a premonition about the airplane exploding. He panics and gets off the plane before takeoff, along with five classmates and a teacher, who are trying to calm him down. Minutes later, in front of the group who missed the plane, it actually blows up with the rest of the class on board. In what follows, each and every one of those who had been spared dies, one by one, as a result of bizarre and complex domestic or traffic accidents. The main character's best friend slips in the bathroom and ends up strangling on a clothesline; other characters are run over by buses or crushed by falling billboards.

In a scene that cleverly translates slapstick's love of detail to the bleak genre of horror, the surviving teacher (Kristen Cloke) becomes the victim of an especially intricate kitchen accident. To make herself some tea, she pours boiling water into a mug, but then she notices that the mug has the school logo on it; traumatized by the death of her students, she quickly dumps the hot water out. Preferring an alcoholic drink instead, she then fills the same mug with cold vodka and ice. The temperature change causes a slight crack in the mug (fig. 4.3a). As she places the mug on her computer monitor, vodka begins to drip unnoticed into it, which causes the monitor to short circuit. It explodes right in front of her face (fig. 4.3b), shooting a shard of glass from the screen into her neck. Oozing blood, she stumbles back to the kitchen (fig. 4.3c), where she collapses. While lying on the kitchen floor, she reaches for a towel, which happens to be hanging from a knife rack (fig. 4.3d), in order to staunch the bleeding. Of course, the knife rack tips over in such a way that the knives fall blade down, stabbing the woman (fig. 4.3e). Then, while one of her students rushes over to help, the entire kitchen goes up in flames (fig. 4.3f). In the end, the whole house explodes, having been ignited by the stovetop (which is still on) and the alcohol sitting next to it.

What is noteworthy about this scene is its ludicrous chain of escalating mishaps. We are witness to a highly complicated and extremely unlikely domino effect whose complex set up—the towel hanging from the knife rack, the mug dripping on the monitor, alcohol beside the stovetop—could have been avoided from the beginning. Such escalating sequences of coincidences appear not only in slapstick and horror movies but also in those (rather common) catastrophe films in which a harmless electrical short circuit eventually causes an entire building to go up in flames (as in the genre-defining disaster movie *The Towering Inferno*, from 1974).

Seldom, however, are these chains of events spelled out in such thorough (and comical) detail. In *Final Destination*, the apparatus that will lead to the disaster is depicted and set up meticulously by the victim herself. The film also works through the mechanical and technical qualities of each and every object involved: the nature of ceramic, which cracks in response to fluctuating temperatures; the short circuit in the computer monitor; the slow tipping of the knife rack as it is pulled down by the towel; the heating and eventual explosion of the alcohol.[30] In the movie, this long chain of coincidences serves to illustrate one single point: A violent death will soon catch up with those who managed to escape it. The long and complicated development of the accident is always unfolding toward a future in which nothing waits beyond preordained destiny. Yet this tells us something about a modern idea of destiny, to which the title *Final Destination* alludes. Replacing the idea of divine providence, the idea that God has a plan for every individual, destiny—at least in its horror-movie version—is nothing but a coincident ending, a final destination we are all headed to.

Final Destination presents us with a scenario for the perfect domestic accident, a cluster of risky arrangements. In this arrangement of individual factors, the scene contains a sort of didactic message that could have come from an educational film about household safety. Its perspective is

FIGURES 4.3A-F In *Final Destination* (2000), the death of the teacher (Kristen Cloke) unfolds like an educational video about household accident prevention. First, the factors contributing to the unlikely series of events are set up by the victim: an open flame, high-proof alcohol, hot water. What follows is an inexorable chain of accidents: an exploding computer monitor, a glass shard stuck in her neck, knives falling blade-end down, and eventually an explosion in the kitchen while a student tries to help.

Source: Stills from *Final Destination* (2000).

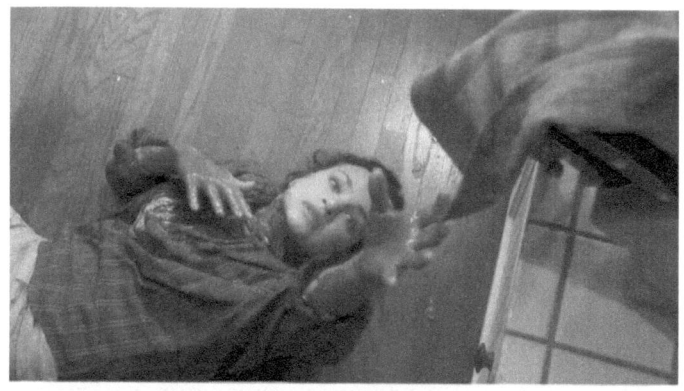

FIGURE 4.3 (*continued*)

that of Vischer's tormented protagonist A.E., full of distrust and prognostic apprehension. Everyday objects become uncanny. The scene interprets things in the light of what they might be capable of, that is, in the light of the malevolent possibilities that might arise from a particular constellation of objects and their material features, physical processes, and mechanical power relations. In this way, they are made part of an epistemology of technical safety. The movie reveals not only the latent potential of a thing or a technology but also the dynamics behind the escalation of the accident, which is both improbable and inexorable. Unlike the car crash's calculable degree of probability, the chain of unfortunate events is a process as uncontrollable as it is incalculable. It follows no coherent rules of its own. It is not the magnitude of the accident that makes it a catastrophe but rather its epistemic complexity, a complexity that the teacher's accident shares with the accidents of megatechnology. The question is how to predict and prevent these fatal developments, which can neither be expected on the basis of statistics nor anticipated on the basis of any underlying regularity.

TECHNICAL SAFETY

The uncanniness of these complex chains of events, spanning from the birth of technical safety associations and Vischer's theory of the malicious object to *Final Destination*'s idea of fate as the outcome of an accident, was born at a specific moment in history and has its own institutions. It is not a coincidence that Vischer lived in the nineteenth century, when safety science was undergoing thorough institutionalization. The discipline started out with safety concerns about one of the most important technologies of the nineteenth century, the steam engine. As early as 1844, a French encyclopedia of trains and steam engines (*Encyclopédie des chemins de fer et des machines à vapeur*) devoted some space to the demonic nature of this technology, which expended entirely novel and dangerous amounts of energy:

> Without strict and ongoing inspections, the most powerful and perfect industrial apparatuses (that is, steam engines and trains) can lead to the

FIGURE 4.4 Boiler explosion of the steam locomotive *Windsbraut* in Leipzig, May 21, 1846. Contemporary depiction.

Source: Public domain.

most horrific catastrophes. The sheer mass of the things that they set in motion, their speed—in short, their total expenditure of energy—can transform into a terrifying destructive force if they are suddenly stopped or diverted. Steam power has opened up new and unknown opportunities for mankind, but it always seems to be in a position that might be most comparable to a person walking on the brink of an abyss whose one false step could send him plummeting down.[31]

The steam engine inspired modernity's first genuine discourse about technical safety. It also triggered the creation of institutions to oversee the technical safety of steam engines. As a universal generator of industrial energy, the steam engine gave rise to a specific and dramatic type of accident: the boiler explosion (fig. 4.4). The latter could be caused by insufficient water levels (that is, by operating errors), material defects (such as small cracks in the walls or calcified safety valves), or inadequate maintenance.

At first, the government mandated certain maintenance routines, but these turned out to be difficult to organize at the regional level. Boiler operators thus instituted regional associations to inspect and maintain the technology on a regular basis. In Germany, the first private steam boiler inspection and review association (*Dampfkessel-Überwachungs- und Revisionsverein*) was founded in 1866. This marked the birth of technical inspection associations (*technische Überwachungsvereine*) as one of the most effective institutions for preventing accidents. The TÜVs, along with other safety-inspection firms, such as the Paris-based Bureau Veritas, founded in 1829, today are internationally operating companies in charge of safety testing and certification. Boiler inspection subjected the object and its potentially hidden malice to painstakingly exact examinations, looking for small cracks, material faults, deformations and leaks, corrosion in the welding seams, and lime scale in the safety valves. To this end, the boiler had to be completely opened up, and all of the bolts in the firebox had to be checked for cracks and (if necessary) replaced. Finally, pressure tests were conducted with cold and hot water, and the valves were tested, adjusted, and resealed. This specialized way of maintaining potentially dangerous technology proved to be highly effective in preventing accidents, and thus the number of maintenance tasks undertaken by the associations quickly began to grow. As early as 1900, the Technical Inspection Association of Cologne-Düsseldorf was commissioned to oversee the maintenance of motor vehicles and to administer driving tests.[32] Safety organizations introduced the professionalization of safety based on keen observation and specialized expertise. Since the smallest detail could be an indicator of imminent harm, it was necessary to employ professional inspectors, whose role quickly expanded from mere inspection to active testing and simulation of accidents. Today, crash tests are conducted for every new car model, and every new household appliance is tested for user safety. In Vischer's terms, the purpose of these tests is to exorcize whatever malice an object might contain. By simulating accidents, we learn something about the potential behavior of a technical object, its potential failures, but also its misuse or dysfunctionality.

Mere inspection, however, is unable to anticipate the complexities of certain types of accidents. Just as in Vischer's story about the wedding disaster, safety measures have to foresee complicated combinations of factors leading up to a chain of unfortunate events. To do this, stories have to be told. The safety science concerned with complex accidents therefore no longer can be limited to an epistemology of statistical risk assessment but has to resort to a narrative epistemology. To understand the "process" of an accident, this accident has to be transformed into a narrative chain of events, unraveling the accident's various factors and coincidences. This is why both safety scientists and disaster sociologists often resort to storytelling.

The disaster sociologist Charles Perrow's famous study of high-risk technologies, *Normal Accidents* (1984), begins with a story about an ordinary breakfast that, through a series of mishaps, leads to someone not getting a desired job.[33] This small private disaster serves as a model for much more complicated accident accounts: an uncontrollable fire in a chemical plant, an accident in a breeder reactor, an explosion on a cargo plane, or a collision between two ships in a canal. These stories not only illustrate the processes behind the accidents in question; they also form the constitutive basis of a systematic analysis of accidents in their dynamic complexity. Stories of this sort can also be found, for instance, in specialized publications such as *Nuclear Safety*, and they are stored in accident databases in an effort to create something like a narrative archive of malfunctions.[34] Knowing the steps that have led to a complex accident makes it possible to understand the factors that played a role in it. A detailed accident narrative, however, does not only unfold in retrospect; it can also be used prognostically: "incident sequence diagrams" can be created to map out the potential consequences of one or more components malfunctioning; a "failure modes and effects analysis" can be drawn up for the malfunction of a single component; or, inversely, one can propose a type of accident and use a "fault tree analysis" (fig. 4.5) to investigate the factors that might lead to that result.[35]

This narrative structure of knowledge makes it possible to arrange individual events into sequences and thus to represent causal connections as well as temporal order. Narratives are the ideal form for analyzing complex, multifactor events and have become an instrumental mechanism of technical safety. What this type of analysis reveals are the couplings that exist between the individual elements of a system—or, to be more precise, the couplings between the dysfunction of one element and the dysfunction of another. Perrow draws a distinction between "tight" and "loose" couplings and thus between "tightly" or "loosely" coupled systems:

> Tight coupling is a mechanical term meaning there is no slack or buffer or give between two items. What happens in one directly affects what

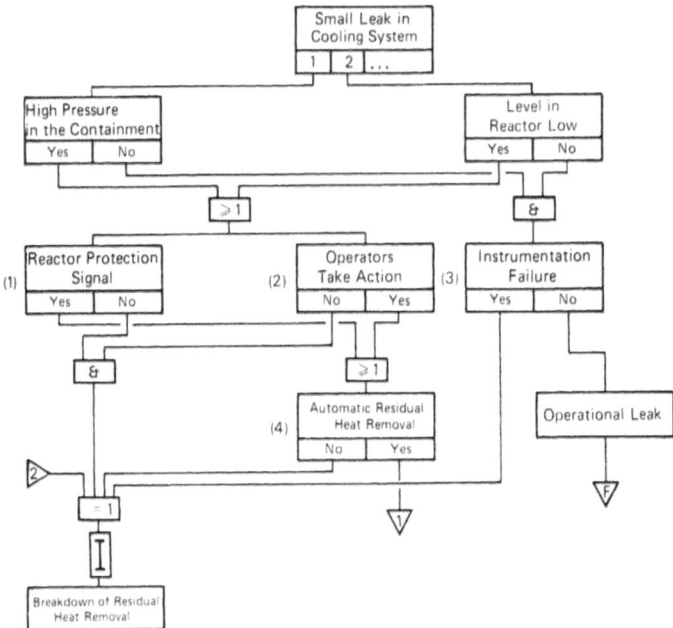

FIGURE 4.5 An example of an incident-sequence diagram from Albert Kuhlmann's *Introduction to Safety Science* (1986). The starting point is a small leak in the cooling circuit of a reactor. The diagram shows the paths of several possible outcomes.

Source: Kuhlmann, *Introduction to Safety Science* (1986). Copyright Springer-Verlag New York.

happens in the other.... Loose coupling, then, allows certain parts of the system to express themselves according to their own logic or interests. Tight coupling restricts this.... Loosely coupled systems, whether for good or ill, can incorporate shocks and failures and pressures for change without destabilization.[36]

In tightly coupled systems, the malfunction of a single element immediately affects everything else, whereas loose coupling allows for replacement, redundancy, or repair. It goes without saying that systems with loose coupling are less risky; if necessary, they can simply be switched off. However, in highly complex technology, loose coupling is not always possible. Complex systems that operate continuously, such as chemical factories or nuclear power plants, do not allow for loose coupling of their components.

Here, every element is tightly connected to other elements, and this means that safety measures such as buffers, redundancies, and possible substitutions have to be incorporated into the very construction of the facility. There is no room for improvisation. Chernobyl, again, is a good example of this: A half-day delay caused the fatal xenon poisoning of the reactor, and a decision made under the utmost pressure, like Akimov's initiation of an emergency shutdown, proved to be the wrong thing to do. When there is no leeway, systems have to be thought through with especially exact precision. All potential malfunctions—and their consequences—and all possible combinations of errors have to be considered in advance. The logic of the chain of unfortunate events has to be anticipated and built into the system itself as a subsystem of safeguards and redundancies. Because motors and pumps can break down, backup motors and pumps have to be in place. This kind of planning gave rise to the concept of the "maximum credible accident" (MCA), the type of accident that can still be "caught" by the system of safeguards before becoming a genuine catastrophe.

Perrow studied tightly coupled technical systems such as nuclear plants, chemical factories, and large oil tankers, coming to the conclusion that they pose risks too large to be acceptable. In highly complex and tightly coupled technical systems, Perrow argues, *accidents are normal*, an intrinsic component of the logic of certain technologies: "We have produced designs so complicated that we cannot anticipate all the possible interactions of the inevitable failures."[37] Whoever still considers them to be tolerable will thus have to secure the tight coupling of the system by means of a safety mechanism that is just as tightly coupled. Yet this conception of technical safety has two blind spots: First, such tightly meshed safety mechanisms make systems even more complex and thus increase the possibility of unplanned and unpredictable accidents. "Because technology," according to the philosopher Michael Hampe,

> is created as a controlled causality against undesirable outcomes and coincidences, it is obvious that the coincidences caused by the complexity of the technology itself also have to be dealt with in a technical manner.... This leads to a constant increase in technical complexities and thus also to the increased possibility of unexpected couplings and unplanned malfunctions.[38]

Second, we overestimate our ability to plan technical systems or, more precisely, to control causal chains. This is based on the idea that everything has a cause that can be easily recognized and managed—and that there must therefore always be a material defect, a design flaw, or a human operating error that can be recognized and isolated. The epistemology of safety underlying the safety sciences is based on the assumption that there will always be an identifiable chain of cause and effect that can be taken into account in designing safety measures. It is also based on the conviction that there will always be someone to be held responsible, a "human error"—someone who slacked off or slept on the job, failed to react or to anticipate the accident in the construction itself. This person can be identified and held responsible. The head engineer and the director of the Chernobyl nuclear plant, for instance, who were not even present during the experiment, were taken to court in the USSR; most of the plant workers who were actually there had died during the meltdown or from its immediate effects. Hampe, however, suggests that this idea of technology as an identifiable and finite chain of causality may be mistaken in the case of complex technological entities:

> If... causal contexts are understood as infinities, as something that can branch out at any given time in an infinite number of ways and can be traced infinitely far back into history and, if its effects are followed, infinitely far into the future, then it becomes clear that uncertainty has to be a necessary component of all causal analyses.[39]

An honest safety assessment of a given system would have to assume that *not* all combinations of malfunctions are known, that *not* all material flaws can be fully anticipated, and that the behavior of employees is likewise unpredictable. Neither stringent technical inspections nor the redundancies of safety systems will ever fully protect people from the malice of things.

LATENCIES: DELILLO'S *WHITE NOISE*

The catastrophic future of things does not necessarily manifest itself in spectacular accidents. Not all futuristic features and effects of things, of technologies, or of materials are perceptible as events, and not all accidents involve explosions or collisions, acute injuries, or visible destruction. Accidents do not necessarily occur in the form of events. The future of things also includes effects that cannot be perceived as an event, such as side effects, aftereffects, and long-term consequences. Again, Chernobyl gives us an example of this specific dimension of accidents. The abandoned city of Pripyat and the aftereffects of nuclear contamination in deformed animals or children with birth defects are the manifestations of a catastrophe that persists to the present and will certainly have consequences beyond those visible today. The damage done to living organisms by nuclear contamination is extremely hard to foresee and still cannot be fully assessed. Published shortly after the reactor meltdown, Christa Wolf's novel *Accident* is a meditation on the invisibility of the threat posed by a radioactive cloud. Narrated from the highly subjective position of the writer, the text depicts the encroachment of a vague, border-crossing danger into the tranquil daily life of East Germany, issuing novel rules of behavior. "No greens. No fresh milk for the children. A new name for danger is being circulated: Iodine 131.... One was supposed to shower the children after they had been outside. Bathing relaxed the skin, opening the pores and washing the radioactivity into the body with a vengeance."[40] A profound and subjective sense of uncertainty begins to take hold. All of a sudden, even the most minor and banal quotidian activities may have fatal consequences that will not be revealed for years to come.[41]

The German sociologist Ulrich Beck identified in these side effects the crux of what he calls the "world risk society." It is marked by a special form of uncertainty and risk awareness that stems from a coupling of knowledge and nonknowledge: "The greater the threat, the greater the gap in knowledge, the more urgent and more impossible is the decision."[42] The spectrum of aftereffects and side effects caused by various technologies, which *could* or *should* be known yet are not taken into consideration, is infinitely broad. It ranges from the toxic or carcinogenic effects of certain materials (asbestos, dioxin, or radioactive material, for instance) to meddling with the ecosystem (with land use or genetically modified life forms) and also includes problems of waste disposal (of radioactive material, of course, but also mere plastic). The broad field of so-called technological-impact assessment is devoted to investigating the *distant* future of things in two respects. First, it is distant because the issues at stake are the medium- and long-term consequences of present technology use, consequences that cannot be anticipated with tests or minimized by safety measures. Only a long expanse of time will bring them to light, and always too late. Second, this future is also distant because the consequences in question cannot easily be traced back to their causes. The causal nexus between a certain practice (unprotected sunbathing or exposure to asbestos, for instance) and a later diagnosis of cancer can only be established by long-term statistical studies. Technological-impact assessment thus suffers from a fundamental dilemma: Only after a certain technology has been widely implemented for a long period of time is it possible to evaluate its actual effects. Yet this also means that it is only possible to do so after its side effects have had time to manifest themselves. They also need to appear frequently enough to be statistically relevant. Even once a technology's risk potential is eventually known, it is usually quite difficult to implement protection laws, and it is already too late, of course, to decide not to implement the technology in the first place.[43] Victims have already been hurt, damages done, technologies established. Some catastrophes have no clearly identifiable beginning and—worse—no ending.

This, too, inspires storytelling. Often, these stories are presented as cautionary tales. They tell of early warning signs that were not taken seriously or misinterpreted and about tragic fatalities that could not be traced back to their real causes. A vivid collection of such cautionary tales is contained in a report commissioned by the European Environment Agency, *Late Lessons from Early Warnings: The Precautionary Principle, 1896–2000*.[44] It consists of fourteen case studies concerned with risky technologies, materials, or epidemics. Each study reconstructs how things developed from the earliest indications of danger to the final implementation of safety measures. The case studies collectively demonstrate how long it took to get from one point to the other. The examples range from the spread of cholera through contaminated drinking water to genetic technologies, overfishing, hazardous materials (such as asbestos, radioactive waste, CFCs, and growth hormones), and manmade illnesses such as mad cow disease. The case of asbestos is especially revealing. In the nineteenth century—ironically enough—asbestos was widely used as a fire retardant in an effort to promote safety. Yet even as early as 1898, a British factory inspector named Lucy Deane reported the "evil effects of asbestos dust," and her observations instigated a microscopic examination of the "sharp glass-like jagged nature of the particles."[45] Shortly thereafter, the first medical report was issued claiming that the inhalation of asbestos particles could lead to lung cancer. Attempts were made to minimize this risk by means of air filters, and subsequent evaluations committed the fallacy of equating "no evidence of harm" with "evidence of no harm."[46] In Germany, cases of lung cancer caused by asbestos were recognized by insurance companies as workplace hazards as early as the 1930s, whereas in England no causal link between cancer and asbestos contamination was officially admitted. The causal connection was in fact difficult to draw because of the growing popularity of another carcinogenic practice: smoking. The industries in question, moreover, did not exactly welcome investigations of their workplace hazards: Doctors and inspectors were treated as disturbers of social peace, an undesirable role that Henrik Ibsen had depicted quite early on in his play *An Enemy of the People* (1882). The difficulty of proving a causal connection between asbestos contamination and certain forms of cancer lies in the latency period between the contamination and the diagnosis, which can be as long as forty years. Only long-term studies spanning two to three decades are capable of ascertaining the problem statistically, by which point employers can simply point to their (long since) improved safety conditions and deny that there is any cause for further action. In other words, by the time that the causal connection has finally been established, the working conditions may have already changed in such a way that there is ostensibly no longer any need for action: "This problem, which might be called the 'latency lacuna,' characteristic of all long-latent-period hazards under conditions of technological change, is a major reason why preventative action is often too late."[47] The latency period obscures the causal link between the source of danger and the harm it causes to the point of unrecognizability. It was not until the end of the 1990s—a century after Lucy Deane's report—that most European countries had banned all three types of asbestos. In the United States, asbestos was phased out in 1989 but only banned in 2003. Even today, there are still many buildings in need of sanitization from asbestos, and patients with lung cancer or mesothelioma are still suing for damages on account of having been exposed to the substance.

These kinds of stories provide lessons about the epistemological and political difficulties on the path between early warnings and safety measures. As early indications of workplace hazards lead to improved workplace safety, a good argument can always be made that the danger in question has already been averted, even if these measures—in hindsight—will prove to be insufficient or inadequate. The lesson these case studies wish to impart is that it remains difficult, if not impossible, to gauge the full extent of certain dangers. As stories, they compress the time between the causes and effects of damage by leaping over the latency period and jumping straight to the diagnosis in order to make causal connections obvious. To do so, they use a narrative trick. The laborious process of investigating potential harm is presented from the perspective of its end result. What organizes the stories is a point at which everything has already been understood, be it the highly carcinogenic effects of asbestos or radioactive materials, the ozone-damaging effects of CFCs, or the ecological consequences of overfishing. As precautionary tales about a bygone future of uncertainty, these stories can only function by being told in retrospect, that is, from a final position of full and certain knowledge. The distant future of things can only become intelligible in hindsight, once this future is already in the past.

The case studies presented by the European Environment Agency are intended to justify a principle of safety that appears in the title of its report, the *precautionary principle*. In Europe, this principle has become the backbone of safety policy, while in the United States, it is still rather controversial. It asserts that whenever there is any uncertainty about the potentially deleterious consequences of a given technology, this technology should not be implemented until its harmlessness can be demonstrated beyond any reasonable doubt. It is no longer enough to calculate the probability of future damages; rather, according to the precautionary principle, the technology's harmlessness must actively be proved. It enhances the same logic of distrust that underlies Vischer's notion of the malice of objects. In the words of François Ewald:

> The precautionary principle invites one to consider the worst hypothesis (defined as the "serious and irreversible" consequence) in any business decision. The precautionary principle requires an active use of doubt, in the sense Descartes made canonical in his *Meditations on First Philosophy*. Before any action, I must not only ask myself what I need to know and what I need to master, *but also what I do not know, what I dread or suspect*. I must, out of precaution, imagine the worst possible,

the concept that an infinitely deceptive malicious demon could have slipped into the folds of an apparently innocent enterprise.[48]

The precautionary principle is thus based on a fundamental assumption about nonknowledge. As the stories related in *Late Lessons* make clear, however, it operates on the basis of a narrative that talks about the future in hindsight, that is, in the future perfect tense: *damages will have occurred.* This is how knowledge and nonknowledge about the future are bound together by a narrative: only from the end point will the causal link between contamination and illness have become apparent. From the perspective of the end point, we would never have made use of the technology in question—and therefore, the precautionary principle applies, and we should abandon its implementation in the present.

The ethical basis of the precautionary principle is the "imperative of responsibility" promoted by the German philosopher Hans Jonas. He sees it as an essential element of what he called an "ethics of an endangered future": "Act so that the effects of your action are compatible with the permanence of genuine human life [or, expressed negatively:] Act so that the effects of your action are not destructive of the future possibility of such life."[49] For Jonas (whose epistemology of foresight and precaution will also be discussed in the next chapter), the future and its integrity are the genuine ethical standard by which present acts and decisions are to be measured. The future of things must not be harmful to the inhabitants of the future. At least in its strictest formulations, the precautionary principle is a principle about how to act in situations involving unknown or invisible future catastrophes. In this regard, the sociologist Ulrich Bröckling has rightly pointed out that the precautionary principle is always driven by a maximum of catastrophic expectation: It entails that we should "always count on the worst."[50] This means turning *fear* into the foundation of our relation to the future. Jonas thus proposes a "heuristics of fear."[51]

One month after the dioxin disaster in Bhopal and a year and a half before Chernobyl and Christa Wolf's anxious reflections about vegetables, bathing, and the threats of modern technology, Don DeLillo published an entire novel devoted to this heuristics of fear and its effects on daily life, *White Noise* (1985).[52] While scholars have repeatedly discussed this novel as an illustration of "postmodern" life and of media simulacra of the 1980s, they have mostly missed its most obvious topic, life under the premises of a "heuristics of fear."[53] The novel not only depicts the affective structure of permanent anxiety and the subjectivities shaped by it; it also sheds light on its social and epistemic aporias.[54] Whereas the narrative trick of *Late Lessons* eliminates the opacity of the future lying epistemically and affectively ahead of us, DeLillo's characters stare anxiously into a future full of looming but invisible threats. The first-person narrator, a college professor named Jack Gladney, with a patchwork family and an area of expertise called "Hitler Studies," lives in a world obsessed with talking about accidents, hazardous materials, the side effects of medications, contaminated food, and how to protect oneself from catastrophes. His children have conversations about the carcinogens in bubblegum (41). His colleague wants to teach a course about the "cinema of car crashes" (40). His children's school is inspected for harmful substances, but the inspectors are dressed in suits made of Mylex, which might itself be a highly hazardous material (35). An airplane (almost) crashes. Gladney's wife takes Dylar, an experimental medication for those afflicted with the fear of death (one of its side effects is to cause people to confuse things with the words for them). One of their daughters is constantly studying reference works in an effort to learn about the risks and side effects of certain drugs. Gladney's friend Murray pays prostitutes to perform the Heimlich maneuver on them (152).

For the adults and their children alike, safety becomes an ongoing obsession, and in Murray's case it even becomes a sort of sexual fetish. The ubiquitous discussions about threats and safety mention a multitude of dangers, without giving any practical advice. The world of the novel is thus one of endemic fear. Fear is the white noise of existence—indistinct, barely audible, but always present. One of the questions that repeatedly comes up between the couple is "Who will die first?" (15).

In an uncanny and indirect way, the novel suddenly seems to answer this question. A train car containing chemicals derails and tips over at the train station. A chemical called Nyodene Derivative (Nyodene D, for short) spills out and forms a toxic cloud, which people then euphemistically refer to as an "airborne toxic event." As a substance, Nyodene D is the concentrated essence of that which is feared and illuminated by technological-impact assessment and the precautionary principle: While it remains unclear of what it is composed, Nyodene D is the epitome of a byproduct—a side effect become substance:

Nyodene D is a whole bunch of things thrown together that are byproducts of the manufacture of insecticide. The original stuff kills roaches, the byproducts kill everything left over.... In powder form it's colorless, odorless and very dangerous, except no one seems to know exactly what it causes in humans or in the offspring of humans. They tested for years and either they don't know for sure or they know and aren't saying. Some things are too awful to publicize.

(131)

No one knows whether anyone knows anything about these side effects or whether the authorities are simply withholding information. The rising toxic cloud becomes a threat to the area where the Gladneys live, so the family retreats to one of the shelters set up for evacuees—a vacant Boy Scout camp. On the drive there, they traverse an almost allegorical landscape littered with the types of accidents discussed above: skidding cars crashing into one another; the location of the chemical disaster, swarming with helicopters and men in Mylex suits; people fleeing with their children in their arms (115–22). The scene displays the pandemonium of the modern accident and safety discourse—bleak and horrifying images all too familiar from the media coverage of catastrophes. Catastrophes are always happening far away and to other people. Accordingly, Professor Gladney's reaction is that of a disaster sociologist: "These things happen to poor people who live in exposed areas. Society is set up in such a way that it's the poor and the uneducated who suffer the main impact of natural and man-made disasters.... I'm a college professor" (114).

Meanwhile, his introverted teenage son Heinrich is almost euphorically caught up in the event. Like the caricature of a safety expert, he delivers well-informed lectures to the other evacuees about Nyodene D and its rate of decay, the direction in which the poisonous cloud is traveling, and its effects on animals and people. The flipside of the white noise of mortal fear is the eloquent presentation of expert knowledge. "Let him bloom" (131), remarks his father. As it is of no practical use whatsoever, it does not calm anyone down, and it is anyway largely unreliable. The sheer performance of knowledge conveys only an effect of "prophetic disclosure" (130–31).

In Heinrich's euphoric posture of expertise, in Gladney's sociological observations ("These things happen to poor people"), and in Murray's sexual arousal over administering the Heimlich maneuver, we find a reactualization of the "desire for catastrophe" that the Cold War, as we saw in chapter 1, had impressed upon people. This desire pervades the safety discourse as the inverse of omnipresent fear. It is a longing for disaster, for the moment when the inaudible and suppressed white noise of mortal fear suddenly becomes an audible sound. It is a longing for the event to occur finally as a manifestation of the latent and looming threat that, as such, could neither be understood nor experienced.

As the fundamental feeling of Gladney's existence, his ubiquitous fear suddenly begins to take shape on account of the airborne toxic event, though the contours of this shape remain blurry. During their drive to the shelter, Gladney gets out of the car for two and half minutes to fill up the tank. In doing so, he might have become contaminated by the Nyodene D cloud. When he arrives at the camp, he is examined by an emergency unit named SIMUVAC for possible harm. Of course, SIMUVAC is not a "real" emergency unit; the name stands for "simulated evacuation" (here we are truly in the midst of 1980s postmodernity, with its obsession with simulation and simulacra). A member of the SIMUVAC team informs Gladney about the possible consequences of his brief exposure to the toxic substance, and the following dialogue ensues:

> "Am I going to die?"
> "Not as such," he said.
> "What do you mean?"
> "Not in so many words."
> "How many words does it take?"
> "It's not a question of words. It's a question of years. We'll know more in fifteen years. In the meantime we definitely have a situation."
> "What will we know in fifteen years?"
> "If you're still alive at the time, we'll know that much more than we know now. Nyodene D has a life span of thirty years, you'll have made it halfway through."
>
>   . . .
>
> "So, to outlive live this substance, I will have to make it into my eighties."

(140–41)

It is unclear what the contamination exactly means, and it is unclear what its long-term consequences will be. It is even unclear whether anyone will live long enough to die from it. "We'll know more in fifteen years" is the unhelpful but precise formula for the latency period that forms the epistemological crux of technological-impact assessments. The conversations in the book revolve around abstract concepts such as threshold levels, exposure times, and the toxicity of Nyodene D, so far only based on experiments with animals: "One part per million can send a rat into a permanent state" (139). It remains unclear what this "permanent state" consists in or whether the results are even applicable to human beings, nor even of what the ratio one part per million is referring to. None of this gives Gladney any intelligible information about a potential illness or how his health might fare in the future. Rather, it is related to future knowledge that is not yet available, a knowledge in which, at best, Gladney will appear as case data in something that the man from SIMUVAC refers to, with charming vagueness, as "a probability excess." Like the inhabitants of Pripyat, who even today are waiting to find out how severely the contamination from 1986 will have affected their life expectancy, their state of health, and their children, the protagonist of DeLillo's novel is, whether alive or dead, one number in a set of fatality statistics. This, it seems, is the only thing that is certain. The probability structure of a statistic whose very parameters are still unclear is, however, entirely unintelligible for the singular case of a given individual and for the subjectivity of the person affected. The only thing that Gladney understands is this: "Death has entered. It is inside you" (141–42). Death, however, is always inscribed in the life of the body. It is *inside* us—with or without Nyodene D, with or without radioactivity, with or without any of the threats, risks, and side effects that we explore in thinking about safety. Thus Gladney's question—"Am I going to die?"—does not make any sense, for it can only be answered in one way: "Yes." As far as the individual is concerned, the only thing that such statistics bring to light is what is always looming and latent behind the white noise of fear and the safety discourse: the awareness of mortality as the one and only future about which we can be certain.

The large-scale accident in *White Noise* thus represents the arrival of a new and different sort of "desire for catastrophe" in modernity and in the modern approach to thinking about safety. It is no longer, as during the

Cold War, an obscene and ineffable desire for the collective and simultaneous death of a politically divided humanity or even a desire for catastrophe to free us from an ongoing state of emergency. If, at its core, the regime of technical safety is driven by the malice of objects and a heuristics of fear, the catastrophic imaginary associated with it reveals a *desire for the manifestation of the latent.* Disaster fiction revolving around technological catastrophes reveals an underlying wish to make the malice of objects and technologies intelligible and thus accessible to subjective understanding. Only in the accident can the latency of threats and omnipresent risks—at long last—become evident in the form of an *event.* Thus in *White Noise,* too, it is only the airborne toxic event that lends a tangible form to the quotidian and persistent awareness of danger. Only in the event of acute disaster does this fear begin to become graspable as such. Being a concentration of all conceivable, not-yet-conceivable, and inconceivable side effects, DeLillo's Nyodene D is the bête noire of the precautionary principle and technological-impact assessment.

It is therefore no coincidence that one of the symptoms of contamination is a sense of déjà vu. When the accident strikes, it will always do so as the recognition of a future that we have long been imagining, as Gladney's colleague Murray points out.

> Why do we think these things happened before? Simple. They did happen before, in our minds, as visions of the future. Because these are precognitions, we can't fit the material into our system of consciousness as it is now structured. . . . We're seeing into the future but haven't learned how to process the experience. So it stays hidden until the precognition comes true, until we come face to face with the event.
>
> (151)

The airborne toxic event may thus be an allegory of what fiction can do for us, given the permanent white noise of fear. It allows the contents of this fear to emerge from latency; it creates an event—something that can be experienced, narrated, and represented in a way that makes the intangible and threatening future intelligible and subject to affective reaction. Whereas the scientific and political discourses of technical safety analyze potential accidents, they are unable to elucidate them and make them available to our subjective understanding and affective processing.

Accidents in literature and film are thus manifestations of something latent, looming as an *impending* or *remote* catastrophe. Be it the statistical probability of the crash, or a fatal chain of unfortunate events, or an MCA, or a side effect that will not be revealed for decades to come—the dangerous future of things cannot be accessed "as such." As a lurid image, a slapstick routine, a horror scene, a helpless monologue by someone persecuted by the malice of things, or the vague anxiety of a college professor, however, the complicated structure of technological risk and safety can become the object of experience and individual affect. Fiction enables us to behold the uncanniness of malicious technologies. It is from such technologies that our fear—the white noise of modernity—derives its narratives as well as its horror and humor.

5

THE PARADOXES OF PREDICTION

Time is forever dividing itself toward innumerable futures.
— JORGE LUIS BORGES, "THE GARDEN OF FORKING PATHS"

NARRATIVES OF PREVENTION

"The future sucked," declares a piece of graffiti at the Union Street subway station in Brooklyn. The idea that "the future *sucks*" may be little more than a pithy summary of the ideas of a *future as catastrophe*. The Greek word *katastrophē* means "a sudden downward turn."[1] Originally a poetological term, "catastrophe" designates the sudden turn of a plot structure toward a bad ending, a disruption of expectations and continuities. It is precisely in this sense that the future is apprehended today. "The future," writes the reinsurance company Swiss Re, "is what radically differs from the present."[2] The future is no longer a promise but a threat, the "end of the world as we know it." Yet the graffiti says: "The future *sucked*." Speaking about the future in the past tense—not in the future perfect ("the future *will have* sucked")—is logically impossible.[3] Nonetheless, it grasps one of the core tenets of our current relation to the future: the idea that knowledge about the future can only exist in the form of a narrative—a fiction—that looks back on the future as something in the past.

What the future is or will be as the outcome of a given present can only be narrated as a sequence of decisions, actions, and events seen in their totality. Only from the fictional standpoint of hindsight is it possible to see the consequences of a decision or the early signs of a crucial trend.

As long as this specific future is undesirable it must be prevented. The long history of prediction from ancient divination and prophesy to modern forms of prognosis is largely a history of methods and institutions designed to recognize future threats and to circumvent them. In the modern age, *prevention* has become the main purpose of prognostic knowledge. Kant, for instance, made the following comment about foresight (*praevisio*):

> Men are more interested in having foresight than any other power, because it is the necessary condition of all practical activity and of the ends to which we direct the use of our powers. Any desire includes a (doubtful or certain) foresight of what we can do by our powers. We look back on the past (remember) only so that we can foresee the future by it; and as a rule we look around us, in the standpoint of the present, *in order to decide on something or prepare ourselves for it.*[4]

For Kant, knowledge of the future is either the basis for decision making or for taking measures of provision, precaution, and prevention. To "prepare ourselves for it," that is, to envisage imminent misfortune and prevent it, is the existential core of any attempt at prediction. The desire to predict is the desire to preempt. This modern link between prediction and preemption was captured succinctly in a quotation attributed to Auguste Comte: "See in order to know; know in order to predict; predict in order to preempt" (*voir pour savoir, savoir pour prévoir, prévoir pour prévenir*).[5] What sounds like a logical sequence, however, is in fact a highly heterogeneous process involving various forms of knowledge and types of action. It betrays the positivist belief that it is possible to derive an understanding of general regularities from observation and, on this basis, to make assumptions about the future. This approach, however, is premised on a fundamental belief in the continuity between past, present, and future. When Kant (like Comte) maintains that looking back on the past enables us to foresee the future, the future is made to seem like a mildly modified extension of the past and the present. The same laws that have shaped the present will also determine the future.

Such a conception may be practical in certain efforts to "prepare ourselves for it." For the modern era, the sociologist Ulrich Bröckling has identified three fundamental "regimes of prevention" and has associated their political and social strategies with particular epistemic structures of prediction.[6] There is, first, a regime of "hygiene" that claims to identify future "agents of harm," whether in the form of "germs" or in the form of "social vermin." It seeks to track these down and eliminate them in the present in order to prevent future damages. This mechanism undoubtedly corresponds quite closely with the optimistic nineteenth-century belief that it is possible to move directly from seeing to foreseeing and preventing. In this regime, prediction is above all an extrapolation of the present, a projection of the familiar onto the future.[7] A second, more contemporary regime of prevention, which Bröckling refers to as "immunization," concentrates less on eliminating threats than on *managing* them. It thus does not rely so much on the possibility of identifying the causes of future damages in the present but operates instead by, for instance, calculating and reducing risks, implementing safety regulations, strengthening immune systems, or creating insurance programs. The epistemology of this regime is based on what strategic planners call "known unknowns": a hypothetical knowledge derived from probability calculations (such as accident statistics), trends, and estimates (such as, for example, the green, yellow, orange, and red "threat levels"). The "immunization" regime aims at *managing the future* via a cybernetic system of modulation. It relies on risk management by nudging, insuring, preparing, and steering. While it does not know exactly what will happen, it claims to know what is likely and unlikely to happen—and it aims at reducing the probability of damages (as in the "safety" regime discussed in chapter 4) or to compensate for future damages (as in insurance). Today, this regime of prevention can be seen as predominant, and it is relatively effective in predicting "normal" or "everyday" accidents or incidences such as car crashes or illnesses that, considered at a sufficient scale across a broad population, exhibit calculable statistical trends.

It cannot, however, account for rare and immense catastrophic events, such as, for example, the damage done by the terror attacks of September 11, 2001, or the case of a devastating epidemic. For such huge events, about which we know (almost) *nothing* and that, therefore, exceed the scope of any possible immunization, Bröckling describes a third regime of prevention.[8] This type of improbable yet broadly damaging event calls for methods of "thinking the unthinkable," as the Cold War strategist Herman Kahn put it. The regime of prevention for this type of catastrophic future is the so-called precautionary principle. It is based on the assumption that we might simply not be able to tell what type of event will threaten us in the future or, indeed, may already be threatening our future.

Based on this principle, the politics of technical safety, examined in the previous chapter, sets out to estimate the long-term or latent consequences of certain technologies or products. It is, as Bröckling points out, based on a "heuristics of fear," as outlined by Hans Jonas.[9] The precautionary principle suggests forgoing the advantages of uncertain technologies (such as climate engineering or genetically modified crops), rather than facing their potentially dangerous and unpredictable long-term effects. In the realm of political security, however, the precautionary principle inclines toward a sort of preventive or preemptive activism. As we know nothing about the form and extent of a future attack or crime, precaution calls for a maximum of countermeasures that extend even to preemptive strikes. "The risks of inaction are far greater than the risk of action," as Dick Cheney put it, articulating the principles of the so-called War on Terror.[10] While in terms of *safety* the precautionary principle calls for the forgoing of unsafe practices and technologies, in terms of *security* it calls for a maximum of preventive action. The precautionary principle operates on the supposition of a structural condition of ignorance captured in Donald Rumsfeld's infamous phrase "unknown unknowns" and therefore calls for a constant state of being "prepared for the worst."[11] It is this self-reflexive orientation toward *not knowing* that accounts for the epistemic complexity of preventive knowledge about the future.

Knowledge about the future is structurally always knowledge under the condition of not knowing. This connection between knowing and not knowing may, in certain cases, lead to optimism, for instance, to the belief in progress and thus the hope that we will soon know more. Here, not knowing is understood as not *yet* knowing.[12] While this idea of epistemic progress might have dominated the nineteenth century, today not knowing is felt as radical uncertainty in the face of unpredictable dangers. This pessimism generates a specific form of knowledge, "security knowledge," which maintains an inseparable relation to nonknowledge. "Security," according to J. Peter Burgess, "concerns precisely *what we do not know. Its entire rationality, politics, and normativity revolve around just this epistemological aberration: security is by nature a relation to what is unknowable.*"[13] Preventative knowledge of the future thus requires a negative epistemology to conceptualize the connection between knowing and not knowing.

This negative epistemology intrinsically depends on a structural fictionality. For this reason, the precautionary principle is deeply interested in *imaginative* processes of prediction and in what Craig Calhoun has called an "emergency imaginary."[14] The imaginary catastrophic futures in literature and film can thus be seen as a means of illuminating the epistemological darkness that envelops the future. They make it possible to envision improbable disasters such as MCAs (maximum credible accidents) or chains of unfortunate events. Yet fiction (in scientific scenarios as much as in novels or films) also implies that the future is one of many possible courses of events. The "negative epistemology" of prevention has to measure and gauge this space of potential outcomes and expectations.

For at its heart, knowledge of the future, in so far as it aims to prevent or to prepare for potential damage or disaster, possesses, as Peter Fuchs has argued, a "temporal structure that seems paradoxical."[15] On the one hand, the future has to be recognized and depicted as an imminent course of events; on the other hand, steps have to be taken for it *not* ever to occur. "From this it follows," according to Fuchs, "that preventive efforts are always concerned with at least two futures, namely one that will unfold with prevention and one that will unfold without it. Which of these futures will become factual will only be decided once the act of prevention has become the past and the future has become the present."[16] The effectiveness of precautionary measures can only be gauged from the point of view of a narrative that is already closed, looking back on two alternative yet mutually exclusive paths: one with the intervention of preventive measures, the other without. "There is no empirical test that can prove whether a certain future (which does not exist) would have in fact arrived."[17] There may indeed be no test, but there are, in the immunity regime, reliable probabilities, for example, that houses without a lightning rod more frequently catch fire if struck by lightning or that unvaccinated people are likely to face health problems if contaminated. Beyond these patterns of probability, however, that is, in cases too rare or too disastrous, expected or probable future events can only be grasped through a minimal *plot*, a sequence of action that transposes a hypothetical "*if* . . . *then* . . . " structure into a structure of *before* and *after*. A hypothetical narrative must relate the course of events that is *not* supposed to happen.

Prevention is thus dependent on a *narrative* providing an *interpretation* of the present that, at the same time, indicates measures that might be taken against the course of events described. It is based on a structure of the self-defeating prophecy—a prediction of the future whose very performance is supposed to prevent the prediction from becoming fact. Prevention, in other words, hopes to avert what it sees coming.

This is why prevention can only be properly understood through a theory of fiction. It conceives of the present as a branching point that leads to multiple alternative stories. Jorge Luis Borges's story "The Garden of Forking Paths" casts this structure as the essence of time: "Time is forever dividing itself toward innumerable futures."[18] The present, according to one of Borges's characters, has the form of a novel: "In all fiction, when a man is faced with alternatives he chooses one at the expense of the others."[19] Borges provides us with a model for what fiction can accomplish on an epistemological level. His story revolves around a mysterious work of art called *The Garden of Forking Paths*, which is in fact a novel in which the protagonist does not choose just one option but simultaneously chooses all of them: "He thus creates various futures, various times which start others that will in their turn branch out and bifurcate."[20] Borges calls this branching structure of alternative possible worlds "fictions" (*ficciones*).[21] "Fiction" here is not about the difference between reality and an invented or imaginary world; it denotes the realm of possibility containing alternative plotlines, each a plausible variant that thwarts all of the others. Time, according to one of Borges's characters, is a labyrinth of fictions, a "garden of forking paths." For Borges, a "fiction" is one of these paths, one variant of reality among others. There is no such thing as only *one* "fiction" but rather what is referred to in the sciences as a "working hypothesis," a "heuristic fiction," or a "scenario" in Herman Kahn's sense. Understanding a story as fiction means to consider its divergence from other possible versions. Understanding the present, in Borges's model, means regarding it as a branching point of multiple potential futures. The present "bifurcates" into multiple, yet mutually exclusive, realities.[22]

This concept of fiction, I believe, is at the epistemic basis of any theory of prevention. Prevention sees the present as a branching point of multiple futures, some of them desirable, others noxious. If everything goes as planned, the noxious versions will remain nothing more than possible worlds that never came into being. Yet these possible worlds were necessary for the very decision to take preventive measures. According to Aristotle's definition of literature (as opposed to historiography), it relates how things *might have been* or *what might have happened*.[23] Literary narratives explore realms of possibility that, just like Borges's forking paths, could always have been otherwise.

This structural affinity between fiction and prediction is the reason why knowing the future has always been a classic topic of literature. Prediction is often linked to a tragic structure in which foreknowledge typically refers to a catastrophic future that needs to be thwarted. The narration of the tragedy of prediction is not, however, just one topic among others (such as war, love, jealousy, and so on). To elucidate the negative epistemology of the inextricable conjunction between knowledge of the future and blindness toward it, literature has to incorporate this conjunction into its very structure of representation. And although the protagonist must remain unconscious of this conjunction, the reader must become aware of it. This is how literature shares the darkness in which the future lies: It casts light on it but must also remain within it.

NEGOTIATING WITH THE FUTURE: CROESUS AND OEDIPUS

> *How dreadful knowledge of the truth can be*
> *When there's no help in truth!*
> —SOPHOCLES, *OEDIPUS REX*

The idea of prevention belongs to a genuinely modern understanding of the future. The future is seen as something contingent, anchored in the present, changeable, plannable, and *preventable*. We constantly make decisions that will determine the course of things to come. We bear the constant weight of responsibility for a future that is—as modernity has come to see it—largely in our hands. It calls for planning, provision, and prevention—and even if we forgo our duty to shape the future, this decision, too, carries its own weight of responsibility. This modern attitude toward the future as manmade notwithstanding, it is necessary to look back to antiquity and its very different relation to the future and to the possibilities and paradoxes of prevention.

Classical antiquity was preoccupied with the possibility of possessing knowledge about the future, and it produced some of the most powerful narratives about the aporias of foreknowledge. It focused on the ineluctable and often fatal connection between *foreknowledge* and *the imperative to act*. In the form of tragedy, it found an aesthetic form that intricately entwines knowing and not knowing the future. This is an idea that continues to afflict our relation to future security: prophesy or prediction may be accurate but can always be misinterpreted. And this misinterpretation will lead to catastrophe.

The main difference between antiquity's relation to the future and today's is the idea that the future *can* be known. For the ancient societies of Mesopotamia, Egypt, or China, and from the Hebrews to the Greeks and Romans, it was self-evident that knowledge of the future could be attained through specific practices such as divination, prophetic trance, or divine inspiration.[24] The ancient world was not concerned with the (modern) question of the possibility of foreknowledge but rather with the question of how to handle this knowledge. Ancient techniques for divination or prediction thus relied heavily on interpretation. Their methods involved either semiotic interpretations of natural signs (as in the entrails of sacrificed animals, the flight of birds, the stars, or the drawing of lots) or of divine utterances conveyed through a medium such as the oracle of Delphi or a prophet.[25] While in the semiotic methods experts explained the prophetic signs, in the case of prophecy or oracle, on the contrary, the interpretation of the god's obscure words was usually left to the addressees. The world of divination is one of endless interpretation. The future may always already be predestined, but it is not apparent to the perspicacity of human beings. God or the gods, in contrast, oversee this world, and their omniscient perspective is the source of the opaque information conferred to the living.

In this need for interpretation lies the hope, and danger, in using foreknowledge as a basis for decision making. The obscurity of signs or words allows for interpretative leeway in the ways human plans can be brought into harmony with divine will. This enables oracles to be used pragmatically and politically as an aid to decision making and political rule.[26] The ambiguity of oracles, however, also carries the danger of misinterpretation, often of a self-serving kind.

The most famous example of this is King Croesus, whose entire life, according to Herodotus, was an ongoing dialogue with the oracle at Delphi. He was also a highly demanding customer of Apollo's extremely expensive services. He tests a number of oracles with a difficult question and is only satisfied by the responses offered by the oracles of Delphi and Amphiaraus.[27] The subsequent gifts he sends to both sites are accompanied by another inquiry. Croesus wants to know whether to wage war against the Persians. To this question, both oracles provide the following famous response: "They told Croesus that if he made war on the Persians, he would destroy a great empire."[28] Here, foreknowledge is used as a basis for decision making but clearly also as the confirmation of preexisting plans. To get the outcome he desires, Croesus pays gold for a favorable oracle. After his defeat against the Persians, the disappointed king sends a delegation to Delphi to complain that the god "used his oracles to encourage Croesus to march against the Persians by leading him to believe that he would put an end to Cyrus's empire." Croesus tends to view the god as a contractual partner; for him, foreknowledge is a good that can be purchased, and he feels entitled to customer satisfaction. Apollo's response to this is highly instructive for understanding the ancient attitude to the future:

> Not even a god can escape his ordained fate. Croesus has paid for the crime of his ancestor four generations ago.... In fact, Loxias [Apollo's appellation as the god of prediction] wanted the fall of Sardis [Croesus's empire] to happen in the time of Croesus's sons rather than of Croesus himself, but it was not possible to divert the Fates. However, he won a concession from them and did Croesus that much good.... Moreover, Croesus has no grounds for complaint as regards the oracle. Loxias predicted that if he invaded Persia, he would destroy a great empire. Faced with this, if he had thought about it he would have sent

men to enquire whether Loxias meant Cyrus's empire or his own. Because he misunderstood the statement and failed to follow it up with another enquiry, he should blame no one but himself for what happened.[29]

Apollo "Loxias" (that is, "the Ambiguous") explains to his disappointed customer not just the course of a future that was entirely unavoidable. He also points out that the ambiguity of the oracle places the responsibility for its use firmly on the side of the person asking. Thus the oracle's prediction can easily accommodate a different interpretation in the event that things turn out differently. The practice of oracles thus integrates the possibility of error within its own system.

Apollo also explains the status of prophesied future knowledge: The future is planned ahead, woven like a thread, and it lies in the hands of the goddesses of fate, the three Moirai, Clotho, Lachesis, and Atropos. A god like Apollo may *know* about this future, but he can only postpone it temporarily or slightly modify it. He is not a lord of destiny but a medium of knowledge, though one of boundless knowledge about the past, the present, and the future—about the infinite and the impossible. This was the way in which the oracle defined its specific type of knowledge in its reply to Croesus's initial test: "I know the number of grains of sand and the extent of the sea; I understand the deaf-mute and hear the words of the dumb."[30] This kind of total knowledge, which includes the future as well as the most unfathomable details, such as the number of grains of sand on the shore, does *not* mean, however, that the oracle can help its customers intervene in these things. The future already exists and will necessarily happen, regardless of whether men like Croesus are able to purchase divine prophecies. The thread of fate is complete before it is unwound by the Moirai. For this reason, the value of a human life can only be evaluated after death, when it is possible to survey all of its twists and turns in hindsight. Croesus experiences this early on when, at the height of his powers, he asks the philosopher Solon of Athens about the most fortunate person on earth—hoping, of course, that Solon would name him, Croesus. Instead, Solon names people who died happily or heroically. These alone, he claims, can be judged as truly fortunate, as their lives can be viewed in their totality.[31] In ancient thought, humans are always limited in their knowledge, and thus the future can only be evaluated in terms of final closure. Only when a life has come to an end and its meaning is clear can its value be recognized. In antiquity, life is a path that does not fork. With their total knowledge, only the gods are aware of this story before it is lived through.[32] But beyond that, they are powerless. The gods are not makers but ideal (omniscient) narrators of human fate. The problem faced by human beings is that of correctly deciphering the fragments and prolepses the oracle offers them.

The most tragic case of this structure of foreknowledge in the Delphic oracle was the Theban royal family. With rare clarity, the myth of Oedipus reveals a fundamental aporia of foreknowledge and its conjunction with preventive action. Knowledge of the future does not imply knowledge about the consequences of preventive measures. Prevention operates blindly, even if there is no possible way *not* to try to avert the terrible fate of the family predicted by Apollo. The Oedipus story is about the blindness that engulfs those with foreknowledge. Whereas Croesus simply could have refrained from going to war with Cyrus, the oracles given to King Laius and later to his son and murderer Oedipus are so atrocious that they *demand* immediate action in the form of an attempt at prevention. Knowing that their son will kill his father and marry his mother, Laius and Jocaste *must* try to escape this destiny. Likewise Oedipus, who receives the same oracle, *has to* flee from his foster parents in Corinth in order to protect them from himself, and in doing so he comes to Thebes, of all places, where he is unwittingly reunited with his natural parents. Like a pair of pliers, the respective oracles grip the parents and their son and force them to meet, ironically through their efforts to prevent the prophesied evil. The myth thus demonstrates one of the central problems of preventive action based on foreknowledge: by announcing future misfortune, foreknowledge impels a decision to act. Even doing nothing and letting destiny run its course would be an act for which the parents and the son would have to bear responsibility. This is why Oedipus, in Sophocles's account, eventually blames himself for the deeds he unknowingly committed.[33] By taking responsibility for his actions, Oedipus reveals the inherently tragic structure of foreknowledge. *It forces* action to be taken and decisions to be made for the sake of the future, yet these decisions are taken without knowing where this *alternative* path might lead. Prevention always comes at a price that is constitutively unknown. For Laius and Jocaste, this price is more than obvious at the very moment they decide to abandon their newborn child. Oedipus, on the other hand, believes that he can simply escape his destiny unscathed and innocent by fleeing from the Corinthian court.

Oedipus's blindness regarding the ambiguity of foreknowledge is precisely the subject of Sophocles's tragedy. In this play, however, the story unfolds retrospectively, beginning at the moment when Oedipus, while ruling Thebes as the successor of King Laius and the husband of Jocaste, has to rid his kingdom of a plague. He requests another prediction from the oracle, which tells him that the plague will only come to an end when the murderer of the previous king has been found. At the end of the subsequent investigation, Oedipus understands that he is the murderer of his predecessor. It is also revealed that this was caused by the very measures taken to prevent the family's fate from taking its course. In this inherent failure of prevention, Peter Szondi identified what he saw as the pivotal aspect of tragedy, namely, the "unity of salvation and annihilation":

> It is not annihilation that is tragic, but the fact that salvation becomes annihilation; the tragic does not take place in the hero's downfall, but rather in the fact that man meets his demise along the very path he took up to escape this demise. . . . That the gods bestow something dreadful on humanity is, however, not tragic. Rather it is tragic when the dreadful occurs *through man's own doing*.[34]

This self-defeating intention gets to the heart of the classical conception of foreknowledge and prevention: Foreknowledge is precisely possible to the extent that prevention is *impossible*. The tragedy of this structure lies in the fact that this type of foreknowledge is a form of knowledge that forces one into action.

The attempt to evade prophesied misfortune must be blind to this. It is the blindness of the Theban royal family that forms the central object of Sophocles's text. Here, the relation between knowing and not knowing the future is reflected early on in the semantics of seeing and not seeing. As his first step toward clarifying the murder of his predecessor, Oedipus summons the seer Tiresias. The blind seer knows the identity of the murderer (and thus also Oedipus's hidden identity as the son of Laius and Jocaste), but despite the king's lengthy provocations he refuses at first to reveal his knowledge. Unsurprisingly, Oedipus does not believe his hints, instead berating Tiresias for being incompetent in his craft, shameless, and above all *blind*. Knowledge is discussed here as the ability to see, and the question is raised about who is truly blind—that is, ignorant:

> OEDIPUS: There is [power in truth]: But not for you, not for you,
>   You sightless, witless, senseless, mad old man! . . .
>   You child of endless night! You cannot hurt me
>   Or any other man who sees the sun.[35]

Tiresias responds only briefly to Oedipus's insinuations that he might be part of a conspiracy against him. He responds at length, however, to being insulted as a blind man by inverting the relationship between sight and knowledge, blindness and ignorance:

> TIRESIAS: Listen to me. You mock my blindness, do you?
>   But I say that you, with both your eyes, are blind:
>   You cannot see the wretchedness of your life,
>   Nor in whose house you live, no, nor with whom.
>   Who are your father and mother? Can you tell me?
>   You do not even know the blind wrongs
>   That you have done them, on earth and in the world below.
>   But the double lash of your parents' curse will whip you
>   Out of this land some day, with only night
>   Upon your precious eyes.
>   Your cries then—where will they not be heard? . . .
>   A blind man who has eyes now; a penniless man, who is rich now;
>   And he will go tapping the strange earth with his staff.[36]

In the conflict between the knowing Tiresias and the ignorant Oedipus, the semantics of blindness and sight is evoked when the king ventures to equate seeing with knowledge. Tiresias instructs him that it is precisely the opposite: It is the seeing man who is truly blind, blinded, and incapable of knowledge, and it is the physically blind man who knows and understands the circumstances at hand. This separation of knowing and seeing is Sophocles's first reference to the relation between knowing and unknowing regarding the future. Whereas seeing implies a form of knowledge that essentially consists in misunderstanding (as it is based on appearances), blindness enjoys a deeper and nonevident insight, the recognition of truth. Everything is different from what it seems: "A blind man who has eyes now; a penniless man who is rich now."[37] The juxtaposition of seeing and knowledge, however, refers not only to Thebes but also to the essence of foreknowledge: To *see* the future always means to *misunderstand* something essential in it. Knowing the future is a shadowy and deceptive type of knowledge, and its greatest deceit lies in conveying the illusion of knowing more than anybody else.

Both Oedipus's and Jocaste's reaction to Tiresias's remarks demonstrates this misunderstanding, this ignorance-in-knowledge. Oedipus, for his part, suspects a plot by his brother-in-law Creon, who, he believes, wishes to remove him from power with the help of fraudulent prophecies. Jocaste, for her part, doubts the reliability of the oracle by stressing the fact that the prophecy came not from the god directly but only from his servants. What becomes apparent in Jocaste's and Oedipus's blindness is the self-fulfilling structure of classical foreknowledge. It is diametrically opposed to the self-defeating structure of modern prevention, which, in essence, aims at being proven wrong. Once expressed, it manifests itself necessarily and inexorably in the urge to prevent the future.

The self-fulfilling power of knowing the future is best expressed in the words used by Jocaste and Oedipus to reinforce their own narrative. Affirming their innocence, they speak without knowing what they are really saying. Precisely by arguing that Apollo's prediction never became fact, Jocaste provides Oedipus with the missing piece of evidence that it did indeed become true. The most striking case of this speaking without knowing about the implications of one's words is Oedipus's unintentional ambiguity when he puts a curse on the murderer of his predecessor—and thus on himself:

> OEDIPUS: I solemnly forbid the people of this country,
>   Where power and throne are mine, ever to receive that man
>   Or speak to him, no matter who he is, or let him
>   Join in sacrifice, lustration, or in prayer.
>   I decree that he be driven from every house,
>   Being, as he is, corruption itself to us: the Delphic
>   Voice of Zeus has pronounced this revelation.
>   ....
>   Now I, having the power that he held before me,

> Having his bed, begetting children there
> Upon his wife, as he would have, had he lived –
> Their son would have been my children's brother,
> If Laius had had luck in fatherhood! . . .
> I say I take the son's part, just as though
> I were his son, to press the fight for him
> And see it won! . . .[38]

Although expressed in hypothetical terms ("as though I were his son"), Oedipus states with stunning precision the full extent of his relation to Laius: Laius is his father, he married his own mother, and his children with Jocaste are his siblings. The ambiguity of Apollo Loxias's pronouncements, which had already misled Croesus, is radically intensified by Sophocles. He lets the oracle's well-known ambiguity penetrate the protagonist's utterances themselves. Their speech unknowingly tells the truth; their words *contain* a knowledge that they cannot comprehend. This ambiguity gives rise to an irony inherent in the tragic structure of prevention. This "tragic irony," according to Menke, consists in doubling the protagonist into both an actor and an observer: "By his action the hero brings about his own fate, because this action consists in a discourse in which not only he himself, or he not only as himself, speaks—in which he unconsciously speaks as his other, as his author and spectator."[39] In his ambiguous curse, "Oedipus not only unconsciously predicts his fate, he also prescribes it for himself; the ironic double meaning of his speech not only mirrors his fate, it *makes* his fate."[40]

The retrospective discovery of the past undertaken by Oedipus can thus be interpreted as the creation of foreknowledge in reverse, or upside down. Solon was right never to praise a living man before his death, as the chorus concludes at the end of the tragedy:

> Let every man in mankind's frailty
> Consider his last day; and let none
> Presume on his good fortune until he find
> Life, at his death, a memory without pain.[41]

It is only at the end of a life's story, in hindsight, that it will it be possible to understand what knowledge of the future *will have been and achieved* in this life. Yet unlike Herodotus's narrative of Croesus's life, Sophocles stages this process of understanding in a drama, that is, in the speeches of the dramatis personae. These speeches become the locus of the play's tragic irony, the collusion between knowledge and blindness. As they speak their truths, they do this before an audience that, given the popularity of the Oedipus myth, *always already knows the final truth*. The audience's perspective is thus exactly that of a god who knows in advance the protagonists' past, present, and future—and thus his and her blindness. The audience knows and thus sees through Oedipus's and Jocaste's blindness, enacted in their speech. It can thus also see how they know the truth without consciously having access to it. Foreknowledge, according to Tiresias, is therefore inherently useless to the person who knows: "How dreadful knowledge of the truth can be / When there's no help in truth!" It is good for nothing because oracular speech is, as the sociologist Elena Esposito remarks, *performative* speech: "Prophetic knowledge does not describe the world from the outside but rather is an active element in this world, striving for its realization."[42] This performativity of knowledge about the future, however, is inaccessible to those seeking foreknowledge; rather they become characters in a drama written by the oracle. The tragic irony within the speech and (speech) acts of his characters highlights the aporia that the ancient world sees in foreknowledge and prevention. Man bears his future within himself (as Oedipus does his past and his identity). It is like an organ inaccessible to him, part of his existence, but one that can neither be changed nor removed.

For antiquity, foreknowledge and the urge to thwart prophesized disaster is thus the epitome of tragic action. While forcing people to take action, it leaves them blind to the consequences of these preventive actions, generating a deadlock of unavoidable guilt. Knowing the future, everything one does—be it by way of action or by letting things take their course—is *self-produced*. The classical model thus touches upon a fundamental paradox of prevention even in the modern sense: the fact that we never really know about its "costs," the potential tragedy of a path not taken.

This performative dimension of foreknowledge is the point that antiquity grasps much more clearly than present-day ideas of prevention. It is, however, occasionally discussed, in, for instance, cases of medical prevention, when certain forms of prophylaxis are regarded as potentially more dangerous than the illnesses they are designed to prevent.[43] They also loom large in the insurance industry, where the existence of certain types of insurance can trigger particularly dangerous behavior. It is a statistical fact that drivers of cars with advanced safety technology tend to drive more aggressively. And in the world of finance, the global crisis of 2008 has shown that protection against risk can lead to an extreme recklessness regarding potential losses. These are just a few examples of where the "costs" of prevention become evident in the modern world, which so heavily relies on regimes of prevention. Like the coercion to act it imposes on those in the know, prevention comes with a price, both in the present and in the future. As we will see, modernity has found its own forms and narratives to deal with the tragedy of prediction and prevention.

SEEKING SECURITY: KAFKA'S "THE BURROW" AND NICHOLS'S *TAKE SHELTER*

> *True caution demands—as, unhappily, it does so often—that you should risk your life.*
>
> — KAFKA, "THE BURROW"

What distinguishes modernity's from antiquity's conception of the future is the idea of the *future as a garden of forking paths*. The modern understanding is no longer based on the notion of a thread of life that unravels inexorably and can only be apprehended or misapprehended. It presupposes an open and malleable future that can be predicted in the present and also altered. Prognoses are no longer self-fulfilling but seen as a form of pragmatic knowledge. They envision a contingent future subject to change. This secular future, however, excludes the divine perspective of absolute knowledge just as it seems to exclude the tragic blindness of Oedipus, who has no access to the knowledge he bears within himself. As individual lives are no longer seen as scripted stories, for the modern age, history is no longer a preordained path toward the Last Judgment but rather an unforeseeable horizon. Time, in the modern era, is "open for the new and without limit."[44] It thus opens up a space of infinite possibilities. Yet for this reason the present is also burdened with the need for constant vigilance and permanent decision making in order to "secure" the future. If the future is made, we are always called upon to take responsibility for what is to come. As Niklas Luhmann ironically remarked, "We no longer belong to the family of tragic heroes who subsequently found out that they had prepared their own fates. We now know it beforehand."[45] Therein lies the problem. Our actions and plans are always just one factor among a multitude of other actions and plans. The ancient protagonists' blindness has been replaced by a fragmented view overlooking an infinity of open possibilities and contingencies. Thus, as Bröckling argues, "prevention is the dominant logic under which contemporary societies negotiate and organize their relation to the future."[46]

The "dark side" of this open future, according to Elena Esposito, is the culture of worry, care, or concern (*Sorgekultur*) that it brings about.[47] Concern (in German: *Sorge*) is the attitude that shifts responsibility for the future onto the present. It is both a need to plan, to shape desirable futures, and an urge to prevent undesirable futures. Heidegger understood care and concern (*Sorge*) as "the characterization of man's essence ... which dominates his *temporal sojourn in the world*."[48] It characterizes our sojourns (*Wandeln*) as well as our transformations and activities. According to an old fable by Hyginus, Cura (care, concern), here cast as a personification, owns human beings *in time*, while they dwell on earth.[49] The Latin word *cura* can mean anxiety, concern, and sorrow as well as carefulness, circumspection, and devotion—that is, both positive and negative attitudes toward the future.[50] The German terms for "care," *Sorge* and its many compounds, however, mainly carry connotations of constant and fearful effort, permanent vigilance and attentiveness, constant anticipation. As modern humans create the future, they spend every waking moment worrying about it. *Securitas*, the Latin word for security, derives from *cura* (*se-cura* denotes the absence of care or concern): "The syntagma *se-cura* vividly conjures a scene in which care has been taken away or one has moved away from care."[51] To achieve security would be to free oneself from all care or concern. However, security also presupposes care and concern. Security's carelessness can only be possible on the basis of concern and prevention.

No text has captured modernity's worrisome relation to the future as vividly as "The Burrow," a late prose text by Franz Kafka. Written in the last year of his life, over the winter of 1923 and 1924, and thus at nearly the same time that Heidegger was working on *Being and Time*, the text presents an inner monologue about concern and the aporias of care/security. The work presents the worried thoughts of an unidentified animal living in a self-constructed burrow. The burrow serves the animal as sanctuary and storage space, bunker, and a trap for all the "small fry" (*Kleinzeug*) the animal feeds upon. "I have established my burrow, and it seems to be a success"[52]—so begins the monologue, which goes on not only to describe the burrow and recapitulate its painstaking creation but also relentlessly to probe its adequacy and safety. The question is whether the burrow, as a materialization of ongoing care and concern, is really such a "success" after all.

For the animal, the burrow is a matter of concern, provision, and protection—a safeguard against the dangers of the future, "the enemies from outside" as well as "the enemies from the bowels of the earth" (163). It is a "life-saving hole," in the event of being hunted down by other predators; a supply room, in the event of a "siege" (164); a place to retreat and hide; and a "labyrinth" in which intruders will lose their way (168). Yet the burrow is not only a protective space but also a place to retire to in the animal's old age: "It is a beautiful thing to have such a burrow in advancing age, to have put a roof over your head at the approach of fall" (164). Inside the burrow, the animal hopes to protect himself against events that threaten to encroach upon his finely structured world—be it "the teeth of my persecutor in my thigh" (163), hunger, or the frailty of old age. Kafka's animal is fully equipped for an unknown kind of emergency. His thoughts circle obsessively around all conceivable dangers; his monologue is a restless search for problems in a world full of threats: "Irresolutely it flits from one worry to the next, it nibbles at every anxiety with the fickleness of despair," Walter Benjamin observed.[53] As the future is open, it is an unpredictable realm of looming danger. Security, which the burrow is supposed to provide, cannot be created in a single act of calculation and effort; rather, it requires *a constant effort*, an unrelenting "epistemology of suspicion," as Elisabeth Strowick has pointed out.[54] As an expert in workplace safety and accident avoidance, Kafka knew that prevention is never a singular measure but rather something that demands "continuous caution."[55] This concerns not only the "weaknesses . . . imposed on the burrow by nature," which can only be recognized "after the fact" (168); it also concerns the construction of the burrow as such. As the animal knows, even the utmost vigilance can only detect those dangers whose nature can be imagined. The real danger, however, lies in the unexpected, the "unknown unknowns," in what is "structurally unknowable."[56]

With remarkable insistence, Kafka's animal reflects on such "structurally unknowable" things, which pose the fundamental problem to all security projects. While its activity in the burrow promises security by controlling space and keeping intruders at bay, the burrow's closed-off structure itself contains potential danger. In the event of an emergency, the animal would be trapped beneath the earth. For this reason, the burrow needs an easy exit, which is concealed beneath just a thin layer of moss:

> True, someone can step on the moss or poke into it, then my burrow would lie open; and whoever desires . . . can break in and destroy the whole thing forever. I fully understand as much, and even now at its high point my life hardly knows an hour of complete peace: there, at that one place on the dark moss, I am mortal, and often in my dreams a lascivious snout sniffs incessantly around it. It can be argued that I could have filled in this real entrance hole as well . . . so that it would never take me more than a slight effort to excavate the exit whenever I wanted. That, however, is not feasible, caution demands that I should have an immediate possibility of escape, *true caution demands—as, unfortunately, it does so often—that you should risk your life*; all these are very laborious calculations, and the delight that the sharp-witted mind takes in itself is sometimes the sole reason why it continues its calculations. I must have the immediate possibility of escape, since, despite all my vigilance, isn't it possible that I could be attacked from a completely unexpected quarter? I live peacefully in the innermost part of my burrow, and meanwhile slowly and quietly from somewhere or other the enemy is boring his way toward me.
>
> (162–63; my emphasis, translation amended)

The security provided by perfect isolation is no security at all. Thus, the burrow needs an exit, which, however, represents its greatest security risk. It is precisely a threat from an "unexpected quarter" that requires the burrow to be equipped with a vulnerable opening, a feature that goes entirely against its stated purpose. The price of security is fundamental insecurity.⁵⁷ The constant awareness of vulnerabilities justifies the permanent concern and readiness without which security would be unthinkable.

Kafka thus demonstrates the way in which security and care/concern are inseparably connected. Total security is not an achievable or even desirable goal, as it would imply either complete isolation, which, as in the burrow or bunker, can become a trap and a grave. Or it would mean total carelessness—a reckless state of insouciance. Kafka's animal knows that this is precisely where the danger lies. There is nothing left for it to do but to ponder, incessantly, the paradoxes of security, an interminable project.

The point of Kafka's analysis of security, however, is not only expressed by the animal's mutterings. It is also expressed by the *form* of the text, which suddenly breaks off. The solipsistic inner monologue of the animal, not addressed to any interlocutor, is caught up in an inescapable temporality, which is reflected in the grammatical tense of the story. Brief forays into the perfect tense—"I have established my burrow"—occasionally allow the animal to look back at things recently completed. But the narrator makes special use of the peculiar feature of the German present tense to denote not only singular events but also ongoing activities or persisting facts, the iterative present tense. Beyond that, the present tense can also serve as a colloquial substitute for the future tense. The animal is trapped in the solitary sphere of its musings just as it is in the iterative present tense of its soliloquy, which refers to repetitive or habitual processes.⁵⁸ This tense is the specific temporal nature of *cura* and the desire for security. In the temporal structure of the text, security is revealed as a desire to fix the present into the future. It is a self-entrenchment in the here and now in order to secure the persistence (or eternal repetition) of the status quo and to isolate oneself against any unforeseen event, be it an enemy or an accident. Precaution means to preserve the present, to ward off the irruption of the event. As John T. Hamilton points out: "The longing for security—the concern to be without concern—is driven by the wish to render the future motionless, to wrest it from its own futurity and set it firmly in the present, where it could be safely assessed."⁵⁹

Kafka's animal is well aware of this essential paradox of security. Caught in the iterative present tense of its ruminations about security, it has to consider what it is *unable* to see from this present perspective. It has to attempt, in other words, to observe itself in the act of observation in order to see "what will happen all around me behind my back" (171). The animal tries again and again to achieve this self-reflexive, second-order observation: to observe itself observing. To do so, it must step outside the burrow. This (maximally vulnerable) position outside, however, plunges the animal into a second-order reflection about the eventual security of the burrow: "I was seized by the childish desire not ever to go back to the burrow but to settle down here, near the entrance, and spend my life observing it, finding my happiness in perpetually realizing how securely the burrow, were I inside it, would protect me" (170). While being stuck in first-order observation, which means a state of permanent vigilance and calculation about the dangers to come, the animal dreams of a reflexive, that is, second-order perspective beyond its own line of vision. The desire for absolute security entails the impossible task of simultaneously inhabiting the burrow and observing it from outside—that is, of living in the present while being able to ascertain it, from a reflexive position, in the future. Technically, that would mean to narrate a story simultaneously in the present *and* past tense, as still ongoing *and* already finished. It is precisely the form of the text as an inner monologue, however, that denies its narrator/protagonist this reflexivity. The animal is confined to the first-person perspective and thus to first-order observation. By observing its own observation, it would be able to consider its blind spots. It would come to terms with its unknown unknowns.

This desire for second-order observation lies at the heart of the modern relation to the future. As Niklas Luhmann remarked, the modern quest for security strives to achieve the "dual perspective," which "encompasses both what observers see and what they do not see."[60] In the modern era, the ancient god's omniscient perspective has become the imperative for the mortals themselves. Not only are modern humans obliged to view the future with constant vigilance; they also have to reflect permanently on their own blind spots. In the modern regime of security, the ancient tragic irony is transmuted into a hyperreflexivity about one's own blind spots. Kafka's animal is fully aware of this: "Of course, trickiness of so fine a weave can be suicidal, I know that better than anyone" (162).[61] Yet neither the animal nor the modern human can see further than the "present future"—that which is visible, conceivable, and to be expected from the perspective of the here and now.[62]

The impossibility of taking into account one's own blind spots causes Kafka's animal to become "suspicious of itself," of its own ability to interpret signs of danger.[63] It is not the animal's isolation that makes it profoundly lonely but its inability to achieve the dual perspective allowing it to observe its own observation. This, however, gives rise to a fundamental undecidability in the text. Is the animal's "suspicion"—against the "hisser," for instance, which it interprets toward the end of the text as an approaching enemy—actually based on signs of a real threat? Or are all the speculations about lurking predators nothing more than the symptoms of basic anxiety, which may not have any defined object? The animal's cause of anxiety, as the driving force of concern and care, is entirely unspecific. What Kafka points out is that its object of concern and anxiety is *being alive* as such. The desire for security is not aimed at any particular form of life but at nothing but the perpetuation of life as *mere life*.[64]

The undefined object of anxiety in the desire for security raises the question of the subjectivity attuned to this desire. Is the perception of danger valid or just a construction? Surely it is a construction, a heuristic fiction meant to assist in the establishment of measures against a possibly dangerous situation. Is the danger of a situation just a projection, hallucination, or autosuggestion? Is the desire for security maybe the paranoid worldview of an existentially anxious subject? A more recent kinsman of Kafka's burrow builder takes the mindset of the security-searching subject as his main topic. Jeff Nichols's film *Take Shelter* (2011) is an adaptation of Kafka's "The Burrow" under the conditions of the contemporary American welfare system.[65] Here, too, building is a metaphor for a desire for security. Its protagonist, Curtis LaForche (Michael Shannon), is a construction worker living in a small town in Ohio with his wife (Jessica Chastain) and deaf young daughter (Tova Stewart). His life is, as Kafka's animal would have it, "established" and "seems to be a success" when he begins to have unsettling dreams about accidents and catastrophes. First there is an attack by his dog, then a car crash. Later his visions become more surreal and violent: A strange intruder creeps around his house, his furniture levitates for a moment, his best friend Stuart (Shea Whigham) attacks him at work, and his wife threatens him with a knife. Each of these visions is associated with a huge, incoming storm. An immense cloud (resembling a mushroom cloud) forms on the horizon; tornados sweep across the countryside; he hears thunder that sounds like the distant growls of a predator; and a thick, yellow, oily rain begins to fall (fig. 5.1).

The visions incite Curtis to take security measures: First he bans his dog from the house, then he begins to clean out a small storm shelter in

FIGURE 5.1 In *Take Shelter* (2011), Curtis LaForche (Michael Shannon) beholds a coming storm. He wonders, "is anyone seeing this?"
Source: Still from *Take Shelter* (2011).

his backyard. Ultimately, he expands this shelter into a large subterranean bunker and equips it with gas masks, water, and food supplies. Although the family's finances are tight and tied up in expensive therapies for their deaf daughter, Curtis nevertheless spends more and more of his time, attention, and money on building the shelter. All of this effort in the name of safety, however, makes him increasingly unsafe, by undermining his social and financial existence. To construct the bunker, he takes out a risky loan that even his banker advises him not to take. Without permission, he uses his company's construction machines and thus loses his job. In short, the future for which Curtis prepares is destroying the present. More and more isolated socially and more and more unsettled, in a fit of rage he prophecies the devastating storm to his horrified colleagues: "Well, listen up! There is a storm comin' like nothing you have ever seen. And not one of you is prepared for it!"

The storm predicted by Curtis LaForche is clearly an allegory of the radical social and economic destabilization experienced by so many middle-class Americans after the 2008 financial crisis. Time and again, the film discusses the symptoms of crisis, in which jobs are harder to find and home loans have become increasingly risky. The conversation about the "home-improvement loan" Curtis requests from his bank reveals that everything the family owns—their two cars, the house—was bought on credit. The world of the impending storm is the world before the financial crisis, a world much more fragile than anyone could have imagined. The storm of the crisis, which had been caused by faulty mortgage credits, exposed the fact that the promises of social security—such as home ownership, a job, health insurance, creditworthiness—could crash within weeks. Middle-class families such as Curtis's could suddenly wind up unemployed and homeless. Not one of them, as the protagonist puts it, was prepared for it.

Yet what are the systems of preparedness and securitization society offers its members? The film addresses at least one such system: health care and health insurance. Not only Curtis's daughter is in need of costly therapies requiring the approval of insurers; Curtis too feels that he needs therapy for his anxiety attacks and hallucinations. Many conversations in the film revolve around the family's health plan. To forgo expensive therapy with a specialist, Curtis begins to attend counseling sessions. These sessions, mostly with friendly but not very competent health workers, reveal the underlying logic of the health care system dealing with mental health. The individual's anxiety about the future, the insistent desire for security, are all treated as symptoms of an individual (mental) illness, especially as there is a case of paranoid schizophrenia in Curtis's family. The logic of therapy forgoes the question whether there might be a storm coming and whether society is prepared for it. The only questions discussed are why Curtis *feels* such anxiety and whether this is a first sign of incipient schizophrenia. Staring into a lightning-seared sky at night, Curtis wonders whether he is losing his mind: "Is anyone seeing this?"

This is Kafka's animal on the psychiatrist's couch. It's about the individualizing and pathologizing of the desire for security and the obsession about the future. At first, Curtis's behavior proves the doctors and health workers right. When a heavy storm does in fact come to the small town, the family flees into the shelter and spends the night wearing gas masks. However, in the end, it was nothing more than a strong wind, and Curtis's preoccupation with the storm seems completely exaggerated. To overcome his security-fixated paranoia, Curtis and his family take a vacation to the ocean on the advice of the psychiatrist he eventually visits. His desire for security is recognized, even by himself, as an individual pathology. Obsessive anxiety over future catastrophes, that seems to be the ultimate conclusion, are an individual problem, not that of a society or even of the modern mindset.

FIGURE 5.2 In the end, far away from their bunker and Curtis's "unhealthy" obsession with security, the entire family sees what Curtis's dreams have long foretold: the catastrophic storm. The windows of their flimsy vacation house reflect the gathering clouds and the shore. The water has strangely receded, as though before a tsunami. Viscous yellowish raindrops fall on their skin.

Source: Still from *Take Shelter* (2011).

Yet the film does not end with this comforting conclusion. In the final scene, while Curtis is building a sandcastle with his daughter, the yellow and oily drops of rain he saw in his vision begin to fall (fig. 5.2). The storm that has been haunting his dreams, with its tornados and mushroom clouds, appears on the horizon, and his family sees it as well. Now that there is no shelter to speak of, the storm is coming.

There are two possible readings of the film's ending. On the one hand, one can conclude that catastrophes will ironically become real once we realize that they are mere pathological fantasies. Foreknowledge is confirmed at the very moment when one has received enough therapy to dismiss that knowledge as sheer paranoia, that is, as nonknowledge. However, there is a second possible reading of the end. In the final scene, both the family and the audience come to share Curtis's vision and to believe in the coming storm. The audience is no longer an outside observer to the story but is trapped in Curtis's mind. The erosion of the possibility of an outsider's perspective, that of a mere spectator, is central to the modern relation to the future. It is no longer possible for anyone to adopt the perspective of the gods. The narrative does not allow for the audience outside the fictional world to see more than what the protagonists see.

They too are blinded by their *cura*, their concern and anxiety. As a garden of forking paths, the modern notion of the future has become a labyrinth in which insanity and foresight can no longer be distinguished.

It is not a coincidence that both Kafka and Nichols use the same metaphor for the modern state of *cura*, concern and anxiety: the burrow. To build is to create security in the sense of preparedness—to be prepared for the unspecified by designing a controllable space, building defense systems, and storing supplies. As I discussed in chapter 3, this is the attitude of today's survival movements. It is an attempt to preserve the present state of affairs, as it were, to "cement" the present in time. In this effort to secure the future into a perpetual present, knowing and unknowing the future are intrinsically intertwined, yet in this modern regime of security, the weight of this epistemological structure is shifted entirely onto the individual. Today, the subject of foresight must endeavor to observe his own observations and see his own blind spots. Unlike Oedipus, who does *not know* that he is ignorant/blind (while Tiresias and the audience can see this), modern subjects of concern are *all too aware* of their ignorance.

TIME MACHINES: MEDIA OF FOREKNOWLEDGE

This leads us to the question of the media of knowing the future. The negative epistemology of foreknowledge is deeply tied to the techniques used to produce and convey such knowledge. In antiquity, foreknowledge was produced either by the semiotics of constellations in the skies, birds' flight, the reading of the entrails of sacrificial animals, or, as we have seen, by the intricate interpretation of Loxias's oracles. In all these cases, the margin between insight and error lies in the act of transmission or interpretation. Everything comes down to the media of transmission or the person interpreting the oracle's words, never to the source itself. In contrast, the modern notion of the future as something that can be shaped, altered, or prevented in the present poses entirely different problems. As a garden of forking paths, any conceivable future is only a *possible* world, one subject to human decisions and errors. Thus the methods and media of foresight have to contain (in both senses of the word) a degree of uncertainty to account for the virtuality of any assumption about the future. Every prediction has to incorporate its own contingency, its possible deviation from itself.

This virtuality of the future enters the methods and techniques of prediction at the beginning of the modern age. Interestingly, the philosophical and literary *descriptions* of the future, as we find them in the genres of utopian and dystopian films or novels, are less apt to include this structure than the mathematical methods used to *calculate the probability* of future events. In fact, descriptions of the future—as in many classical examples of futuristic novels, from Mercier's *L'an 2440* (1770) to Orwell's *1984* (1949)—are not so much forms of prediction as critical mirrors of the present. The eighteenth century gave rise not just to a secular philosophy of history and a secular understanding of catastrophe. It also developed statistical methods to represent and analyze regularities in births, deaths, sicknesses, and food consumption—and thus the methods to understand future trends. However crude, Malthus is a groundbreaking example of such a statistical glance into the future. The nineteenth century not only depicted utopias of technical and social progress. It also invented the mathematical construct of the "average person" (Adolphe Quetelet's *homme moyen*), which, by recording the frequency of certain qualities or events in a larger population, made it possible to predict certain social processes and trends (such as the rise of certain illnesses in the population or of a certain type of accident). In fact, this approach is the basis of the prevention regime of "immunization," as pointed out by Bröckling. The twentieth century, finally, not only realized dystopian and totalitarian societies but also created, with the help of modern computers, the capacity to develop highly complex models of future developments (of the economy, the climate, ecological systems, etc.). Predicting the future is no longer done by semiotic or interpretive processes but by methods of computation and simulation. These methods operate by means of processing large amounts of data or, as in simulations or scenarios, by imagining several alternative futures. The future now is cast in terms of probabilities, risks, trends, and projections that never claim to represent the ultimate and singular truth about what is to come. The future has become abstract, dispersed, and virtual; it can only be represented in a form that acknowledges the difficulties or even impossibility of such a "representation" of the future.

In the modern age, history, experience, or perception no longer count when it comes to dealing with the future. This, however, is exactly the reason why imaginary narratives of the future—of a possible future—have such an appeal. Imaginary futures enable an experience of what cannot be experienced, a narrative of what cannot be narrated anymore. Yet they can do so only by reflecting on their complicated conditions of possibility—that is, their epistemology and their media. For this reason, modern visions of the future almost always refer to certain media of foreknowledge. Byron, for instance, writes about "*a dream* that was not all a dream"; Mary Shelley, in her novel *The Last Man* (1826), bases her story on allegedly ancient notes found on leaves in the cave of the Cumaean Sibyl, the Roman prophetess. The futuristic novels since the age of Enlightenment can rarely come into being without the help of some magic slumber that gently catapults their heroes into a not-so-distant future, as in Mercier's *L'an 2440*, Wells's *The Sleeper Awakes* (1910) or Bellamy's *Looking Backward: 2000–1887* (1887). The technologically most advanced novels base their prognostications on a source of inspiration coming from a remote time in the future. They imagine a transmitter, as it were, broadcasting from the future to a receiver in the present, as in Olaf Stapledon's influential *Last and First Men: A Story of the Near and Far Future* (1930) or Gregory Benford's *Timescape* (1980), which delves deeply into the technicalities of such a transmission system.

The core epistemological and medial ideas of such an "access" to the future were developed by H. G. Wells in his novel *The Time Machine* (1895). He imagines a machine that enables time to be traversed just like space. What this machine makes possible as a result is *time-axis manipulation*. It can move forward and backward in time, it can accelerate and decelerate, and it can disappear from a room without moving (by leaving the timeframe of the bystander). This notion of time as an arrow that can be stopped, sped up, or bypassed is the epistemic basis of numerous modern stories that wish to do more than describe the future. Their concern is rather to ask about the conditions under which the future can be accessed or seen. Time machines represent the possibility to explore the future as one would explore a foreign country.

Already in Wells's work, the idea of the time machine had a *media a priori*: film. It is not a coincidence that the publication of *The Time*

Machine, in 1895, took place during the era of the earliest film experiments with the manipulation of the time axis. In fact, such techniques as the substitution splice or "stop trick" were first used in the very year of *The Time Machine*'s publication. Film makes time-axis manipulation possible as a visual illusion: Movements can be accelerated or slowed down, they can be shown in reverse, and things can be made to appear or disappear suddenly without being moved in space. Wells, according to Keith Williams, was fully aware of the cinematic origins of his time machine.[66] In the novel, the machine even creates the same flicker typical of early film: "As I went on, still gaining velocity, the palpitation of night and day merged into one continuous greyness."[67]

But time travel does not just have a *media a priori*. It also raises complicated logical implications, which Wells rather neglected. It implies the possibility of intervening proactively in the future and retrospectively in the past. Wells's time traveler intervenes in the very distant future year AD 802,701, when he saves an Eloi woman. The logical paradoxes of time travel, however, hinge on trips to the past. Time travel implies a disjunction between the personal time of the time traveler and the external time of the rest of the world. This can lead to the time traveler meeting himself as a child in the past or as an old person in the future. Furthermore, going into the past can lead to the time traveler altering certain things that would make his own later existence impossible—the famous "grandfather paradox."[68]

As long as these obvious paradoxes are avoided (that is, if a character does not go back in time to kill her grandfather or father in order to prevent her own birth), time travel is in fact a heuristically useful construction. It is the construction underlying every prognosis and every act of prevention. It relies on the simple claim that it is possible, from a future perspective, to identify catastrophic tendencies in the present. Every nontrivial and correct prognosis, according to Nassim Taleb, must contain some element from the future: "To understand the future to the point of being able to predict it, you need to incorporate elements from this future itself."[69] At least hypothetically in using a prediction, we have to assume that it does contain such elements from the future. This perspective from the future onto the present is also the epistemic basis of the precautionary principle. Hans Jonas's groundbreaking treatise on a "future-oriented ethics" (*Zukunftsethik*) in his *The Imperative of Responsibility* (1978) proposes exactly this: to adopt a hypothetical point of view in the future in order to *look back* on the present.

> What can serve us as a compass [for a future-oriented ethics]? The envisioned threat itself! It is only in its *lightning flash from the future*—in the recognition of its planetary scope and profound implications for mankind—that it is possible to discover the ethical principles from which we can derive the ethical principles that our newfound powers call for.[70]

Jonas's idea is that we must imagine the evils of the future (most notably the potential destruction of mankind by a nuclear apocalypse) in order to prevent them. Other theorists have understood this act of anticipation as adopting a viewpoint in the future in order to understand the present and its looming dangers: "It is only from the perspective of the future that we are able to judge how far-reaching the causal effects of our present activity have been, and even then it is impossible to know conclusively," as the philosopher Dieter Birnbacher put it.[71]

The construction of a possible perspective from the future is thus not simply a matter of science fiction. It is the heuristic fiction that underlies the epistemology of the precautionary principle. Yet it has to face the difficulties posed by modernity's contingent future. To consider the present as it is illuminated by a "lightning flash" from the future means to encounter the very unpredictability of danger that the precautionary principle assumes. The hypothetical view from an anticipated future is supposed to allow us to scrutinize the present for the signs of unknown, latent dangers. It demands that we decipher the present for threats that *have not yet become visible*. This perspective, whose technical symbol is the time machine, is the necessary fiction inherent in every notion of prevention and precaution. As we have seen in the previous chapter, this perspective can adopt the form of a retrospective narrative, as was the case in the collection of case studies *Late Lessons from Early Warnings: The Precautionary Principle, 1896–2000*. As a narrative that reconstructs the history of unrecognized warnings about the dangers of asbestos, the book allows the present to be treated as a past that can be looked upon retrospectively.

The implications of such a view from the future, however, can only really be illuminated through fictions. It is no coincidence that the idea of time travel into the future gained prominence in the literature and film of the 1980s, only a few years after *The Limits to Growth* (1972) or Jonas's *The Imperative of Responsibility*. Doubtless, the 1970s and 1980s were a time of intense anxiety about the future, from ecological crises (for example, acid rain and deforestation) and the long-term effects of nuclear technology (Chernobyl) to the possibility of nuclear war in the final phase of the Cold War (the arms race). In 1984, Jacques Derrida spoke ironically of an "apocalyptic tone recently adopted in philosophy," taking up a similar title and historical moment from Kant.[72] The 1980s imagine an imminent future that will be catastrophic and that needs to be prevented here and now. And this is why it is necessary to establish a form of communication between the future and the present. Gregory Benford's *Timescape* (1980), for example, depicts a complicated experimental arrangement involving tachyon rays, which travel faster than light. With these, scientists from the year 1998 (a future plagued by ecological catastrophes brought about by artificial fertilizers) attempt to send messages to their predecessors in the year 1962 in order to warn them about the disastrous algal blooms that the overuse of fertilizer will have caused.[73] Interestingly, Benford takes into account the fact that a change in the past might have effects beyond the ecological catastrophe it is supposed to prevent. It will in fact generate an alternate history. Thus in Benford's novel, for example, John F. Kennedy will have survived the November 1963 assassination attempt. Benford thus creates a "fissured historical universe" of alternative historical developments.[74]

Less complex but much more well known in this respect are the Terminator films—*The Terminator* (1984), *Terminator II: Judgment Day* (1991), *Terminator III: Rise of the Machines* (2003), and *Terminator Salvation* (2009). *The Terminator* hinges directly on the grandfather paradox: the possibility of killing someone's ancestor in the past and thereby preventing his or her existence in the present.[75] In the near future of the year 2029, humans are engaged in a brutal war for survival against intelligent machines, which threaten to eradicate their creators. The machines' plan is to send a cyborg (Arnold Schwarzenegger) back in time in order to thwart the birth of John Connor, the leader of the human resistance movement. They hope to achieve this by sending the robot to kill John's mother, Sarah Connor (Linda Hamilton), before her son is conceived. Despite the android's superior technology, however, the future of mankind is not annihilated but rather generates itself: Kyle Reese (Michael Biehn), a man from the future, is sent back in time to save Sarah Connor, and the two have a son—John. Moreover, Kyle convinces Sarah to attack the computer lab that is developing the first generation of the future evil robots. Like no other piece of time-travel fiction, *The Terminator* preaches a very American optimism about the possibilities of intervening in the future. Sarah Connor is a luckier and more aggressive version of the security-obsessed beings in Kafka or Nichols. The film's mantra: "The future's not set. There's no fate but what we make for ourselves." Sent from the future, Kyle Reese, her savior and the father of her child, clearly defines the status of his temporal origins: It is just "one possible future." (The film is careful, however, to sweep aside the paradoxes to which it gives rise: The possible future from which Kyle Reese comes can no longer exist, because he dies in the present of the movie.) Though it may disregard some of the paradoxes involved with alternative futures, *The Terminator* is based on the fundamental hope of all modern time-travel fiction: the idea that the future can be changed if we know about it. Even on the verge of doom, lucid foreknowledge ensures that something can be done in the present to redirect the course of events. The future would thus change itself or, more precisely, make itself impossible. *The Terminator* presents the happy dream of prevention and avoids its logical and epistemic paradoxes. Yet this optimism about prevention in time-travel fiction has its blind spots because it ignores the connection between blindness and insight in foreknowledge, a connection that had already been recognized in antiquity. What if the gaze of the future does not fully comprehend the present? What if well-intentioned interventions do not help but rather cause unforeseen problems? What if retroactive meddling changes the future for the worse?

SEEING THE FUTURE: GILLIAM'S *12 MONKEYS* AND SPIELBERG'S *MINORITY REPORT*

These paradoxes are not only logical problems. They also lead us back to the question of the *media* of foreknowledge. If film is, generally speaking, time-axis manipulation, then it is the ideal medium to think about the mediality of foreknowledge.[76] I will consider only two films here, films that demonstrate with extraordinary profundity the medial problems that knowledge of the future poses: *12 Monkeys* (Terry Gilliam, 1995) and *Minority Report* (Steven Spielberg, 2002). Both consider not only medial formats in which blindness and insight are interconnected in foreknowledge; they also, self-reflexively, treat *film* as the medium of foreknowledge. If we look into the future, the future, these movies say, *looks like film*. Tellingly, both movies also raise questions about the possibilities and limitations of preemption. However, their takes on the possibility of knowing the future are completely at odds. Whereas Spielberg's movie, despite all of its apparent skepticism regarding the politics of preemption, maintains an underlying faith in prevention, Gilliam's work takes up Sophocles's insights about the tragic irony of foreknowledge and transplants them into the modern age of the 1990s.

In *12 Monkeys*, Terry Gilliam presents a pessimistic, that is, European counterpart to the optimism of the *Terminator* series.[77] Its disaster scenario is typical of films from the 1990s: an act of bioterrorism. The story begins with a catastrophe announced in the opening credits, predicted by "a clinically diagnosed paranoid schizophrenic, April 12th 1990—Baltimore County Hospital": "Five billion people will die from a deadly virus in 1997 . . . The survivors will abandon the surface of the planet . . . Once again the animals will rule the world." Just as in the *Terminator* series, the film's present is a postapocalyptic 2025. Humanity has fled into sterile underground compounds. To find out what really happened, the prisoner James Cole (Bruce Willis) is sent above ground to look for evidence regarding the virus's origin. As in Alan Weisman's later fantasy of a world without people, lions and bears roam freely through the abandoned city.[78] By means of time-travel technology (which operates on a trial-and-error basis and first sends Cole to a battlefield of the First World War), Cole is sent back to the time before the outbreak, first to the year 1990 and then to the fall of 1996, immediately before the onset of the pandemic. His objective is to seek out information about its cause. By maintaining that he has come from the future, he is (not surprisingly) locked up in a psychiatric ward, where an attractive doctor named Kathryn Railly (Madeleine Stowe) takes an interest in his case and tries to help him. During his visit in 1990, Cole tries in vain to explain the coming catastrophe to his doctors. During his second visit, he unceremoniously abducts Railly and attempts, with her assistance, to locate the source of the epidemic or at least to send some information about it into the future. In the present, knowledge of the future can only be perceived as insanity.

Cole is alone in knowing about the catastrophic future. Yet although he knows how things will turn out, he does *not* know exactly what happened or who was responsible for the pandemic. He knows the future but cannot read the present. His impossible task is to collect preventive knowledge, which entails decoding the future's traces in the present. Unlike Sarah Connor in *The Terminator*, who knows how everything came about, Cole is not an agent of prevention but rather an instrument of retroactive recognition. As he explains to Railly and her colleagues in the psychiatric hospital, "I'm supposed to be getting information.... It won't help you. You can't do anything about it. You can't change anything." Cole raises the same question as Tiresias: Can knowledge about the future even be useful in the present? Even if we were to know how everything will turn out, would we possess the necessary understanding and ability to make decisions that will alter the course of events? Or, at the very least, would we even be able to comprehend what is really going on *now*? As Gilliam's protagonists Cole and Railly desperately follow the clues leading to the potential culprits—the so-called Army of the 12 Monkeys—in fact they (as well as the audience) miss the true villain throughout the entire movie, until its final moment, at which point insight comes too late.

Unlike *The Terminator*, *12 Monkeys* not only confronts the paradoxes of time travel but also makes them a central principle of its design. The return to the past enables the time traveler to encounter himself in a kind of strange time loop. This moment—a scene in which Cole as a child comes across himself as an adult—is the central moment around which the movie is built. The scene, overexposed and filmed in slow motion, reminiscent of a dream sequence, opens the movie and is repeated six times, each time from a different angle, always in slow motion, and so bright that it is difficult to make out what is really happening. Only at the end do we understand the sense of this scene—the end meaning both the end of the story and the end of Cole, who has been recalling this scene throughout his life.[79] The scene shows a man in a tropical shirt (revealed later on to be Cole in disguise) breaking through security at the Baltimore-Washington International Airport, drawing a weapon, and getting shot by police officers in civilian clothing (fig. 5.3b). A red-haired man with a briefcase and a yellow jacket flees in the tumult. A blonde woman (Dr. Railly, likewise in disguise, wearing a blond wig) screams and kneels beside the dying man, pressing her hand on his wound (fig. 5.3a). A boy standing nearby (the young Cole) observes the events, and his eyes meet Railly's for a moment (fig. 5.3c). Cole keeps dreaming this scene repeatedly, a trauma that consists in a blurry film scene shot from different angles.

This idea of a recurring, traumatic scene from someone's memory that only becomes intelligible at the end is, as Gilliam readily admits, borrowed from Chris Marker's experimental film *La Jetée* (1962).[80] The latter begins with the following line: "This is the story of a man marked by an image from his childhood." And this is exactly the story of James Cole: He is marked by the recurring memory of the scene at the airport, witnessed as a child. Caught up in a time loop, Cole encounters himself in this very scene, as the ten-year-old observer and as the grown man who is shot. From *La Jetée*, however, Gilliam borrowed not only the fundamental structure of his plot and the scenario of a global catastrophe (in *La Jetée*, this is a global nuclear war) but, and more importantly, the idea of film as a medium of time-axis manipulation. Marker's film restructures time in an aesthetically radical manner: It does not consist of moving images but rather of a sequence of stills with a narrator's voiceover. *La Jetée* is not just "the story of a man, marked by an image." Above all, it is the story of a man whose existence is fragmented into individual frames and whose time travel is not only a matter of entering another temporal dimension but primarily a matter of life being transformed into motionless individual moments. This is *La Jetée*'s reflection on media: It is a fragmentation of the medium of film into disassociated images and a soundtrack in which the extradiegetic voice of the narrator confusingly overlaps with intradiegetic sounds and language (itself split between German and French). In *La Jetée*, film as the medium of time-axis manipulation is broken down into its original elements (single frames, audio tracks) only to tell a story about what time-axis manipulation might mean if it were possible outside the medium.

Measured against the standard of Marker's radically experimental film, Gilliam's aesthetic is far more conventional. Yet *12 Monkeys*, too, is concerned with demonstrating that time travel is a *cinematic operation*. When Cole is sent back in time, the screen flickers like a movie being played too

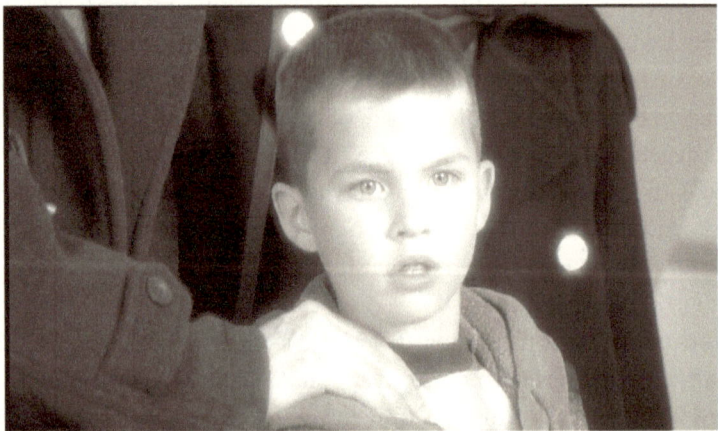

slowly, its individual frames suddenly becoming visible. When, at first, he inadvertently lands in the First World War, he lands in a different film genre. Even the childhood memory/dream scene, which haunts Cole until he eventually becomes a part of it, emphasizes its own cinematic character through its overexposed images, slow motion, and the interrupted, blotchy soundtrack, not to mention the protagonists' disguises—they are suddenly dressed in the style of the 1950s. The traumatic scene, at once a memory and a prediction of the future, looks like a clip from a midcentury film noir. Our knowledge of the future, as Gilliam seems to be arguing, is like a film—or at least like a movie in which we are simultaneously viewers and actors.

This is Gilliam's gist when it comes to the media of foreknowledge. Despite its intensity, the traumatic scene remains unintelligible to Cole and to the audience until the bitter end, when it enters the movie's plot. After Railly and Cole have followed, without much success, the countless clues leading to the Army of the 12 Monkeys, to its crazy founder Jeffrey Goines (Brad Pitt), and his father (a famous molecular biologist played by Christopher Plummer), they realize that they will not be able to solve the puzzle of the impending catastrophe. All the signs they have pursued turn out to be tracks they themselves have left. Frustrated, Cole simply decides to stay in the present: "This is the present. . . . This is right now! . . . I'm staying here! You got that?" What he ultimately wants is to regain the happy condition that defines every present, namely, the condition of not knowing the future: "I want to become . . . a whole person. I want this to be the present. I want the future to be unknown." Cole and Railly decide to fly to Key West together for a holiday. As they are being pursued wherever they go, they put on disguises in a movie theater (which happens to be playing Hitchcock's *Vertigo*) and then go to the airport. There, another time traveler hands Cole an old-fashioned pistol—clearly a prop from another movie entirely. While picking up their plane tickets, they notice

FIGURE 5.3 *12 Monkeys:* Images from the dream sequence in an airport that haunt Cole throughout his life: (a) a blond woman screams; (b) an unknown man in a tropical shirt is shot; and (c) a young boy looks on in horror. The sequence is repeated throughout the movie.

Source: Stills from *12 Monkeys* (1995).

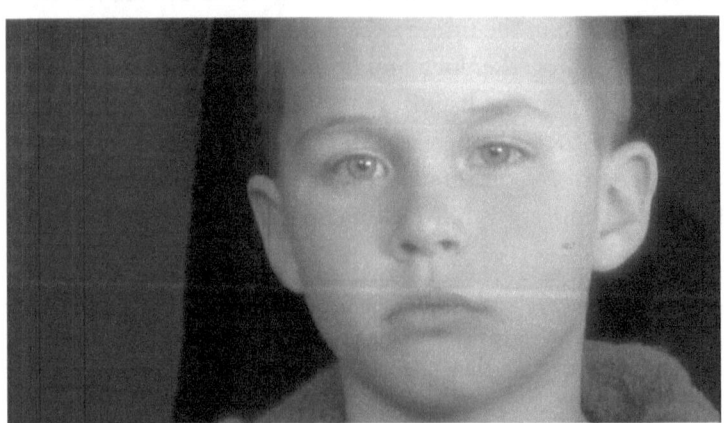

the molecular biologist's red-haired assistant embarking on a trip to the very group of cities in which the pandemic first broke out. Only now do Cole and Railly realize that it was not Jeffrey Goines's army of animal-rights activists that released the virus but rather this assistant, who, though present throughout the whole movie, goes unnoticed by the protagonists and audience alike. Cole is killed in an attempt to shoot the inconspicuous yet murderous assistant (fig. 5.4a), who escapes and goes on to release the virus. Humanity's downfall is set underway, and Cole will never be able to communicate what he knows about the true causes of the catastrophe.

Unlike the audience of *Oedipus Rex*, in *12 Monkeys* the audience participates in the protagonist's blindness. Just as Cole is unable to decipher his own memory in order to recognize the true threat in the present, the audience only recognizes at the end what they have overlooked throughout the entire film. Distracted by the beauty of Dr. Railly, the touching confusion of James Cole, and the exuberant hysteria of Jeffrey Goines, the spectator ignores the quiet, red-haired minor character who happens to be the solution to the puzzle. He escapes attention even though, in one scene, he says to Dr. Railly that humanity ought to be eradicated, even though he is the only person in Goines's laboratory who is working with the highly dangerous virus, and even though he is the person in charge of the lab's security.

This misconception remains with the viewer until the end of the film. Once Cole is dead and the assistant smilingly has opened his biohazard test tubes at the security guard's request (fig. 5.5), the audience is confronted with something that does not exactly follow the logic of the plot. The information provided at the beginning of the movie—"Five billion people will die"—by then has long been forgotten. The hopeless future,

---

FIGURE 5.4 At the end of the movie, it becomes clear that the dream sequence shows Cole's own death. (a) Cole is shot by security guards as he attempts to stop the assistant. At this point, the scene is presented in a realistic manner and eventually understood both by the protagonists and the audience. (b) What we see is always just an individual tragedy. Cole dying in the arms of Dr. Railly. (c) The young Cole becomes a witness to his own dramatic death. In the end, the horrified eyes of the boy meet those of Dr. Railly. Here, Cole is simultaneously acting and observing.

Source: Stills from *12 Monkeys* (1995).

FIGURE 5.5 In the end, an overlooked minor character in the movie proves to be the solution to the puzzle. The assistant of the Nobel laureate Professor Goines releases the deadly virus. Ironically, he opens the glass vessel containing the virus at the request of a security official at the airport.

Source: Still from *12 Monkeys* (1995).

from which Cole has been sent back, will now begin. However, we see none of this in the movie. Instead, what we see is what the ten-year-old Cole sees: the death of a man and the tears of a beautiful blond woman (fig. 5.4b), the tragedy of a man who has brought about his own death before his own eyes, the trauma of a child witnessing his own future death (fig. 5.4c), and the end of a love story that was never given a chance even to begin. What we see is thus not the catastrophe of global megadeath; what we see is the individual's tragedy. Even at its end, the film actively operates with an aesthetics of blindness that the audience shares with the movie's characters.

Knowledge of the future is good for nothing. Gilliam's tragic—and very European—objection to the voluntarist American preventionism of the *Terminator* series has a point. Even if the modern conception of the future is not that of an unraveling thread but rather that of a garden of forking paths, knowledge about the future still does not automatically allow us to decipher latent threats in the present. Paradoxically, it is precisely to the extent that we *see* the future—that we have media to anticipate, prognosticate, and represent the future—that we continue to misunderstand it. Or rather, by staring at the future, we miss the point of the present. Gilliam ultimately points to the *present*—not the future—as the darkness that any attempt at prevention would have to enlighten.

An American response to this tragic take is Steven Spielberg's *Minority Report* (2002). It presents one of the most prominent cinematographic reflections on the possibility and mediality of prevention and preemption.[81] While Gilliam questions the possibility of recognizing the latent signs of a catastrophic future in the present, Spielberg is concerned with the politics of prevention and preemption. To this end, he narrows the wide spectrum of prevention and prediction to an intricate case study, that of *preempting murder*. Here the idea of security is not a matter of protection, as is the case with Kafka, Nichols, or the architects of technical safety. In *Minority Report*, preemption involves a politics of security whose goal is to apprehend the perpetrator of a murder before the deed can be committed. In the time of the War on Terror, this notion of security has become virulent, even though Spielberg's prescient script was written long before the year 2001.

The basic idea of the movie is the establishment of a government institution called Precrime, which is able to foresee imminent murders and intervene at the last moment. Precrime relies on the precognitive visions of three "precogs," adolescents in some kind of lucid coma who are able to visualize crimes before they take place. Preemption is a *political* measure enacted to protect the community from major crime. Spielberg thus inextricably links the question of the possibility of foreknowledge with the problem of employing this knowledge politically. This becomes clear in an advertisement for Precrime, which, after a six-year trial period in Washington, DC, is now ready to be implemented nationwide: "That which keeps us safe also keeps us free. Precrime: It works!" Yet it is precisely this connection between safety and freedom that the film calls into question. Do prescience and the possibility of intervention really leave the idea of freedom intact? Is it permissible to punish someone for a crime they never even had a chance to commit? Is preemption an intervention in the free will of the potential offender, who might choose to act differently at the last moment? Is the system capable of making mistakes? And might it be abused?

Spielberg ties these political questions to the complicated medial machinery that is used to generate foreknowledge. The precogs, on whose visions Precrime depends, are kept unconscious, floating in a nutrient solution, while they dream about the future. These dreams are recorded, stored, and evaluated by Precrime, which then urgently deploys an intervention team to the prospective crime scene. The thwarted murderers are anaesthetized on site into a coma and taken to a giant depot for the delinquent. The beginning of the film depicts the interpretation process of the precogs' visions in detail. In flickering, fragmented, and barely decipherable images, they envision a husband murdering his wife and her lover, whom he has caught together in bed. The movie's protagonist, John Anderton (Tom Cruise), who is head of Precrime, receives this material, identifies the offender and the victims, and begins to sort out the precogs' visions on a large, transparent screen. The goal is to identify the crime scene as quickly as possible in order to send out the intervention team. In the movie's most famous scene, to a soundtrack of Schubert's Eighth Symphony, Anderton analyzes video material on the giant glass touchscreen by playing it forward and backward, slowing it down, zooming in, picking out details (fig. 5.6a). On the touchscreen in *Minority Report*, film is no longer just a sequence of images but rather a three-dimensional, searchable space. Whereas Gilliam's reflections about media are still oriented toward the flickering aesthetics of optical film, Spielberg has arrived in the age of video and electronic image processing.

Once again, the future is film. But here it is fragmentary, accelerated, dark, and unintelligible—a shaky, distorted, three-dimensional video (fig. 5.6b). What Anderton engages in to decipher this future is, as one of his colleagues calls it, "scrubbing the image." The core goal of this analysis is to find clues about the exact scene of the crime. Anderton quickly lists all of the details that he sees: the architectural style of the house, the type of façade, the cement between its bricks, details about the neighborhood, and so on. Spielberg's point is clear: If the future is film (though a highly distorted and unclear one), then foreknowledge is the result of analyzing this material as a body of evidence. It has to be enlarged, decelerated, fast forwarded, rewound (fig. 5.7). The evidence of the event and its future location has to be extracted from the visual fragment at hand. Here, too, time-axis manipulation is the method of choice, but this time it is being applied to a future that has already been conveyed through media.

FIGURE 5.6 (a) Standing in front of a large transparent touchscreen, John Anderton (Tom Cruise) analyzes the footage of a future crime. (b) Footage from the first murder vision. The precogs may be able to see the future, but their visions of crime are obscure, distorted, fragmentary, and utterly illegible unless subjected to comprehensive analysis.
Source: Stills from *Minority Report* (2002).

Richard Grusin has suggested the term "premediation" to describe the phenomenon of an already mediated future whose sole function is to prevent itself (in this case, murder) from taking place. According to Grusin, premediation is not an invention of *Minority Report* but is characteristic of any regime of preemption, especially of the post-9/11 security politics in the United States: "Premediation entails the desire to remediate the future *before it happens*, the desire that catastrophic events like those of 9/11 never catch us unawares, the desire to avoid the catastrophic immediacy of watching live on TV a plane crash into the World Trade Center."[82] In Grusin's view, premediation is the always preexisting medial

218 THE PARADOXES OF PREDICTION

FIGURE 5.7 Anderton analyzes the muddled video clips of the precogs for evidence about future crime scenes. This process, which is referred to as "image scrubbing," is necessary to make the future legible in the present.

Source: Still from *Minority Report* (2002).

formatting of future events. No catastrophe will ever happen that we haven't already seen on TV. Like Spielberg's fictional Washington, DC, in the year 2054, in which the future is always mediated in advance, Grusin sees a nexus behind the preemptive politics of the Bush era and the media-based anticipation of potential catastrophes. Its goal is to soften the blow of real catastrophes by constantly disseminating new visual material of potential, near, or remote disasters. Medial anticipation of disasters engenders, according to Grusin, a permanent "low level of anxiety among the American public," and this serves to prepare the people for "preemptive" wars like the campaigns in Iraq and Afghanistan.[83] The medial anticipation of catastrophe and the politics of preemption that defined the War on Terror (with its indefinite detentions, preemptive strikes, and threat-level color codes) are thus two sides of a security policy that reinterpreted the precautionary principle as the radical imperative to act: better to detain the wrong man than risk a terrorist attack, better to launch a military strike on civilians than fail to destroy a Taliban training facility. Seen in this context, Precrime would be the Department of Homeland Security's wildest dream.

Into this all-too-perfect world of smoothly running preemption, however, Spielberg and his screenwriters Scott Frank and Jon Cohen now set in motion a plot whose resemblance to that of *Oedipus* is hard to miss: a man has to solve a crime of which he himself is guilty. As the references to Sophocles are absent from the short story by Philip K. Dick upon which the movie was based, they are entirely the work of Spielberg and his collaborators.[84] John Anderton, the head of Precrime, who, in the movie's opening successfully preempts a murder, is suddenly identified by the precogs as the murderer of a man named Leo Crow (Mike Binder), whom he does not know. Having briefly viewed the video material that shows him shooting Crow in a hotel room, Anderton flees the Precrime facility and is hunted by his former colleagues. Like Oedipus, he has to explain a crime committed by himself; although he knows its outcome, its circumstances remain a puzzle. Again like Oedipus, Anderton is at the height of his power at the beginning, and this power begins to crumble the closer he comes to an explanation. As in Sophocles's play, the film revolves around the motif of blindness and sight: Eyes are constantly shown opening and closing. The movie begins with the lines: "I forgot my glasses. You know how blind I am without them." One of the precogs, moreover, wishing to have Anderton understand her vision of her mother's murder, asks him insistently: *"Can you see?"* Here, too, seeing is not understanding the truth—it is rather to misunderstand it. As Tiresias knows, one has to be blind truly to *see*. In a milder yet nevertheless gruesome form of self-blinding than Oedipus, Anderton has his eyes removed and replaced with transplants in order to escape the omnipresent surveillance based on iris scans. "Sometimes in order to see the light you have to risk the dark," is the advice offered to Anderton by Dr. Iris (!) Hineman (Lois Smith), the inventor of the precog system and a worthy successor to the ancient seer.

Despite the many allusions to *Oedipus Rex*, the modern world of *Minority Report* does not share its notion of an inevitable future. As Hineman explains to Anderton, there are occasional deviations between the visions of the three precogs, so-called minority reports that suggest an alternative future. In the mind of the most talented of the precogs, Agatha (Samantha Morton), Anderton hopes to find just such an alternative future for his own prospective crime. His contact with Agatha adds yet another puzzle to the plot: beyond Anderton's future murder of the unknown Crow, there is the unexplained murder of Agatha's mother, a vision of which haunts her relentlessly. Anderton abducts Agatha from the Precrime facility and downloads her visions concerning his murder of Crow in the hope of finding his own alternative future. But there is none to be found; as Hineman perplexingly insists, "The precogs are never wrong." As determined as Oedipus heading toward his own ruin, Anderton now follows the clues from Agatha's future visions to a hotel room, where his future victim Crow is in fact waiting for him. In the following scene, however, it is revealed that the situation has been intentionally staged. Crow confesses to being the abductor of Anderton's son Sean, who had disappeared years ago. Photographs of numerous children are strewn across the bed, including some of the missing Sean. Although Anderton, enraged, at first really does want to kill him, he decides at the last second to arrest Crow. We now realize that the entire "orgy of evidence," the photographs of children demonstrating Crow's apparent child abuse, has been a trap: Crow had consented to being killed by Anderton in order to provide for his family. When Anderton moves in to arrest him, the despondent Crow reaches for the weapon in Anderton's hand, pulls it toward him, thereby triggering a shot that kills him—just as the precogs had seen (fig. 5.8).

This scene ultimately clarifies a number of the contradictory statements that are made about the precog system. On the one hand, it is claimed that they are never wrong; on the other hand, the possibility exists for an alternative future. Even Agatha, who is present during the scene with Crow, exhorts Anderton again and again: "You have a choice. Walk away. Right now!" But Anderton stays because he *wants to know*. He is less interested

FIGURE 5.8 When the scene predicted by the precogs between Anderton and Leo Crow actually occurs, it becomes clear that everything is different from how it seemed in precog vision. Anderton does not kill Crow—although it appears that he does.

Source: Still from *Minority Report* (2002).

THE PARADOXES OF PREDICTION 221

in *what* will happen than in *why*. This gets to the heart of the kind of foreknowledge the precogs' visions produce. They merely *see* the future. They see, as it were, the future's *footage*. But as is the case with any visual material, it shows something that may in fact be entirely different. Like videos made with a defective hand camera, the precogs' visions are composed of short, spotty clips that create only the *appearance* of evidence. It is only in the extended scene in the hotel room that the context becomes clear: the fact that Anderton, at the last moment, decides not to kill Crow; that the orgy of evidence was in fact staged; and that Crow kills himself with Anderton's weapon. Suddenly, even if the outcome, Crow's death, is the same, the entire story changes. No act of scrubbing these obscure images could have brought this to light, as the scrubbing process cannot distinguish, for instance, between a man present at the crime scene and a picture of a man on a billboard, as the unfolding scene reveals. The two contradictory truths that we learn about the precogs' video visions, that there are alternative futures and that they are never wrong, are reconciled by the visions' poor visual quality. What they present is just an incomplete and obscure *image of the future*. What the precogs see is how the future will have *looked* (fig. 5.9).

FIGURE 5.9 According to the precogs' vision of the future, Anderton will murder an unknown man named Leo Crow (Mike Binder). He is analyzing on the touchscreen the vision of his own crime. The man with the glasses wearing an overcoat, who seems to be standing behind the murder victim, is in fact a picture on a billboard that is being lifted past the window.

Source: Still from *Minority Report* (2002).

The disjunction between an image of and the truth about the future is underscored by the way in which Spielberg stages the difference between the visions and the linear and easily intelligible quality of the rest of the movie, best exemplified in the scene with Crow. This difference in visual quality also resolves the puzzle of Agatha's mother's murder. Here, too, the precogs' visions had led down the wrong track. A very precise decipherment of the footage's details (the shallow waves in which the woman is drowned) reveals that even the precogs' visions can be manipulated, just like the photographs that Anderson finds on the bed of the presumed child abuser. Anderton eventually finds out that none other than the founder of Precrime, Lamar Burgess (Max von Sydow), manipulated the footage in order to get away with a crime. It turns out that he had killed Agatha's mother in order to recruit Agatha as a precog. Anderton realizes in the end that media may lie and conceal things, rather than serve as a body of evidence. At the very heart of the ostensibly infallible principle of preemption there is a secret crime and the fallibility of the media upon which it is based.

If the Precrime system is fallible, this raises questions about the ontological status of what the precogs see. As we saw, they do not see the future but only images of it. This in turn raises questions about the contingency of the futures they see. If the precogs possess certain foreknowledge, this would imply that the crime is not a perpetrator's own decision but the result of an ineluctable process. This is precisely how Anderton understands Precrime: as a system to recognize the paths of predetermination. However, he thereby not only misunderstands Precrime but also his own activity within it. Preemption is not meant to prevent predetermined futures but contingent acts driven by free will. To put it more precisely: These acts *would be* executed so long as their actors are allowed to act freely and are not hindered from doing so. Foreknowledge in this sense is not a matter of knowing a predetermined future but rather of knowing about a *conditional* future, a future that will emerge if certain conditions are met.[85] A good example is the crime of passion that takes place at the beginning of the film: *If* a man finds his wife in bed with another man *and* happens to have a pair of scissors in his hands, *then* he will (or is likely to) make an effort to stab them. The scene with Anderton and Crow, however, shows that a different decision can be made. What the precogs *see* is thus how things will turn out if no other factors intervene. There is thus no contradiction in the film's repeated insistence that, even in the most heated situation, there is room to make a different decision: "You have a choice," stresses Agatha to Anderton, and the latter says the same to his corrupt mentor Burgess, who is threatening to shoot him. The precogs' visions contain advance knowledge about the infinite complexity of contingent, causal connections, nothing more. This complexity may also account for the fact that their foreknowledge is limited to a very short time span: they see the future a few minutes before it is likely to happen. The precise structure of this precognition becomes clear in the scenes where Agatha, fleeing the Precrime facility aided by Anderton, gives him instructions about how to evade their pursuers: He should grab an umbrella that will be needed five minutes later in order to avoid being spotted from above; he should then stand still, because in a few moments that precise place would not be observable, and so on.

If foreknowledge is knowledge about a *conditional* future, then people's actions are not *predetermined* by the predicted future; rather, the more foresight one has, the more freely one can make decisions. Precognition provides a reflective advantage that, as Dean Kowalski has noted, actually *enables* freedom: "The more you know about your future, the freer you are to act. Being privy to the relevant prevision, we get a chance to rethink what we are about to do, thereby making us freer with respect to our choice."[86]

Seen in this light, Precrime certainly has its flaws: misinterpretation, misuse, the suspension of the legal process, etc. But as one of Anderton's counterparts remarks, "If there's a flaw, it's human." Precrime can be seen as a dream of regulatory foresight that brings state conceptions of order (no crime, no chaos, no accidents) into harmony with individual free will. Security and freedom, as Precrime's advertisement promises, are no longer contradictory. That said, the film nevertheless goes to some lengths to disavow the world of 2054. It is a world of permanent surveillance, ubiquitous identity control, and brutal state invasions of the private sphere. Electronic spiders creep through homes to subject all inhabitants—whether they are sleeping, watching television, fighting, or having sex—to iris identification scans. It is (nearly) impossible to flee, despite Anderton's comment to his pursuers that "everybody runs." Ultimately, the world of Precrime is a world of martial law. There is no due process and no presumption of innocence, and citizens are locked away without trial for crimes they have never had the chance to commit.

Superficially, the ending of *Minority Report* is satisfying in every respect. The deceitful father figure Lamar Burgess, Anderton's mentor, is exposed for having manipulated a number of cases. The Precrime program is shut down. Anderton returns to his estranged wife, and the couple has another child together. The precogs no longer have to dream about crimes but become "normal" teenagers, sitting at the seaside, reading books. So the movie's happy ending implies a media shift away from the evil video visions of the future back to the good old medium of the Enlightenment, the book. According to Spielberg's conclusion, preemption is nothing more than an unacceptable intervention of the state into private affairs, a suspension of the rule of law based on unreliable media of prediction. Spielberg's liberal motto would be the exact opposite of Precrime's. Not *what keeps us safe also keeps us free* but *what keeps us free also keeps us safe*.[87] It is not Precrime but civil rights that will guarantee safety and freedom: "Spielberg's answer is that, ultimately, our political system, not the divine, orders our lives and keeps us safe. To paraphrase the language of the film: 'The American Constitution: It works.'"[88]

Despite his frequent allusions to *Oedipus Rex*, Spielberg thus comes to a conclusion diametrically opposed to Sophocles's. Whereas Sophocles demonstrates that the oracle is always right, Spielberg calls into question the authority of foreknowledge.[89] Whereas the seer and the oracle in Sophocles utter the truth that remains veiled to the royal family, Spielberg argues that foreknowledge is afflicted with medial and institutional flaws. Whereas Sophocles bars his protagonist from any escape and has him stumble ineluctably toward disaster, Spielberg insists on the individual's ability to save him- or herself through freedom of moral choice. This is why, at close inspection, Precrime's flaws are merely accidental: personal corruption, medial distortion, legal gray areas. Such problems could be solved by hiring upright staff, improving image quality, and instituting a more orderly legal process to deal with potential criminals.

Spielberg's reliance on the truth in images is manifest in the aesthetics of the movie itself, in spite of its neo-noir appeal. Just as we understand the scenes with Crow in the main story more accurately than those in the precogs' clips (see fig. 5.8 versus 5.9 and 5.6b), we also understand *Minority Report*'s general message: preemption is bad. Set as it is in 2054, the movie is itself a form of preemptive knowledge, intent on saving us from omnipresent surveillance and preemptive strikes. *Minority Report* is thus not merely a demonstration of premediation, as Grusin suggests. The film itself *is* premediation—a cautionary, medial anticipation of a future whose terror lies in the fact that we will be able to anticipate, via media, everything that is to come. Spielberg's recommendation at the end may be that we should simply refrain from precognition and preemption because we have no control over the side effects of our systems of foreknowlege.

The point Spielberg entirely misses is the ineluctable link between blindness and insight in foreknowledge, as this is not just a question of the reliability of images or the integrity of the institution of prevention. Sophocles's Oedipus, Kafka's animal, Curtis LaForche, and James Cole all gain insight into the negative epistemology of foreknowledge in the horrific moment when they become aware of their own blindness. Ultimately, there are situations in which freedom of action may not be simply a decision between good and evil (as in Anderton's choice between murder and lawful action). The freedom to choose preventive action might instead involve killing someone for the benefit of mankind (as, for example, Cole's attempt to shoot the mad scientist at the last minute) or abandoning one's own child (as Oedipus's parents do). The American voluntarism of free choice and the security politics of liberalism, as preached in movies such as *The Terminator* and *Minority Report*, willfully ignore or misconstrue the paradoxes of prevention. They rely on the assumption that there will or that there should be good evidence to guide our behavior; that the consequences of our actions will be straightforward; that the decisions facing us will be those between good and evil; and that, in the garden of forking paths, there will be moral, political, legal, and scientific signposts to show us the way.

The modern idea of prevention fundamentally overturns the ancient belief in a preordained future. It hinges on an open future that can be shaped by the means of our prescience. While the ancient and the modern understanding of foreknowledge and prevention are diametrically opposed, they nevertheless mutually illuminate each other. Whereas the people of antiquity could not conceive of an open future and the individual's freedom to make contingent choices, modern societies tend to underestimate the tragic element of prevention: that it may dictate decisions with high moral (not to mention economic) costs. One thing, however, is common to both: their recourse to a narrative that analyzes a sequence of events in the light of its eventual outcome, be it as the superior knowledge of the gods or the seer, the desire for second-order observation, or the possibility of time-axis manipulation. Prevention depends on a proleptic narrative, and here, I believe, lies the epistemological function of films and literary texts. By showcasing *that* and *how* the future enters and guides the narrative, they expose the necessity of a position that looks back on the present from the future. By elucidating both the insight and the blindness of prevention, they demonstrate the costs of knowing and unknowing the future.

CONCLUSION

In modernity, the future is no longer part of an eschatological history or of divine providence, and the end of the world is not a moment of ultimate justice. The end of the world has instead become nothing but a sudden drastic "turn downward" (the original sense of the word *katastrophē*), a disruption of the present, the biological annihilation of both nature and humankind. As such, the future as catastrophe is not only a medium of self-reflection but also an imperative for preventive action. The flash of disaster highlights the human condition. By offering a glimpse of its potential end, it illuminates the present, its limitations, aporias, and flaws. Yet the open future of modernity also shifts the weight of responsibility for this future entirely onto human shoulders, subjecting us to a permanent state of *concern* (*Sorge*).

The catastrophic imagination has not simply replaced the modern attitude toward the future, an attitude marked by optimism and the belief in growth, progress, and improvement.[1] The tradition of catastrophic thought we have examined in this book has been, throughout the modern age, a constant antagonist to modernity's progressive mindset, cast in the literary figure of the Last Man. Since the end of the eighteenth century, authors including Jean Paul, Byron, and Malthus discarded the classic conception of apocalypse as divine judgment. Byron and Malthus, for their part, brutally destroy the Enlightenment's idea of human perfectibility and progress. Progress and growth, according to Malthus, will not bring forth a brighter future but will lead to a massive subsistence crisis: famine. Malthus is thus the first author to think the "limits to growth," an idea famously brought back into political thought by the Club of Rome a hundred and seventy years later. In the nineteenth century, the fear of a cooling world resonated with a new knowledge about the history of the planet: the discovery of the ice age. The cooling scenario looks like the flipside of the steam technology that was driving the Industrial Revolution. And Darwin's theory of evolution is, in the catastrophic imaginations of the time, answered by images of devolution and degeneration that will be brought forth by irreversible cooling.

The Cold War's Last Men eventually embody humanity's option actively to bring forth the end of the world through nuclear weapons. The philosopher Günther Anders sees a modern "apocalypse blindness" at work, a human inability to take account of technology's consequences.[2] Underneath the ideology of deterrence, the Last Man of the nuclear age reveals an unavowable desire for collective suicide, as Kubrick and Lumet point out. On a different note, ideologies of preparedness and survival skills have outlasted the Cold War and persist to the present day, influencing social movements as much as Hollywood blockbusters. These survival scenarios present us with highly problematic "tragic choices" and a biopolitical agenda that links the survival of one group to the sacrifice of others. Finally, the modern narrative about ever-improving technological safety is countered, as we have seen, by the aesthetic fascination with all kinds of accidents, from the car crash and the "malice" of the most mundane objects to the spectacular and complex failures of big technology (such as nuclear or chemical plants) and the unfathomable long-term effects of certain substances or technologies.

From the end of the eighteenth century to today, fiction has been a favorite, yet not the only, medium of this insistent counterdiscourse. Modernity's optimism in anticipating and planning the future has—from its onset—been contradicted by a fictional "what if?" pointing out all the dangers and contingencies threatening the idea that a bright future lies ahead. What if we can't really see what is coming? What if we are blind to the minute details that hint at the catastrophe lurking in the future? What if the price of prevention is too high? The fictional figure that embodies this perspective is, as we have seen, the Last Man, who is both a figure of insight into the causes of the catastrophe and its victim. His is the gaze of hindsight, projected into the future: What will we have known about the present, seen from a vantage point of the future? Both seeing and not seeing, knowing and not knowing, both observer and observed, the Last Man is the ultimate personification of the intricate entanglement of insight and blindness that characterizes our relation to the future.

Why do we imagine ourselves as Last Men? It's not as though we have *lost* the solid old optimism toward the future and developed a sense of wariness and latent fear. Rather, this sense—brought to us by images, narratives, and movies—has always been there throughout the history of the modern age. Nonetheless, this feeling of a looming catastrophe seems to be both more intense and more ungraspable than ever before. While the nineteenth century indulged in visions of natural disasters that were—in most cases—overcome by human ingenuity and technology, and while the Cold War saw a future that was, at least, graspable in a specific apocalyptic scenario, the present seems to be lost in a maze of multiple and unfathomable disasters, a catastrophe without event.

Even today's most popular disaster scenario—global warming—is still just *one* version of a catastrophic future. Other scenarios involve natural catastrophes (such as droughts and floods, avalanches, storms, etc.), technical failures or accidents, epidemics, and much else. What is significant for the current disaster imaginary is the idea of a catastrophe without event, a slow and imperceptible transformation leading up to an unforeseeable multitude of potential disasters. Today's anticipation of a catastrophe without event conjoins two contradictory expectations: The idea that everything will continue the way it has in the past but that, within this very continuity, a major disruption lies in wait, an "end of the world as we know it," as a widely used book title suggests.[3]

A *National Geographic* website from 2010 advertises "How to Survive (Almost) Anything" and then lists an array of potential scenarios, both natural and technological. These include: "A Tsunami Hits the Northwest," "An Avalanche Strikes . . . Inbounds!" "Drought: West Runs Dry!" "Megafires Ignite the Backcountry," "A Pandemic Traps You Overseas," "The Power Grid Crashes," "The GPS System Winks Out," "Caught in Bandit Cross Fire," etc. It further offers "14 Survival Skills."[4] The present feels as if it is drifting toward a disaster, one almost impossible to anticipate, for it will consist not in a "big bang" but in nothing more than inadvertently crossing a critical threshold or reaching a tipping point.

What we are consciously or unconsciously expecting is the "tipping over" of a situation that once offered stability. But, as Walter Benjamin so aptly wrote: "The concept of progress is to be grounded in the idea of the catastrophe. That things 'just go on' *is* the catastrophe. It is not that which is approaching but that which is."[5]

The current idea of a future as catastrophe binds together continuity and discontinuity, stability and disruption. This paradoxical structure accounts for the epistemological problems in anticipating and preventing the coming catastrophe. Many of the current concepts of unpredictable types of events—such as the tipping point or the black swan—imply that we have to prepare for highly improbable, unforeseeable, yet system-changing events.[6] Other such concepts, like the side effects or latency lacunas of certain types of technology or substances, emphasize the temporal and causal rift between cause and effect.[7] The uncanniness of these concepts is that the indicators for disaster are given in the present yet are likely to be systematically overlooked. Tipping points are hidden behind the continuous functioning of self-regulating systems (such as global climate or water cycles but also markets or the financial system), right up until a threshold is reached. Then, in a virtually unforeseeable manner, the system "tips over," collapsing or changing into an entirely new state. Similarly, side effects and aftereffects are shrouded in long latency periods that separate a causal factor from its deleterious consequences (such as the outbreak of certain diseases, the poisoning of soil and water, etc.). Very often, the system's flaws and breaking points aren't even visible in the present but only become manifest in the catastrophic event, or even only in hindsight. Our current fascination, even obsession, with catastrophe scenarios, I have argued, stems precisely from this unpredictability. While we don't know what is ahead of us, we indulge in imagining it.

This book has analyzed the way fiction and narrative relate to these epistemological problems of foreseeing and conceptualizing a looming disaster. If the signs of catastrophe are veiled in a latency that keeps them both present and hidden, fiction is a way of giving shape to the catastrophe without event. This shape might be an imaginary scenario, fleshing out a potential disaster situation in all its minute detail and consequence; it might be a narrative to understand the temporal and causal concatenation of events; it may be an image or a figure providing a fictional vantage point from which a final truth can be envisioned. The fictions discussed here open up a hypothetical space in which to analyze, dissect, even experience the future—to brace ourselves against it, to give fear a shape, to process it emotionally, or to understand the elements of the approaching danger in order to prevent it. The epistemic value of fictional disaster scenarios might thus lie in the possibility of assuming a viewpoint in the future in order to look back on the present as a past. Fiction allows for hindsight, albeit a hypothetical yet epistemologically effective one.

Nonetheless, this glance into the future, or from the future back into the present, does not necessarily trigger a reflex of preventive action. On the contrary, many of the more popular disaster fictions seem to leave us with a rather comforting sense of passivity, a secret pleasure in watching the world go up in flames—while, fortunately, the nice guys survive. Our concern for a looming catastrophe is linked to an astonishing lack of individual or collective activism. The fixation with catastrophe seems in fact to inhibit us from taking matters into our own hands—whether in the form of a political movement for climate politics, by adopting more responsible forms of consumerism, or by taking personal safety measures. The catastrophe without event makes it difficult to decide against what exactly to protest, how specifically to behave, and how effectively to prepare. What is left is an attitude of diffuse concern (*Sorge*) coupled with a profound cluelessness about what to do, about how best to "take care" of (*sich sorgen um*) the future. Except, perhaps, for the self-help books that promise to teach us "365 ways to save the earth" or paradoxically lecture us to "think for ourselves."[8]

To take specific and efficient measures of prevention, we not only need a clearer scenario but also a designated agency to hold responsible for the looming danger. And this should be more than an abstract concept such as "capitalism," "*Homo sapiens*," or "technology." Rather, we need to hold *ourselves* responsible as participants in a Western lifestyle that is endangering the earth's entire life system, as the concept of the Anthropocene suggests. Bruno Latour has described the complicated nature of human agency in the Anthropocene, insofar as we are both agents and victims of our own demise. He writes:

> The ecological end of the world is special in the sense that it is billions of humans who are responsible (very unequally needless to say) for the

misery of billions of other humans. The waters of the Flood are not coming from above to drown the sins of men; rather, it's the sinful men themselves whose manifold actions are going to drown the sinful men. We are bringing the end of times on ourselves by a stunning effect of blind reflexivity. Each one of us—to a very different extent depending on whether we are rich or poor, influential or helpless, wasteful or ascetic—we are, at once, the innocent victim, the sinful perpetrator, and the exterminating angel.[9]

This is the position of the Last Man today: agent, victim, and observer of a catastrophe he or she saw coming but did not recognize as such. What Latour calls "blind reflexivity" concerning global ecology echoes Anders's "apocalypse blindness" regarding the Cold War. The "blind reflexivity" of our time, however, is not just a blindness or a lack of imagination but a highly reflexive inertia, an inability or disinclination to taking action here and now. It consists in seeing the danger but not knowing what to do about it. At one extreme, it expresses itself in the insistence that we do not know if anything needs to be done—as, for instance, the climate skeptics claim. At the other, there is a sense that something more radical is needed than the "365 ways to save the planet"—bicycling, recycling trash, avoiding plastic bags, driving an electric car. The task, as Latour has pointed out elsewhere, would be to constitute a political entity that would be able to take responsibility for the changing state of the planet's life system.[10] Man as the agent of the Anthropocene would have to understand that he might end up being the Last Man, a situation in which inaction and action, indecisiveness and decision making, and knowledge and nonknowledge blur into indistinctness.

This is why we depend on fictions to elucidate the structure of this blind reflexivity. There are, however, two different attitudes toward this kind of fiction: On the one hand, it can be understood as "proactive," or "alarmist," a way of imagining a worst case in order to prevent it, to prepare for it, or even to adopt a policy of preemption (including the infamous "preemptive war"). Such a reading of disaster fiction, sometimes even an overt alarmist intention of the text or movie itself, calls for immediate action, often at the cost of thorough investigation, by targeting potentially "harmful" factors or even social groups. On the other hand, we can also adopt a passive, hyper-reflexive attitude to the images and narratives of a catastrophic imaginary, even going so far as to dismiss them as alarmist in the derogatory sense. This attitude consists in distancing oneself as an observer external to the situation yet enjoying the adventure and thrill the protagonists are going through in their fight for survival.

Slavoj Žižek has suggested the term "interpassivity" for this type of aesthetic experience. "Interpassivity" means to experience something (sometimes even to do something) vicariously, through the medium of another person. The examples Žižek gives of such interpassive experience include "canned laughter" in sitcoms (laughter in the place of the actual viewer) or the Greek chorus (commenting on the play's action on behalf of the audience) but also the "interpassive suffering" that had Western intellectuals fascinated by the war in Yugoslavia.[11] Interpassivity seems an apt concept for the audience's attitude to catastrophe fiction, for the strange enjoyment of disaster in the realm of fiction. Watching a disaster movie, we experience the disaster vicariously through the protagonist/victim. Letting a fictional someone live through the disaster in one's place offers the possibility of both experience and reflexivity, involvement and distance at the same time.

At first glance, a lot of popular disaster fiction seems to call for a proactive attitude. Watching the world being destroyed by Cold War deterrence ideology and its underlying, disavowed, obscene desire for collective suicide is as much a call for pacifist action as Emmerich's or Gore's attempts to mobilize an ignorant audience to combat global warming. Even Spielberg's profound meditation on the benefits and dangers of preemptive policing in *Minority Report* in the end feels like an alarmist warning against preemptive surveillance and its legal and epistemological pitfalls. The same holds true for the narratives warning against the catastrophic effects of technology, as in the "cautionary tales" of the *Late Lessons* report by the European Environment Agency. These types of fictions want to teach a lesson that should immediately translate into a political call for action. The call for action, as we have seen here, can be ironic and playful, as in Kubrick's and Lumet's movies; entertaining, as in Emmerich's cli-fi; aesthetically brilliant, as in Spielberg; or at least well-meaning and instructive, as in Gore's slide show. However, it can also carry highly problematic messages. Claiming to unveil a reality hidden underneath the appearances of everyday life, the alarmist discourse might also call for the identification of dangerous groups, for security through preemption, or even the establishment of a state of exception in the face of imminent danger. Alarmism uses compelling narratives and scenarios to draw lines of distinction, to separate the dangerous and the innocuous, friends and enemies. And it may call for decisions to be taken in the absence of sufficient evidence or due process.

Most of the fictions we have dealt with here, however, do not aim at conveying this kind of alarmist message; they tend, rather, to distance themselves from it. They count on the audience's interpassive attitude toward disaster, succinctly expressed by Professor Gladney in DeLillo's *White Noise*: "These things happen to poor people who live in exposed areas. Society is set up in such a way that it's the poor and the uneducated who suffer the main impact of natural and man-made disasters. . . . I'm a college professor."[12]

We can enjoy the end of the world in all its horror because we shift our latent fears about the future onto the manifest terror of fictional characters. Reading McCarthy's *The Road* or Byron's "Darkness" in our armchairs, we can both take in the texts' insights about the destruction of nature and humankind—even empathize with the distraught protagonists—but also distance ourselves from the situations presented in order to ask theoretical questions about the origin of the catastrophes or the deep meaning of the books' last paragraphs. This structure might explain both our current fascination with catastrophe scenarios and our striking unwillingness to draw any kind of practical conclusion from the latent fears to which they give shape.

Taking Lacan's famous "subject supposed to know" as his model, Žižek elaborates on the relation between interpassive experience and belief: We attribute a belief that we do not or no longer have to another person or instance, who in turn becomes *"a subject supposed to believe."*[13] Žižek's example for this kind of interpassive delegation of belief are parents who do not believe in Santa Claus but enact the Santa Claus mumbo-jumbo because they want (or believe) *their children to believe in him*. Interpassivity thus relies on an instance of naivety or deep involvement to which the belief can be attributed, instead of identifying with this belief oneself.

Dealing with a future that we both know and do not know, a future we fear yet do not want to believe in, the interpassive experience of catastrophe within fiction allows us to delegate this belief or this fear to the fictional protagonist or to a supposedly naive viewer. The literary protagonist will have to live through the disaster; produce all the reactions of anguish, surprise, and suspicion; and even be forced to make questionable "tragic choices"—but not us, the audience. A supposedly naive viewer would absorb the immediate message of alarm: "be afraid, be prepared, take action immediately!" If catastrophe is, as in many of the examples analyzed here, understood as the revelation of an underlying truth (about humankind, about technology, about society) hidden under the surface of the present, we distance ourselves as readers and viewers of this fictional catastrophe from believing in this truth through interpassive delegation. While we are affectively identifying with the protagonists in their plight, we are also adopting a distanced position of contemplation and analysis. As an interpassive audience, we are all like DeLillo's college professor: Watching others perish in fiction, we assume that we will not be affected by disasters, will not have to make difficult choices, and will not succumb to an alarmist panic about the latest catastrophe scenario.

If alarmism calls for immediate action and the suspension of reflexivity, interpassivity, on the other hand, encourages the blind reflexivity Latour decries, a reflexivity that suspends every urge for action. Both attitudes toward disaster fiction, however, seem to miss a crucial dimension of the examples discussed here. They do not just convey a truth revealed in the moment of catastrophe; they also provide us with an insight into the epistemic conditions of this revelation. Not only do they make us enter the catastrophic world, to investigate it from an insider's perspective. They also allow us, from an outside perspective, to understand this world's ethical and political aporias. Finally, they present the epistemic paradoxes of foreknowledge and prevention for analysis, by adopting a viewpoint that tragically understands the disaster only in hindsight, from a viewpoint both inside and outside the story. Through this double perspective, modern disaster fiction, in contrast with the ancient view that bound the possibility of foreknowledge to a future already set, demonstrates the *contingency* of a disastrous course of events. None of the fictional catastrophes we analyzed was fixed in advance as a pure destiny. All of them were contingent (think of Jean Paul's "insane chance"),[14] most of them theoretically preventable. They would have been preventable had a slightly different view on things been taken in the moments leading up to the disaster; they might have taken a different course if certain decisions had been made differently. In the modern age, the only insight that is noncontingent in the wake of disaster is that this insight always comes too late.

Herman Kahn called scenarios "aids to the imagination."[15] I believe that, beyond an alarmist or interpassive approach, disaster fictions can be used as such aids, that is, as tools for dealing with a contingent future the weight of which is laid on our shoulders. The novels and poems, movies and metaphors, models and images analyzed in this book can serve as tools for thinking about the future, overcoming the reflexive blindness that lets us know about a looming disaster yet inhibits definitive action by distancing such insights from ourselves. The question is how we can integrate these fictional insights into our reality without succumbing to the epistemic, political, and ethical pitfalls of alarmism or remaining stuck in comfortable interpassivity. The French philosopher Jean-Pierre Dupuy has described this distancing between our insights and our concept of reality—that which we believe in as being "real"—as the core problem of our relation to given dangers, be they technological, economical, or ecological. He writes:

> Let's suppose we are certain, or almost certain, that catastrophe lies ahead.... The problem is that we do not believe it. *We do not believe what we know.* What challenges our cautiousness is not the lack of knowledge about the inscription of the disaster in the future, but the fact that this inscription is not credible.... Everything leads us to think that we cannot extend indefinitely, in time or space, our current mode of development. But questioning what we have learned to see as progress would have such tremendous repercussions that *we do not believe what we know for a fact.* There is no uncertainty here, or only very little. Uncertainty is at most an alibi, not an obstacle, definitely not.[16]

Dupuy makes a case for an "enlightened catastrophism"—hence the title of his book—based on *believing* that which we already *know*. What does it mean to believe—or not believe—in one's own knowledge? If interpassivity consists in distancing ourselves from our belief and delegating it to someone else as a "subject supposed to believe," Dupuy argues for an overcoming of this distance. He claims that we should integrate our knowledge about looming disasters into our lifeworld and our definition of reality. He suggests we treat the catastrophic imagination like a prophecy. For him, the case in point is the prophecy of Jonah, one of the few in the Bible that are not self-fulfilling. The prophet Jonah was sent by God to predict the destruction of Nineveh. After an attempt to escape this risky assignment—the famous episode with the whale—Jonah goes to Nineveh, preaches, and admonishes its inhabitants to give up their sinful lifestyle. To Jonah's surprise, they comply, repent, and cover their heads with ashes. In turn, the city is spared by God. Jonah argues with God because God—by sparing the city—has proven Jonah a false prophet. But this, Dupuy argues, is precisely the point. Precisely by *believing* in the veracity of Jonah's prophecy, they saved themselves from the prophecy coming true. Dupuy picks up the ancient insight into the performativity of prophecy that we have observed in Sophocles's *Oedipus Rex*. Predicting the future always already intervenes into the present by the very act of prophecy, if, that is, the prophecy is taken seriously.

Believing in the certainty of a looming disaster would turn prophecy or foreknowledge into truly preventive knowledge, precisely by making the prophecy *self-defeating*. It would mean giving the future—the catastrophic future—the same degree of reality and factuality that we grant our present. This, however, would mean depicting the disaster in all its lurid concreteness—and to believe in it—not as a potential but as a *given* yet preventable future. Jorge Luis Borges, who coined the image of time as "a garden of forking paths," that is, as a contingent and open structure, captures this paradox of a future both open (contingent) and given (subject to the laws of nature): "The future is inevitable and exact, but it may not happen. God lies in wait in the intervals."[17] What lies in wait in the intervals—in the modern age—is the possibility of intervention, human or divine, into the "inevitable and exact" future.

Fictions can present the future meticulously, realistically. They can make a future situation accessible to experience, almost, as Dupuy argues, like a "memory of the future."[18] They also, however, elucidate the conditions of a gaze into the future, the conditions of foreknowledge in the shape of a warning prophecy. This kind of reflexivity is neither an alarmist call for immediate and heedless action nor a blind reflexivity that only beholds the future without assuming responsibility for it. This reflexive attitude regarding the aesthetic gaze into a catastrophic future involves both a consciousness of and a suspension of its fictionality. It would mean using fictional scenarios of catastrophe as self-defeating prophecies. Yet, come what may, catastrophe fictions will always teach us a lesson about the frailty of the present. They convey a view from a future in which we will know we missed the moment at which we could have prevented it.

NOTES

INTRODUCTION

1. *I Am Legend*, dir. Francis Lawrence (Los Angeles: Warner Bros. Pictures, 2007).
2. Initially, the topic was invented in Romanticism (see chapter 1) and resurged in post-apocalyptic novels and films after World War II, in books such as George A. Stewart, *Earth Abides* (London: V. Gollancz, 1949); Arno Schmidt, "Schwarze Spiegel," in *Brand's Haide: Zwei Erzählungen* (Hamburg: Rowohlt, 1951), 153–259; Nevil Shute, *On the Beach* (1957; New York: Vintage, 2010); Pat Frank, *Alas Babylon* (London: Constable, 1959), Kurt Vonnegut, *Cat's Cradle* (New York: Dell, 1963), and J. G. Ballard, *The Drowned World* (1963; New York: Norton, 2012). For recent fiction with this theme, see Michel Houellebec, *The Possibility of an Island* (2005), trans. Gavin Bawd (New York: Vintage, 2007); Thomas Glavinic, *Night Work* (2006), trans. John Brownjohn (Edinburgh: Canongate, 2009); the many adaptations of Richard Matheson's *I Am Legend* (1954, 1964, 1971, 2007); and Margaret Atwood, *Oryx and Crake: A Novel* (New York: Anchor, 2003), and *The Year of the Flood* (New York: Random House, 2007), to name just a few.
3. Alan Weisman, *The World Without Us* (New York: Thomas Dunne, 2007), 7.
4. Jan Zalasiewicz, *The Earth After Us: What Legacy Will Humans Leave in the Rocks?* (New York: Oxford University Press, 2008), prologue.
5. Jan Zalasiewicz et al., "Are We Now Living in the Anthropocene?" *GSA Today* 18 (2008), 4.
6. Weisman, *The World Without Us*, 3. It is remarkable that the book, which is in fact based on an impossible and fictitious scenario, has been advertised as a work of "narrative nonfiction." See the book's homepage: http://www.worldwithoutus.com/index2.html.
7. Aleida Assmann, *Ist die Zeit aus den Fugen? Aufstieg und Fall des Zeitregimes der Moderne* (Munich: Hanser, 2013).

8. See Jacques Derrida, "No Apocalypse, Not Now (Full Speed Ahead, Seven Missiles, Seven Missives)," *Diacritics* 14 (1984): 23.
9. Ulrich Beck, *World at Risk*, trans. Ciaran Cronin (Cambridge: Polity, 2009).
10. Jared Diamond, *Collapse: How Societies Choose to Fail or Succeed*, 2nd ed. (New York: Penguin, 2011); Harald Welzer, *Climate Wars: What People Will Be Killed for in the Twenty-First Century*, trans. Patrick Camiller (Cambridge: Polity, 2012).
11. James E. Hansen, "Climate Change Is Here—and Worse Than We Thought," *Washington Post*, August 3, 2012, https://www.washingtonpost.com/opinions/climate-change-is-here--and-worse-than-we-thought/2012/08/03/6ae604c2-dd90-11e1-8e43-4a3c4375504a_story.html.
12. James Lovelock, *The Revenge of Gaia: Why the Earth Is Fighting Back, and How We Can Still Save Humanity* (London: Penguin, 2006).
13. Quoted from page 11 of a promotional booklet titled *The Risk Landscape of the Future* (2004), http://www.swissre.com/library/The_Risk_Landscape_of_the_Future.html.
14. Aristotle, *Poetics*, trans. George Whalley (Montreal: McGill-Queen's University Press, 1997), 87 (§36).
15. See Olaf Briese and Timo Günther, "Katastrophe: Terminologische Vergangenheit, Gegenwart und Zukunft," *Archiv für Begriffsgeschichte* 51 (2009): 155–95.
16. Briese and Günther, "Katastrophe," 167.
17. David Hume, *An Enquiry Concerning Human Understanding* (1777), ed. Tom L. Beauchamp (Oxford: Clarendon, 2000), 97.
18. Briese and Günther, "Katastrophe," 188.
19. Samuel Beckett, *Endgame: A Play in One Act, Followed by Act Without Words: A Mime for One Player* (New York: Grove, 1958), 13.
20. Walter Benjamin, "Central Park," trans. Lloyd Spencer, *New German Critique* 34 (1985): 50.
21. Malcolm Gladwell, *The Tipping Point: How Little Things Can Make a Big Difference* (New York: Little Brown, 2000).
22. Charles Taylor, *Modern Social Imaginaries* (Durham, NC: Duke University Press, 2004), 23.
23. Beck, *World at Risk*, 10.
24. See Peter Sloterdijk et al., *Das Raumschiff Erde hat keinen Notausgang* (Berlin: Suhrkamp, 2011).
25. Slavoj Žižek, *Welcome to the Desert of the Real! Five Essays on September 11 and Related Dates* (London: Verso, 2002).
26. See Isak Winkel Holm, "The Cultural Analysis of Disaster," in *The Cultural Life of Catastrophes and Crises*, ed. Carsten Meiner and Kristin Veel (Berlin: Walter de Gruyter, 2012), 15–32.
27. Cormac McCarthy, *The Road* (New York: Knopf, 2006), 24.
28. Lord George Gordon Byron, "Darkness" (1816), in *Lord Byron: The Complete Poetical Works*, ed. Jerome J. McGann, 7 vols. (Oxford: Clarendon, 1980–1993), 4:41 (lines 8–9).
29. Walter Benjamin, *The Arcades Project*, trans. Howard Eiland and Kevin McLaughlin (Cambridge, MA: Harvard University Press, 1999), 462–63.

30. Clifford Geertz, "Thick Description: Toward an Interpretive Theory of Culture," in *The Interpretation of Cultures: Selected Essays* (New York: Basic Books, 1973), 3–30.
31. Richard Grusin, "Premediation," *Criticism* 46 (2004): 17–39.
32. Herman Kahn, *Thinking About the Unthinkable* (New York: Horizon, 1962), 143.
33. Étienne Souriau, "La structure de l'univers filmique et le vocabulaire de la filmologie," *Revue internationale de filmologie* 7/8 (1951): 232. It was Souriau who introduced the term "diegesis" to film theory.
34. Gérard Genette, *Narrative Discourse Revisited*, trans. Jane E. Lewis (Ithaca, NY: Cornell University Press, 1988), 17.
35. McCarthy, *The Road*, 307.

1. LAST MEN

1. Eugen Weber, *Apocalypses: Prophecies, Cults, and Millennial Beliefs Through the Ages* (Cambridge, MA: Harvard University Press, 2000).
2. Reinhart Koselleck, *Futures Past: On the Semantics of Historical Time* (New York: Columbia University Press, 2004).
3. Marcus Tullius Cicero, *On the Ideal Orator*, trans. James M. May and Jakob Wisse (Oxford: Oxford University Press, 2001), book 2, 36.
4. Jorge Luis Borges, "The Garden of Forking Paths," trans. Helen Temple and Ruthven Todd, in *Ficciones* (New York: Grove, 1962), 89–101.
5. See Günther Anders, *Die atomare Drohung: Radikale Überlegungen* (München: Beck, 1981), 207 and *passim*; Klaus Vondung, *Die Apokalypse in Deutschland* (München: Deutscher Taschenbuch Verlag, 1988), 12, 106, and *passim*; Morton Paley, *Apocalypse and Millennium in English Romantic Poetry* (Oxford: Clarendon, 1999).
6. See Paley, *Apocalypse and Millennium in English Romantic Poetry*.
7. For the literary history of the Last Man in Romanticism, see Morton Paley, "Envisioning Lastness: Byron's 'Darkness,' Campbell's 'The Last Man,' and the Critical Aftermath," *Romanticism: The Journal of Romantic Culture and Criticism* 1 (1995): 1–14; and Werner von Koppenfels, "Le coucher du soleil romantique: Die Imagination des Weltendes aus dem Geist der visionären Romantik," *Poetica* 17 (1985): 255–98.
8. Matheson's novel was adapted as *The Last Man on Earth* in 1964, *The Omega Man* in 1971, and *I Am Legend* in 2007.
9. Jean Paul, "Speech of the Dead Christ," in *Jean Paul: A Reader*, ed. Timothy Casey, trans. Erika Casey (Baltimore, MD: Johns Hopkins University Press, 1992), 182, translation amended.
10. Jean Paul, "Speech of the Dead Christ."
11. Jean Paul, "Speech of the Dead Christ," 183.
12. Jean Paul, "Speech of the Dead Christ," 182–83.
13. See the excellent catalogue with Martin's most important paintings: Martin Myrone, ed., *John Martin: Apocalypse* (London: Tate, 2011).
14. R. J. Dingley, "'I Had a Dream': Byron's 'Darkness,'" *Byron Journal* 9 (1981): 26.

15. Bernard le Bovier de Fontenelle, *Entretiens sur la pluralité des mondes* (1686; Paris: Ménard et Desenne, 1828), 181–84.
16. Paley, "Envisioning Lastness," 6.
17. Jean-Jacques Rousseau, "Discourse on the Origin and Foundations of Inequality Among Men," in *The Discourses and Other Political Writings*, ed. and trans. Victor Gourevitch (Cambridge: Cambridge University Press, 2012).
18. Jean-Antoine-Nicolas Caritat Marquis de Condorcet, *Outlines of an Historical View of the Progress of the Human Mind* (1795), trans. from the French (Philadelphia: M. Carey, 1796); Gotthold Ephraim Lessing, *The Education of the Human Race* (1760), trans. Fred W. Robertson (London: C. K. Paul & Co., 1881); Johann Gottfried Herder, *This Too a Philosophy of History for the Formation of Humanity* (1774), in *Philosophical Writings*, trans. Michael N. Forster (Cambridge: Cambridge University Press, 2002), 272–358; William Godwin, *Enquiry Concerning Political Justice and Its Influence on Morals and Happiness* (London: G. G. J. and J. Robinson, 1793).
19. Thomas Robert Malthus, *An Essay on the Principle of Population*, 2nd heavily rev. ed. (1803), ed. Patricia James (Cambridge: Cambridge University Press, 1989), 15.
20. Michel Foucault, *The History of Sexuality*, vol. 1: *An Introduction*, trans. Robert Hurley (New York: Vintage, 1978), 143.
21. See Carol Blum, *Strengths in Numbers: Population, Reproduction, and Power in Eighteenth-Century France* (Baltimore, MD: Johns Hopkins University Press, 2002), 152–92.
22. Johann Peter Süssmilch, *Die göttliche Ordnung in den Veränderungen des menschlichen Geschlechts aus der Geburt, dem Tode und der Fortpflanzung desselben* (Berlin: Verlag des Buchladens der Realschule, 1761).
23. Thomas Robert Malthus, *An Essay on the Principle of Population as It Affects the Future Improvement of Society with Remarks on the Speculations of Mr. Godwin, M. Condorcet, and Other Writers . . .* (London: Johnson, 1798 [1st ed.]; repr., Oxford: Oxford University Press, 1966), 14.
24. Malthus, *An Essay on the Principle of Population*, 139.
25. Gillen D'Arcy Wood, *Tambora: The Eruption That Changed the World* (Princeton, NJ: Princeton University Press, 2015).
26. Ernest Lovell Jr., ed., *His Very Self and Voice: Collected Conversations of Lord Byron* (New York: Macmillan, 1954), 299.
27. For Europe and North America, see John D. Post, *The Last Great Subsistence Crisis in the Western World* (Baltimore, MD: Johns Hopkins University Press, 1977). For a global perspective, see D'Arcy Wood, *Tambora*.
28. In 1816, science was still unable to trace the causal relation between the Tambora eruption and the global change in weather. Only in 1883, with a global telegraph network and a better understanding of climate mechanisms, were scientists able to establish the link between the eruption of the volcano Krakatau (Indonesia) and a change in weather in Europe.
29. Jonathan Bate, "Living with the Weather," *Studies in Romanticism* 35, no. 3 (1996): 435.

1. LAST MEN   243

30. Karl Jaspers, *Die Atombombe und die Zukunft des Menschen. Politisches Bewusstsein in unserer Zeit* (Munich: Piper, 1962), 21–22. This book is the extended version of a radio essay that was broadcast in October 1956 in Germany. Translation mine.
31. Günther Anders, "Thesen zum Atomzeitalter" (1959), in *Die atomare Drohung. Radikale Überlegungen* (München: Beck, 1986), 93. Translation mine.
32. For early testimony on the apocalyptic discourse about radiation, see S. R. Weart, *Nuclear Fear: A History of Images* (Cambridge, MA: Harvard University Press, 1988), 17–35.
33. Frederick Soddy, "Some Recent Advances in Radioactivity," *Contemporary Review* 83 (May 1903): 712.
34. H. G. Wells, *The World Set Free* (London, 1914), 108–9.
35. S. R. Weart and H. G. Szilard, eds., *Leo Szilard: His Version of the Facts* (Cambridge: MA: MIT Press, 1978), 18.
36. Bernard Brodie, ed., *The Absolute Weapon: Atomic Power and World Order* (New York: Harcourt, 1946).
37. Mary Kaldor, *The Imaginary War: Understanding the East-West Conflict* (Oxford: Blackwell, 1990).
38. Hugh Seton-Watson, *Neither War nor Peace: The Struggle for Power in the Postwar World* (New York: Praeger, 1960).
39. Günther Anders, *Die Antiquiertheit des Menschen. Über die Seele im Zeitalter der zweiten industriellen Revolution* (1956; Munich: Beck, 1961), 283. Translation mine.
40. Anders, "Thesen zum Atomzeitalter," 96.
41. See Robert Jungk, "Die Entwicklung sozialer Phantasie als Aufgabe der Zukunftsforschung," in *Ansichten einer künftigen Futurologie. Zukunftsforschung in der zweiten Phase*, ed. Dietger Pforte and Olaf Schwenke (Munich: Hanser, 1973), 121–35.
42. Herman Kahn, *On Thermonuclear War* (Princeton, NJ: Princeton University Press, 1960). For an extensive biographical and intellectual assessment of Kahn's work and impact, see Sharon Ghamari-Tabrizi, *The Worlds of Herman Kahn* (Cambridge, MA: Harvard University Press, 2007).
43. Kahn, *On Thermonuclear War*, 113.
44. Kaplan, *The Wizards of Armageddon* (Stanford, CA: Stanford University Press, 1991), 222.
45. Kahn, *On Thermonuclear War*, ix.
46. Kahn, *On Thermonuclear War*, 228.
47. Arthur Herzog, "Report on a Think Factory," *New York Times Magazine*, November 10, 1963.
48. Jacques Derrida, "No Apocalypse, Not Now (Full Speed Ahead, Seven Missiles, Seven Missives)," *Diacritics* 14 (1984): 23.
49. William Poundstone, *Prisoner's Dilemma* (New York: Doubleday, 1992), 91–92.
50. Bernard Brodie, *Strategy in the Missile Age* (Princeton, NJ: Princeton University Press, 1959), chap. 8: "The Anatomy of Deterrence," 264–304.
51. See Anatol Rapoport, *Game Theory as a Theory of Conflict Resolution* (Dordrecht: Reidel, 1974), 17–34.

52. See Nicholas Thompson, "Inside the Apocalyptic Soviet Doomsday Machine," *Wired*, September 21, 2009, https://www.wired.com/politics/security/magazine/17-10/mf_deadhand.
53. *Dr. Strangelove or: How I Learned to Stop Worrying and Love the Bomb*, dir. Stanley Kubrick, script by S. Kubrick, P. George, and T. Southern, based on P. George, *Red Alert* (1958), 90 minutes, b/w, USA 1964. For a more detailed reading of Kubrick's film, see Eva Horn, *The Secret War: Treason, Espionage, and Modern Fiction* (Evanston, IL: Northwestern University Press, 2013), 238–50.
54. *Fail-Safe* (1964), dir. Sidney Lumet, script W. Bernstein, based on E. Burdick and H. Wheeler, *Fail-Safe* (1962), 112 minutes, b/w, USA 1964.
55. Weart, *Nuclear Fear*, 276.

2. CATASTROPHE WITHOUT EVENT: IMAGINING CLIMATE DISASTER

1. *The Day After Tomorrow*, dir. Roland Emmerich (Los Angeles: Centropolis Entertainment, 2004).
2. Robert Heinlein, *Time Enough for Love: The Lives of John Lazarus* (New York: G. P. Putnam's Sons, 1973), 371.
3. On the historical discourse of "climate as judgment," see Michael Hulme, "The Conquering of Climate: Discourses of Fear and their Dissolution," *Geographical Journal* 174 (2008): 5–16.
4. Ulrike Brunotte, "Die Bühne der Götter: Figurationen religiöser Meteorologie," in *Zwei Grad: Das Wetter, der Mensch und sein Klima*, ed. Petra Lutz and Thomas Macho (Göttingen: Wallstein, 2008), 44–49.
5. In a passage I quote at greater length later, Michel Serres remarks that weather phenomena ("meteora," in his terms) bear an "exceptional knowledge" (*savoir inouï*). Michel Serres, *The Birth of Physics*, trans. Jack Hawkes (Manchester: Clinamen, 2000), 67.
6. Wilhelm Capelle, "Μετέωρος—μετεωρολογία," *Philologus* 71 (1912): 416.
7. Serres, *The Birth of Physics*, 67–68.
8. Serres, *The Birth of Physics*, 68.
9. August Schmauß, *Das Problem der Wettervorhersage* (Leipzig: Becker & Erler, 1945), 2.
10. Jacques Lacan, "Psychoanalysis and Cybernetics, or On the Nature of Language," in *The Seminar of Jacques Lacan—Book II: The Ego in Freud's Theory and in the Technique of Psychoanalysis, 1954–1955*, trans. Sylvana Tomaselli (Cambridge: Cambridge University Press, 1988), 296.
11. Quoted from a brochure available on the National Oceanic and Atmospheric Administration's homepage: http://www.nws.noaa.gov/om/csd/graphics/content/outreach/brochures/Weather&Climate_General_Public.pdf.
12. See Michael Hulme, *Weathered: Cultures of Climate* (London: Sage, 2017).
13. Hippocrates, "Airs, Waters, Places," in *Hippocrates*, vol. 1, trans. W. H. S. Jones (1923; repr., Cambridge, MA: Harvard University Press, 1957), 65–137; Aristotle *Poetics* 1327b.

14. Eva Horn, "Klimatologie um 1800: Zur Genealogie des Anthropozäns," *Zeitschrift für Kulturwissenschaften* 10 (2016): 87–102; James Rodger Fleming and Vladimir Jankovic, "Revisiting Klima," *Osiris* 26, no. 1 (2011): 1–15.
15. Johann Gottfried Herder, "Ideas for a Philosophy of the History of Mankind," in *J. G. Herder on Social and Political Culture*, trans. F. M. Barnard (Cambridge: Cambridge University Press, 1969), 288.
16. Herder, "Ideas for a Philosophy of the History of Mankind," 290–91.
17. Julius von Hann, *Handbook of Climatology*, trans. Robert Ward (London: Macmillan, 1908), 1.
18. Quoted from the IPCC Fourth Assessment Report: Climate Change 2007: https://www.ipcc.ch/publications_and_data/ar4/wg1/en/annex1sglossary-a-d.html.
19. For a critique of this abstract, globalized concept of the climate, see Eva Horn, "Being in the Air," in *Breathe! Investigations Into Our Environmentally Entangled Future*, ed. Klaus Loenhart (Berlin: Birkhäuser, 2018).
20. See Spencer R. Weart, *The Discovery of Global Warming*, rev. and expanded ed. (Cambridge, MA: Harvard University Press, 2008), 63–85.
21. George Gordon Lord Byron, "Darkness" (1816), in *Lord Byron: The Complete Poetical Works*, ed. Jerome J. McGann (Oxford: Clarendon, 1980–1993), 4:40 (ll. 4–5).
22. Byron, "Darkness," 42–43 (ll. 69–74).
23. Byron, "Darkness," 43 (ll. 78–82).
24. John Playfair, "Hutton's Unconformity," in *Transactions of the Royal Society of Edinburgh* 5, no. 3 (1805): 73.
25. See Stephen Jay Gould, *Time's Arrow—Time's Cycle: Myth and Metaphor in the Discovery of Geological Time* (Cambridge, MA: Harvard University Press, 1987).
26. Georges-Louis Leclerc Buffon, *Epochs of Nature* (1778), in *Natural History, General and Particular*, trans. William Smellie, 2nd ed. (London, 1785), 9:401–4.
27. Frederick L. Jones, ed., *The Letters of Percy Bysshe Shelley*, vol. 1: *Shelley in England* (Oxford: Clarendon, 1964), 499.
28. See Peter Schnyder, "Paläontopoetologie: Zur Emergenz der Urgeschichte des Lebens," in *Die biologische Vorgeschichte des Menschen*, ed. Maximilian Bergengruen et al. (Freiburg: Rombach, 2012), 109–31.
29. Georges Cuvier, *Essay on the Theory of the Earth*, 5th ed., trans. Robert Kerr (Edinburgh: William Blackwood, 1827), 15.
30. Charles Lyell, *Principles of Geology*, 3 vols. (London: John Murray, 1830–1833).
31. Camille Flammarion, *Omega: The Last Days of the World* (New York: Cosmopolitan, 1894), 226. See Eva Horn and Urs Stäheli, "Nachwort: Eine 'soziologische Spekulation,'" in Gabriel Tarde, *Fragment einer Geschichte der Zukunft* (Konstanz: Konstanz University Press, 2015), 113–44.
32. Flammarion, *Omega*, 240–41.
33. H. G. Wells, "The Time Machine," in *Seven Science Fiction Novels of H. G. Wells* (New York: Dover, 1950), 68.
34. "Deep time" is the concept of a geological time in the modern sense. The idea was first developed by the eighteenth-century philosopher and geologist James Hutton in his *Theory of the Earth, with Proofs and Illustrations* (Edinburgh, 1795).

35. Gabriel García Márquez, "The Cataclysm of Damocles (Ixtapa-Zihuatanejo, Mexico, August 6, 1986)," in *I'm Not Here to Give a Speech*, trans. Edith Grossman (New York: Viking, 2014), 38–39.
36. Samuel Glasstone and Philip J. Dolan, eds., *The Effects of Nuclear Weapons* (Washington, DC: United States Department of Defense, 1957), 71.
37. Paul J. Crutzen and John W. Birks, "The Atmosphere After a Nuclear War: Twilight at Noon," *Ambio* 11 (1982): 123–24.
38. R. P. Turco et al., "Nuclear Winter: Global Consequences of Multiple Nuclear Explosions," *Science* 222 (1983): 1283–92. The coauthors of this study—Richard P. Turco, Owen B. Toon, Thomas P. Ackerman, James B. Pollack, and Carl Sagan—were collectively known as TTAPS.
39. Carl Sagan, *Nuclear War and Climate Catastrophe: Some Policy Implications* (Ithaca, NY: Cornell University Press, 1983).
40. Sagan, *Nuclear War and Climate Catastrophe*, 10.
41. In 1983, too, Soviet scientists published a study that broadly confirmed the results of Turco's research group. See V. V. Alexandrov and G. L. Stenchikov, *O modelirovanii klimaticeskich posledstvij jadernoj vojny* [On modeling the climatic consequences of a nuclear war] (Moscow: USSR Academy of Sciences, 1983).
42. See the civil-defense film *Duck and Cover* (1951), http://www.youtube.com/watch?v=CoK_LZDXpoI.
43. Nevil Shute, *On the Beach* (New York: Vintage, 2010), 202–3.
44. Thomas Brandstetter, "Der Staub und das Leben: Szenarien des nuklearen Winters," *Archiv für Mediengeschichte* 12 (2005): 150.
45. Eliot Marshall, "Nuclear Winter Debate Heats Up," *Science* 235 (1987): 271.
46. Russell Seitz, "In from the Cold: 'Nuclear Winter' Melts Down," *National Interest* 5 (1986): 3–17.
47. R. P. Turco et al., "'Nuclear Winter' to Be Taken Seriously," *Nature* 311 (1984): 307.
48. Brandstetter, "Der Staub und das Leben," 152.
49. Brandstetter, "Der Staub und das Leben," 155.
50. For a political interpretation of these "post-nuclear wolves," see Brandstetter, "Der Staub und das Leben," 153.
51. *The Road*, dir. John Hillcoat (Los Angeles: Dimension Films, 2009).
52. Cormac McCarthy, *The Road* (New York: Knopf, 2006), 45.
53. McCarthy, *The Road*, 149.
54. McCarthy, *The Road*, 149.
55. Turco et al., "'Nuclear Winter,'" 1283.
56. McCarthy, *The Road*, 50.
57. McCarthy, *The Road*, 4.
58. Crutzen and Bricks, "The Atmosphere After a Nuclear War," 123.
59. McCarthy, *The Road*, 24.
60. Such is the interpretation offered by Donovan Gwinner, "'Everything Uncoupled from Its Shoring': Quandaries of Epistemology and Ethics in *The Road*," in *Cormac McCarthy: All the Pretty Horses, No Country for Old Men, The Road*, ed. Sarah L. Spurgeon (New York: Continuum, 2011), 137–55.

61. McCarthy, *The Road*, 241.
62. Michel Serres, *The Natural Contract*, trans. Elizabeth MacArthur and William Paulson (Ann Arbor: University of Michigan Press, 1995), 32.
63. Serres, *The Birth of Physics*, 68.
64. Serres, *The Birth of Physics*, 67.
65. For a similar interpretation, according to which the novel is an engagement with the discourse of theodicy, see Isak Winkel Holm, "The Frailty of Everything: Cormac McCarthy's *The Road* and Modern Disaster Discourse," in *The Cultural Life of Catastrophes and Crises*, ed. Carsten Meiner and Kristin Veel (Berlin: Walter de Gruyter, 2012), 233–48.
66. Bernhard Pötter, "Knapp am Untergang vorbei" (an interview with Paul Crutzen), *taz.de* (September 12, 2007), http://www.taz.de/!5195070/.
67. See Paul J. Crutzen, "Geology of Mankind," *Nature* 415 (2002): 23; and, in greater detail, Will Steffen et al., "The Anthropocene: Are Humans Now Overwhelming the Great Forces of Nature?" *Ambio* 36 (2007): 614–21.
68. James Lawrence Powell, *2084: An Oral History of the Great Warming* (Kindle E-Book, 2011).
69. *An Inconvenient Truth*, dir. Davis Guggenheim (Los Angeles: Paramount Classics, 2006).
70. Carl Sagan, *Pale Blue Dot* (New York: Random House, 1994), 218.
71. See Naomi Oreskes and Erik M. Conway, *Merchants of Doubt: How a Handful of Scientists Obscured the Truth on Issues from Tobacco Smoke to Global Warming* (New York: Bloomsbury, 2012).
72. Paul N. Edwards, *A Vast Machine: Computer Models, Climate Data, and the Politics of Global Warming* (Cambridge, MA: MIT University Press, 2010), 84.
73. Edwards, *A Vast Machine*, 6.
74. Edwards, *A Vast Machine*, xviii.
75. For an analysis of this fallacy, see Bruno Latour, "Why Has Critique Run Out of Steam? From Matters of Fact to Matters of Concern," *Critical Inquiry* 30 (2004): 225–48.
76. J. G. Ballard, *The Drowned World* (London: Fourth Estate, 2014), 7.
77. Ballard, *The Drowned World*, 44.
78. Ballard, *The Drowned World*, 84.
79. Ballard, *The Drowned World*, 86.
80. For a more in-depth discussion of this topic, see Eva Horn, "The Aesthetics of Heat: For a Cultural History of Climate in the Age of Global Warming," *Metaphora* 2 (2017).

3. SURVIVAL: THE BIOPOLITICS OF CATASTROPHE

1. On the history and the varieties of the survival movement, see Uta Kornmeier, "Fit für den Ernstfall? Überleben als Hobby," in *Überleben: Historische und aktuelle Konstellationen*, ed. Falko Schmieder (Munich: Fink, 2011), 395–409.
2. Claudia Aradau has analyzed the inherently artificial structure of this "preparedness." Her study is based on the exercises and tests that are used in various fields to prepare

people to anticipate the future. See Claudia Aradau, "The Myth of Preparedness," *Radical Philosophy* 161 (2010): 1–7.

3. Herman Kahn, *On Thermonuclear War* (Princeton, NJ: Princeton University Press, 1960). This book is discussed in more detail in chapter 1.
4. See http://adventure.nationalgeographic.com/survival.
5. https://en.wikipedia.org/wiki/Survivalism.
6. Guy Oakes, *The Imaginary War: Civil Defense and American Cold War Culture* (New York: Oxford University Press, 1994), 105.
7. John Robb, "The Difference Between Resilience and 'Prepping,'" *Walden Labs: Solutions for Self-Reliance*, August 13, 2013, http://waldenlabs.com/the-difference-between-resilience-and-prepping/.
8. Kornmeier, "Fit für den Ernstfall? Überleben als Hobby," 408.
9. Ulrich Beck, *Risk Society: Towards a New Modernity*, trans. Mark Ritter (London: Sage, 1992).
10. Among other platforms, I have in mind the German forum known as the "Human Survival Project," which is engaged in laying the ground rules for such catastrophe groups: http://www.human-survival-project.de/html/human_survival.html.
11. See, for instance, the right-wing website www.ernstfall.org, which criticizes immigration based on the argument that a culturally heterogeneous society would lack solidarity in the event of crisis. Solidarity can only come from family or, at best, one's own ethnic group.
12. Slavoj Žižek, *Welcome to the Desert of the Real! Five Essays on September 11 and Related Dates* (London: Verso, 2002), 12–32.
13. For a discussion of such films, see Nitzan Lebovic, "The Biopolitical Film (A Nietzschean Paradigm)," *Postmodern Culture* 23 (2012).
14. Georg Seeßlen and Markus Metz, *Krieg der Bilder, Bilder des Krieges: Abhandlung über die Katastrophe und die mediale Wirklichkeit* (Berlin: Edition Tiamat, 2002), 27.
15. Katrin Röggla, *Disaster Awareness Fair: Zum katastrophischen in Stadt, Land und Film* (Graz: Literaturverlag Droschl, 2008), 9 (my emphasis).
16. Lebovic, "The Biopolitical Film."
17. Michel Foucault, *The History of Sexuality*, vol. 1: *An Introduction*, trans. Michael Hurley (New York: Pantheon, 1978), 143.
18. Thomas Lemke, *Biopolitics: An Advanced Introduction* (New York: New York University Press, 2011), 4.
19. Roberto Esposito, *Immunitas: The Protection and Negation of Life*, trans. Zakiya Hanafi (Cambridge: Polity, 2011), 113 (my emphasis).
20. Giorgio Agamben, *Homo Sacer: Sovereign Power and Bare Life*, trans. Daniel Heller-Roazen (Stanford, CA: Stanford University Press, 1998).
21. Michel Foucault, *"Society Must Be Defended": Lectures at the Collège de France, 1975–1976*, trans. David Macey (New York: Picador, 2003), 254.
22. H. G. Wells, *The War of the Worlds* (New York: Bantam, 2003), 181.
23. See especially Carl Schmitt, "Total Enemy, Total War, Total State," in *Four Articles, 1931–1938*, trans. Simona Draghici (Washington, DC: Plutarch, 1999), 28–36.

24. Carl Schmitt, *The Concept of the Political*, expanded ed., trans. George Schwab (Chicago: University of Chicago Press, 2007), 27.
25. See, for example, Werner Sombart, *Händler und Helden: Patriotische Besinnungen* (Munich: Duncker & Humblot, 1915); or Georg Simmel, *Der Krieg und die geistigen Entscheidungen* (Munich: Duncker & Humblot, 1917). For further discussion, see Eva Horn, "Krieg und Krise: Zur anthropologischen Figur des Ersten Weltkriegs," in *Konzepte der Moderne*, ed. Gerhart von Graevenitz (Stuttgart: Metzler, 1999), 633–55.
26. See Eva Horn, *The Secret War: Treason, Espionage, and Modern Fiction*, trans. Geoffrey Winthrop-Young (Evanston, IL: Northwestern University Press, 2013), 275–300.
27. *Independence Day*, dir. Roland Emmerich (Los Angeles: Centropolis Entertainment, 1996).
28. *Deep Impact*, dir. Mimi Leder (Los Angeles: Paramount Pictures, 1998).
29. Onora Nell [O'Neill], "Lifeboat Earth," *Philosophy and Public Affairs* 4 (1975), 273–92.
30. Guido Calabresi and Philip Bobbitt, *Tragic Choices: The Conflicts Society Confronts in the Allocation of Tragically Scarce Resources* (New York: Norton, 1978).
31. Calabresi and Bobbitt, *Tragic Choices*, 32.
32. For a discussion of this very question, see John M. Taurek, "Should the Numbers Count?" *Philosophy and Public Affairs* 6 (1977): 293–316.
33. Weyma Lübbe, "Einleitung," in *Tödliche Entscheidung: Allokation von Leben und Tod in Zwangslagen*, ed. Weyma Lübbe (Paderborn: Mentis, 2004), 23.
34. Agamben, *Homo Sacer*.
35. Dennis L. Meadows et al., *The Limits to Growth* (New York: Universe, 1972).
36. Meadows et al., *The Limits to Growth*, 88–128. Later updates of the Club of Rome's report (published in 1992 and 2004) take into account the additional consequences of climate change. With respect to fuel resources and technological progress, however, their prognoses are far more optimistic.
37. Nell, "Lifeboat Earth," 278–79.
38. William Paddock and Paul Paddock, *Famine 1975! America's Decision: Who Will Survive?* (Boston: Little, Brown, 1967).
39. Paul R. Ehrlich, *The Population Bomb* (New York: Ballantine, 1968). In the first edition of the book, Anne Ehrlich is not credited as a coauthor.
40. Ehrlich, *The Population Bomb*, xi.
41. Ehrlich, *The Population Bomb*, 1.
42. *Soylent Green*, dir. Richard Fleisher (Los Angeles: MGM, 1973).
43. In an essay in response to the Club of Rome's report from 1972, Cesare Marchetti endeavored to refine the concept of the "carrying capacity" of the earth. See Cesare Marchetti, "10^{12}: A Check on the Earth-Carrying Capacity for Men," *Energy* 4 (1979): 1107–17.
44. Alan Weisman, *Countdown: Our Last, Best Hope for a Future on Earth?* (New York: Back Bay, 2013),
45. Johan Rockström et al., "Planetary Boundaries: Exploring the Safe Operating Space for Humanity," *Ecology and Society* 14, no. 2 (2009), http://www.ecologyandsociety.org/vol14/iss2/art32/.

46. The contingency of this process is indicated by the variety of preferences and categorizations that have characterized the different approaches to triage used in various countries and traditions.
47. Elias Canetti, *Crowds and Power*, trans. Carol Stewart (New York: Farrar, Straus and Giroux, 1984), 227.
48. Günther Anders, *Die Antiquiertheit des Menschen* (Munich: C. H. Beck, 1961), 1:216.
49. Anders, *Die Antiquiertheit des Menschen*, 1:213 (this is the title of his chapter on *Waiting for Godot*).
50. For a thorough survey of postatomic fiction, see Paul Brians, *Nuclear Holocaust: Atomic War in Fiction* (Kent, OH: Kent State University Press, 1987). An updated version of this work is available at http://public.wsu.edu/~brians/nuclear/. See also Spencer R. Weart, *Nuclear Fear: A History of Images* (Cambridge, MA: Harvard University Press, 1988); John Canaday, *The Nuclear Muse: Literature, Physics, and the First Atomic Bombs* (Madison: University of Wisconsin Press, 2000); and David Dowling, *Fictions of Nuclear Disaster* (Basingstoke: Macmillan, 1987).
51. An exception is Pierre Temkine, who has argued that *Waiting for Godot* reflects the existence of Jews living in hiding in occupied Paris. According to his interpretation, Godot is meant to be an escape agent for whom Vladimir and Estragon are waiting in vain. See Pierre Temkine et al., *Warten auf Godot: Das Absurde und die Geschichte*, ed. Denis Thouard and Tim Trzaskalik (Berlin: Matthes & Seitz, 2008).
52. Samuel Beckett, *Endgame: A Play in One Act, Followed by Act Without Words: A Mime for One Player* (New York: Grove, 1958).
53. See Christoph Menke, *Die Gegenwart der Tragödie: Versuch über Urteil und Spiel* (Frankfurt: Suhrkamp, 2005), 188–202.
54. Of course, Beckett scholars have repeatedly pointed out the postapocalyptic theme of *Endgame*. There has hardly been any mention, however, of contemporary history and (bio)politics. For the most part, emphasis has been placed on the theological motives behind Beckett's apocalyptic vision. See, for example, James E. Robinson, "Samuel Beckett's Doomsday Play: The Space of Infinity," in *The Theatrical Space*, ed. James Redmond (Cambridge: Cambridge University Press, 1987), 215–27; and Estelle Manette Thaler, "Apocalyptic Vision in Heartbreak House and Endgame: The Metaphor of Change," *Zeitschrift für Anglistik und Germanistik* 34 (1986): 343–51.
55. Theodor W. Adorno, "Trying to Understand Endgame," trans. Michael T. Jones, *New German Critique* 26 (1982): 123.
56. Charles A. Carpenter has thus suggested that the play should be read as a dramatization of the "private fallout shelter dilemma." In the light of the campaigns during the 1950s (especially in England) to build private bunkers, he believes that *Endgame* dramatizes a bunker owner's dilemma between letting in outsiders or only protecting his or her own family. Charles A. Carpenter, *Dramatists and the Bomb: American and British Playwrights Confront the Nuclear Age, 1945–1964* (Westport, CT: Greenwood, 1999), 136–44.
57. Bonnie Honig, *Emergency Politics: Paradox, Law, and Democracy* (Princeton, NJ: Princeton University Press, 2009), 1–11.

58. Cavell argues that the play is about a "normal" unhappy family with typical generational conflicts. See Stanley Cavell, "Ending the Waiting Game," in *Must We Mean What We Say? A Book of Essays* (Cambridge: Cambridge University Press, 1969), 115–62.
59. Adorno, "Trying to Understand Endgame," 122.
60. Cormac McCarthy, *The Road* (New York: Knopf, 2006).
61. See Sara L. Spurgeon, ed., *Cormac McCarthy: All the Pretty Horses, No Country for Old Men, The Road* (New York: Continuum, 2011), 2.
62. George Monbiot, "Civilization Ends with a Shutdown of Human Concern: Are We There Already?" *Guardian*, October 30, 2007, https://www.theguardian.com/commentisfree/2007/oct/30/comment.books.
63. See, for example, Ron Charles, "Apocalypse Now," *Washington Post* (October 1, 2006), http://www.washingtonpost.com/wp-dyn/content/article/2006/09/28/AR2006092801460.html. McCarthy's play *The Sunset Limited* is the work most reminiscent of Beckett's plays.
64. George Gordon Lord Byron, "Darkness" (1816), in *Norton Anthology of English Literature*, ed. Stephen Greenblatt (New York: Norton, 2005), 2:616.
65. Isak Winkel Holm has read this "okay" as a Nietzschean affirmation of the world as it is. At best, however, the father is saying "yes" to his own resignation, for the world is in a state of disintegration beyond any notion of theodicy, which has been the traditional philosophical response to the phenomenon of catastrophe. See Isak Winkel Holm, "The Frailty of Everything: Cormac McCarthy's *The Road* and Modern Disaster Discourse," in *The Cultural Life of Catastrophes and Crises*, ed. Carsten Meiner and Kristin Veel (Berlin: Walter de Gruyter, 2012), 242.
66. Regarding the lack of empathy in the book and the refusal of its characters to help others, see Donovan Gwinner, "'Everything Uncoupled from Its Shoring': Quandaries of Epistemology and Ethics in *The Road*," in *Cormac McCarthy: All the Pretty Horses, No Country for Old Men, The Road*, ed. Sarah L. Spurgeon (New York: Continuum, 2011), 150; and Kenneth Lincoln, *Cormac McCarthy: American Canticles* (New York: Palgrave Macmillan, 2009), 169.
67. I am indebted to Balázs Keresztes for pointing out to me the idea that the utility and value of all objects are reconsidered when survival is at stake.

4. THE FUTURE OF THINGS: ACCIDENTS AND TECHNICAL SAFETY

1. *Chernobyl Diaries*, dir. Brad Parker (Los Angeles: Warner Bros., 2012).
2. Paul Virilio, *The Original Accident*, trans. Julie Rose (Cambridge: Polity, 2007), 5.
3. Stephen Graham and Nigel Thrift, "Out of Order: Understanding Repair and Maintenance," *Theory, Culture & Society* 24 (2007): 4.
4. Guillaume Grandazzi, "Commemorating the Chernobyl Disaster: Remembering the Future," *Eurozine* (April 21, 2006), http://www.eurozine.com/commemorating-the-chernobyl-disaster-remembering-the-future/.

5. Grandazzi, "Commemorating the Chernobyl Disaster."
6. Ulrich Beck, "Risk Society and the Welfare State," in *World Risk Society* (Cambridge: Polity, 1999), 77.
7. Robert Musil, *The Man Without Qualities*, trans. Sophie Wilkens (New York: Knopf, 1995), 1:4.
8. Paul Virilio and Sylvère Lotringer, "Technik und Fragmentierung," in *Aisthesis: Wahrnehmung heute oder Perspektiven einer anderen Ästehtik*, ed. Karlheinz Barck (Leipzig: Reclam, 1983), 72.
9. The journal *Safety Science*, for instance, describes its field as follows: "The journal covers the physics and engineering of safety; its social, policy and organizational aspects; the management of risks; the effectiveness of control techniques for safety; standardization, legislation, inspection, insurance, costing aspects, human behavior and safety and the like." Quoted from the publisher's homepage: http://www.elsevier.com/wps/find/journaldescription.cws_home/505657/description#description.
10. From its beginning, the field of trauma research has been investigating the puzzling consequences of accidents that cannot be traced back to physical injuries. For a foundational study in this regard, see Esther Fischer-Homberger, *Die traumatische Neurose: Vom somatischen zum sozialen Leiden* (Bern: Huber, 1975).
11. On the theological vestiges of "salvation" in modernity, see Hubert Thüring, "Der Unfall und das Rettungswerk: Narrative und Modelle bei Thomas Mann und Adolf Wölfli," in *Rettung und Erlösung: Politisches und religiöses Heil in der Moderne*, ed. Johannes F. Lehmann and Hubert Thüring (Munich: Wilhelm Fink, 2015), 149–67.
12. As a fundamental motif of futurism, the idea of mankind surpassing itself through technology was, from the beginning, closely associated with the accident, which was treated as a sort of heroic sacrifice in the name of progress. See Gabriele D'Annunzio, *Forse che si, forse che no* (Milan: Treves, 1910).
13. Hans Blumenberg, *Shipwreck with Spectator*, trans. Steven Rendall (Cambridge, MA: MIT Press, 1996).
14. See Claudia Lieb, *Crash: Der Unfall in der Moderne* (Bielefeld: Aisthesis, 2009). Lieb interprets the accident primarily as a poetological figure.
15. Among other early polemics against the car, see Michael von Pidoll, *Der heutige Automobilismus: Ein Protest und Weckruf* (Vienna: Manz, 1912).
16. See Matthias Bickenbach and Michael Stolzke, "Die Logik des Zufalls: Zufall und Notwendigkeit," in Matthias Bickenbach and Michael Stolzke, *Die Geschwindigkeitsfabrik. Eine fragmentarische Geschichte des Autounfalls* (Berlin: Kadmos, 2014), 47–64.
17. Karl Marbe, *Praktische Psychologie der Unfälle und Betriebsschäden* (Munich: Oldenbourg, 1926).
18. Musil, *The Man Without Qualities*, 1:3–4.
19. Musil, *The Man Without Qualities*, 1:5.
20. Wolfgang Schäffner, "Das Trauma der Versicherung: Das Ereignis im Zeitalter der Wahrscheinlichkeit," in *Modernität und Trauma: Beiträge zum Zeitenbruch des Ersten Weltkriegs*, ed. Inka Mülder-Bach (Vienna: Universitätsverlag, 2000), 110.

21. Matthias Bickenbach, "Der Alltag der Kontingenz: Crashing Cars. Über Autounfälle, Exempel und Katastrophendidaktik," in *Eigentlich könnte alles auch anders sein*, ed. Peter Zimmermann and Natalie Binczek (Cologne: Verlag der Buchhandlung Walter, 1998), 125.
22. Friedrich Theodor Vischer, *Auch einer: Eine Reisebekanntschaft* (1879; repr. Stuttgart: Deutsche Verlagsanstalt, 1908), 17–18.
23. Vischer, *Auch einer*, 25.
24. For the broader historical and philosophical context, see Jörg Kreienbrock, *Malicious Objects, Anger Management, and the Question of Modern Literature* (New York: Fordham University Press, 2012), 143.
25. Ernst Kapp, *Grundlinien einer Philosophie der Technik: Zur Entstehungsgeschichte der Kultur aus neuen Gesichtspunkten* (Braunschweig: Verlag George Westermann, 1877). Vischer's novel contains a short story within it, "Der Besuch: Eine Pfahldorfgeschichte" ("The Visit: Story of a Stilt Village"). The story is a textbook illustration of Kapp's anthropological theory about the genesis of technology, describing how an early civilization develops tools.
26. See G. W. F. Hegel, *Phenomenlogy of Spirit*, trans. A. V. Miller (Oxford: Oxford University Press, 1977), 111–119.
27. On the history of Murphy's Law, see Joe Smith, "Murphy's Laws: Origin," www.murphys-laws.com/murphy/murphy-true.html.
28. Sigmund Freud, "The Uncanny," in *The Standard Edition of the Complete Psychological Works of Sigmund Freud*, trans. James Strachey (London: Hogarth, 1955), 17:236.
29. On the role of the accident in slapstick films, see Karen Beckman, *Crash: Cinema and the Politics of Speed and Stasis* (London: Duke University Press, 2010), 55–104.
30. Of course, none of these material and technical details would function in reality. Ceramic cracks do not allow intensive dripping; computer screens implode instead of explode; knives fall with their heavy handles facing downward, not their tips; vodka with ice is not flammable, etc.
31. Félix Tourneux, "Accidens" (sic), in *Encyclopédie des chemins de fer et des machines à vapeur* (Paris: Jules Renouard, 1844), 2–3.
32. On the history of this organization, see http://www.tuv.com/de/deutschland/ueber_uns/daten_fakten/geschichte/geschichte_tuev_rheinland.html.
33. Charles Perrow, *Normal Accidents: Living with High-Risk Technologies*, 2nd ed. (Princeton, NJ: Princeton University Press, 1999).
34. On nuclear safety, see Perrow, *Normal Accidents*, 46–49. Perrow is correct to note that exchanging knowledge about malfunctions does not necessarily prevent their recurrence. On the need to develop databases for technical safety, see Albert Kuhlmann, "Was muss die Sicherheitswissenschaft leisten?" in *Leben in Sicherheit: 1. Weltkongress für Sicherheitswissenschaft*, ed. A. Kuhlmann (Cologne: Verlag TÜV Rheinland, 1990), 37.
35. See Albert Kuhlmann, *Introduction to Safety Science*, trans. H. Hermann (New York: Springer, 1986).
36. Perrow, *Normal Accidents*, 89–92.

37. Perrow, *Normal Accidents*, 11.
38. Michael Hampe, *Die Macht des Zufalls: Vom Umgang mit dem Risiko* (Berlin: WJS Verlag, 2006), 106.
39. Hampe, *Die Macht des Zufalls*, 108.
40. Christa Wolf, *Accident: A Day's News*, trans. Heike Schwarzbauer and Rick Takvorian (Chicago: University of Chicago Press, 2001), 15–16.
41. According to Ursula Heise, the strength of this text lies in its stupendous triviality. By fixating on the limited perspective of an individual subject, the work—as she reads it—represents one of the first efforts to address the coupling of local and global danger posed by modern technology. See Ursula Heise, *Sense of Place and Sense of Planet: The Environmental Imagination of the Global* (Oxford: Oxford University Press, 2008), 178–204.
42. Ulrich Beck, *World at Risk*, trans. Ciaran Cronin (Cambridge: Polity, 2009), 117.
43. This has come to be known as the Collingridge dilemma. See David Collingridge, *The Social Control of Technology* (London: Pinter, 1980).
44. Poul Harremoës et al., eds., *Late Lessons from Early Warnings: The Precautionary Principle, 1896–2000* (Copenhagen: European Environment Agency, 2001), http://www.eea.europa.eu/publications/environmental_issue_report_2001_22.
45. Harremoës et al., eds., *Late Lessons from Early Warnings*, 53.
46. Harremoës et al., eds., *Late Lessons from Early Warnings*.
47. Harremoës et al., eds., *Late Lessons from Early Warnings*, 55.
48. François Ewald, "The Return of Descartes's Malicious Demon: An Outline of a Philosophy of Precaution," in *Embracing Risk: The Changing Culture of Insurance and Responsibility*, ed. Tom Baker and Jonathan Simon, trans. Stephen Utz (Chicago: University of Chicago Press, 2002), 286 (my emphasis).
49. Hans Jonas, *The Imperative of Responsibility: In Search of an Ethics for the Technological Age*, trans. Hans Jonas and David Herr (Chicago: University of Chicago Press, 1984), 11.
50. Ulrich Bröckling, "Dispositive der Vorbeugung: Gefahrenabwehr, Resilienz, Precaution," in *Sicherheitskultur: Soziale und politische Praktiken der Gefahrenabwehr*, ed. Christopher Daase et al. (Frankfurt: Campus, 2012), 102.
51. Jonas, *The Imperative of Responsibility*, 26.
52. Don DeLillo, *White Noise* (London: Picador, 1985). Subsequent references will appear parenthetically in the text.
53. Regarding "postmodernity," "simulacra," and other themes in the scholarship devoted to DeLillo's novel, see the overview provided by Stacey Olster, "White Noise," in *The Cambridge Guide to Don DeLillo*, ed. John N. Duvall (Cambridge: Cambridge University Press, 2008), 79–93; and Mark Osteen, ed., *Don DeLillo: White Noise. Text and Criticism* (New York: Penguin, 1998). Ursula Heise, in her *Sense of Place and Sense of Planet*, 160–69, offers a different and very productive reading. She convincingly analyzes the "airborne toxic event" chapter in terms of Ulrich Beck's risk society, in which risks and dangers are evenly distributed on the social level and thus nearly undetectable by the individual.

54. Regarding the intricate connection that exists between prevention programs, their technologies, and their specific manners of subjectivation, see Bröckling, "Dispositive der Vorbeugung."

5. THE PARADOXES OF PREDICTION

1. Regarding the semantic history of Greek *katastrophē* and its cognates, see Olaf Briese and Thimo Günther, "Katastrophe: Terminologische Vergangenheit, Gegenwart und Zukunft," *Archiv für Begriffsgeschichte* 51 (2009): 155–95.
2. Quoted from a promotional booklet published by the insurance company Swiss Re, *The Risk Landscape of the Future* (2004), http://www.swissre.com/library/The_Risk_Landscape_of_the_Future.html.
3. Here, of course, I am setting aside intellectual histories concerned with historical conceptions of the future, such as those by Reinhart Koselleck or Georges Minois. See Reinhart Koselleck, "The Unknown Future and the Art of Prognosis," in *The Practice of Conceptual History: Timing History, Spacing Concepts*, trans. Todd Samuel Presner et al. (Stanford, CA: Stanford University Press, 2002), 131–47; and Georges Minois, *Histoire de l'avenir: Des prophètes à la prospective* (Paris: Fayard, 1996).
4. Immanuel Kant, *Anthropology from a Pragmatic Point of View*, trans. Mary J. Gregor (The Hague: Martinus Nijhoff, 1974), 59 (§35), emphasis mine.
5. In fact, this precise formulation does not appear anywhere in Comte's work, even though he is so often concerned with establishing the foundation for a factually based knowledge of the future.
6. Ulrich Bröckling, "Dispositive der Vorbeugung: Gefahrenabwehr, Resilienz, Precaution," in *Sicherheitskultur: Soziale und politische Praktiken der Gefahrenabwehr*, ed. Christopher Daase et al. (Frankfurt: Campus, 2012), 93–108.
7. An instructive example of this from literature is H. G. Wells's *The Time Machine*, which projects contemporary anthropological and social theories such as Darwinism and Marxism onto the societal and biological conditions of the year AD 802,701.
8. Bröckling, "Dispositive der Vorbeugung," 99.
9. Hans Jonas, *The Imperative of Responsibility*, trans. Hans Jonas and David Herr (Chicago: University of Chicago Press, 1984).
10. Quoted from Bröckling, "Dispositive der Vorbeugung," 100.
11. Bröckling, "Dispositive der Vorbeugung," 102.
12. A clear example of this epistemic optimism can be found in Herder's essay "On Knowing and Not Knowing the Future" (1797). See Johann Gottfried Herder, "Vom Wissen und Nichtwissen der Zukunft," in *Werke in zehn Bände*, ed. Günther Arnold et al. (Frankfurt: Deutscher Klassiker Verlag, 1998), 8:283–96.
13. J. Peter Burgess, *The Ethical Subject of Security: Geopolitical Reason and the Threat Against Europe* (London: Routledge, 2011), 2 (my emphasis).
14. Craig Calhoun, "A World of Emergencies: Fear, Intervention, and the Limits of Cosmopolitan Order," *Canadian Review of Sociology and Anthropology* 41 (2004): 392.

15. Peter Fuchs, "Prävention: Zur Mythologie und Realität einer paradoxen Zuvorkommenheit," in *Moderne Mythen der Medizin: Studien zur organisierten Krankenbehandlung*, ed. Irmhild Saake and Werner Vogd (Wiesbaden: VS Verlag, 2008), 364.
16. Fuchs, "Prävention," 364.
17. Fuchs, "Prävention," 364.
18. Jorge Luis Borges, "The Garden of Forking Paths," in *Ficciones*, trans. Helen Temple and Ruthven Todd (New York: Grove, 1962), 100.
19. Borges, "The Garden of Forking Paths," 98.
20. Borges, "The Garden of Forking Paths," 98.
21. At the same time, of course, *Ficciones* is also the seemingly mundane but in fact highly programmatic title of Borges's first and most significant collection of stories.
22. As regards the past, this distance can be the difference between two conflicting versions of a story, a lie or a secret whose "reality" can only be deciphered indirectly within the text containing the lie itself. On Borges's theory of fiction, see Eva Horn, *The Secret War: Treason, Espionage, and Modern Fiction*, trans. Geoffrey Winthrop-Young (Evanston, IL: Northwestern University Press, 2013), 45–56.
23. See Aristotle *Poetics* 9, 1451a36–38.
24. Jean-Pierre Vernant et al., *Divination et rationalité* (Paris: Éditions du Seuil, 1974), 9; Minois, *Histoire de l'avenir*, 18–46.
25. Raymond Bloch, *La divination dans l'antiquité* (Paris: PUF, 1984), 6.
26. Joseph Fontenrose distinguishes between historical, quasi-historical (that is, invented), legendary, and fictional oracles. Especially those oracles deemed "inauthentic" or "fictional" by Fontenrose offer deeper theoretical insights about the nature of foreknowledge. Joseph Fontenrose, *The Delphic Oracle* (Berkeley: University of California Press, 1978). In *Divination et rationalité*, Jean-Pierre Vernant likewise distinguishes between the pragmatic use of oracles as aids to decision making and the use of oracles to predict a future unforeseen by human beings.
27. Herodotus, *The Histories*, trans. Robin Waterfield (New York: Oxford University Press, 1998), 20–21 (I, 47–49).
28. Herodotus, *The Histories*, 23 (I, 53).
29. Herodotus, *The Histories*, 42 (I, 90–91).
30. Herodotus, *The Histories*, 21 (I, 47).
31. Herodotus, *The Histories*, 13–16 (I, 29–33).
32. See Jean-Pierre Vernant, *Parole et signes muets* (Paris: Éditions du Seuil, 1974), 22–23.
33. According to Christoph Menke's excellent interpretation, *King Oedipus*'s tragic fate lies in the fact that the catastrophe is brought by the king onto himself "not, however, because he *is* guilty, but rather because he *judges* himself to be guilty." Christoph Menke, *Tragic Play: Irony and Theater from Sophocles to Beckett*, trans. James Phillips (New York: Columbia University Press, 2009), 12.
34. Peter Szondi, *An Essay on the Tragic*, trans. Paul Fleming (Stanford, CA: Stanford University Press, 2002), 59 (my emphasis).

35. Sophocles, *Oedipus Rex*, in *The Oedipus Cycle: Oedipus Rex—Oedipus at Colonus—Antigone*, trans. Dudley Fitts and Robert Fitzgerald (New York: Harcourt Brace & Company, 1976), 19–20.
36. Sophocles, *Oedipus Rex*, 23.
37. Sophocles, *Oedipus Rex*, 23.
38. Sophocles, *Oedipus Rex*, 13–14.
39. Menke, *Tragic Play*, 49–50.
40. Ibid., 50.
41. Sophocles, *Oedipus Rex*, 78.
42. Elena Esposito, "Formen der Zirkularität in der Konstruktion der Zukunft," in *Prophetie und Prognose: Verfügungen über Zukunft in Wissenschaft, Religionen und Künsten*, ed. Daniel Weidner and Stefan Willer (Munich: Fink, 2013), 325–40: 338.
43. For examples of this phenomenon, see Werner Bartens, *Vorsicht Vorsorge: Wenn Prävention nutzlos oder gefährlich wird* (Frankfurt: Suhrkamp, 2008).
44. Reinhart Koselleck, *Futures Past: On the Semantics of Historical Time*, trans. Keith Tribe (Cambridge, MA: MIT Press, 1985), 241.
45. Niklas Luhmann, "Describing the Future," in *Observations on Modernity*, trans. William Whobrey (Stanford, CA: Stanford University Press, 1998), 74.
46. Bröckling, "Dispositive der Vorbeugung," 93.
47. Elena Esposito, "Die offene Zukunft der Sorgekultur," in *Gefahrensinn*, ed. Lorenz Engell et al. (Munich: Fink, 2009), 107–14.
48. Martin Heidegger, *Being and Time*, trans. John Macquarrie and Edward Robinson (New York: Harper & Row, 1962), 243.
49. Gaius Julius Hyginus, *Fabulae, XXCC: Cura*, ed. P. K. Marshall (Stuttgart/Leipzig: Reclam, 1992), 171–72.
50. On the broad semantic range of the Latin term *cura*, see John T. Hamilton, *Security: Politics, Humanity, and the Philology of Care* (Princeton, NJ: Princeton University Press, 2013), 10–13.
51. Hamilton, *Security*, 52.
52. Franz Kafka, "The Burrow," in *Selected Stories*, trans. Stanley Corngold (New York: Norton, 2007), 162. Throughout this section, Corngold's translation is occasionally modified.
53. Walter Benjamin, "Franz Kafka: On the Tenth Anniversary of His Death," in *Illuminations*, trans. Harry Zohn (New York: Schocken, 1968), 132.
54. See Elisabeth Strowick, "Epistemologie des Verdachts: Zu Kafkas Bau," in *The Parallax View: Zur Mediologie der Verschwörung*, ed. Marcus Krause et al. (Munich: Fink, 2011), 123–36.
55. See Franz Kafka, "Jubilee Report: Twenty-Five Years of the Workmen's Accident Insurance Institute (1914)," in *Franz Kafka: The Office Writings*, ed. Stanley Corngold et al. (Princeton, NJ: Princeton University Press, 2009), 301–21. Here he notes that, in the case of quarry work, "the main issue is not actually the use of safety devices." Rather, "we must insist that caution be exercised continuously.... The situation ... calls for constant supervision" (316).

56. Burgess, *The Ethical Subject of Security*, 2–3.
57. Hamilton, *Security*, 26. I owe many important insights to Hamilton's brilliant interpretation of Kafka's story.
58. J. M. Coetzee, "Time, Tense, and Aspect in Kafka's 'The Burrow,'" *PMLA* 96 (1981): 556–79.
59. Hamilton, *Security*, 27.
60. Niklas Luhmann, "Risiko und Gefahr," *Soziologische Aufklärung* 5 (1990), 137.
61. According to Hermann Weigand, this passage indicates the animal's recognition of tragic irony; see his article "Franz Kafka's 'The Burrow' ('Der Bau'): An Analytical Essay," *PMLA* 87 (1972): 156.
62. Luhmann, "Describing the Future," 70.
63. This is the convincing interpretation offered in Strowick's "Epistemologie des Verdachts."
64. See Friedrich Balke, "Störungen im Bau," in *Signale der Störung*, ed. Albert Kümmel and Erhard Schüttpelz (Munich: Fink, 2003), 314. For the general distinction between "mere life" and "more life," see Bonnie Honig, *Emergency Politics: Paradox, Law, and Democracy* (Princeton, NJ: Princeton University Press, 2009), 1–11; and my chapter 3.
65. *Take Shelter*, dir. Jeff Nichols (Los Angeles: Sony Pictures Classics, 2011).
66. See Keith Williams, *H. G. Wells, Modernity, and the Movies* (Chicago: University of Chicago Press, 2008).
67. H. G. Wells, *The Time Machine: An Invention* (New York: Henry Holt, 1895), 41.
68. See David Lewis, "The Paradoxes of Time Travel," *American Philosophical Quarterly* 13 (1976): 145–52.
69. Nassim Nicholas Taleb, *The Black Swan: The Impact of the Highly Improbable*, 2nd ed. (New York: Random House, 2010), 172.
70. Hans Jonas, *Das Prinzip Verantwortung: Versuch einer Ethik für die technologische Zivilisation* (Frankfurt: Insel, 1979), 7–8 (my emphasis). This passage, which is from the preface to the original work, is absent from the English translation of the book: *The Imperative of Responsibility: In Search of an Ethics for the Technological Age*, trans. Hans Jonas and David Herr (Chicago: University of Chicago Press, 1984).
71. Dieter Birnbacher, *Verantwortung für zukünftige Generationen* (Stuttgart: Reclam, 1988), 156.
72. Jacques Derrida, "Of an Apocalyptic Tone Recently Adopted in Philosophy," *Oxford Literary Review* 6, no. 2 (1984): 3–37.
73. Gregory Benford, *Timescape* (New York: Simon & Schuster, 1980).
74. For an analysis of the novel's "mantopoetics," see Philipp Theisohn, *Die kommende Dichtung: Geschichte des literarischen Orakels, 1450–2050* (Munich: Fink, 2012), 461–69.
75. *The Terminator*, dir. James Cameron (Los Angeles: Orion Pictures, 1984).
76. On film as a medium of time-axis manipulation, see Friedrich Kittler, "Real Time Analysis, Time Axis Manipulation," trans. Geoffrey Winthrop-Young, *Cultural Politics* 13 (2017): esp. 6–10 (on early film). More recent media, according to Kittler, are designed with the particular aim of making the effect of time-axis manipulation, upon which they are based, invisible.

77. *12 Monkeys*, dir. Terry Gilliam (Los Angeles: Universal Pictures, 1995).
78. Alan Weisman, *The World Without Us* (London: Virgin, 2008).
79. On the aesthetics and function of this scene in the film, see Alain J. J. Cohen, "*12 Monkeys*, *Vertigo*, and *La Jetée*: Postmodern Mythologies and Cult Films," *New Review of Film and Television Studies* 1 (2003): 149–64.
80. *La Jetée*, dir. Chris Marker (Paris: Argos Films, 1962).
81. *Minority Report*, dir. Steven Spielberg (Los Angeles: DreamWorks Pictures, 2002).
82. Richard Grusin, "Premediation," *Criticism* 46 (2004): 36. Emphasis mine.
83. Grusin, "Premediation," 26.
84. See Geoffrey Bakewell, "The One-Eyed Man Is King: Oedipal Vision in *Minority Report*," *Arethusa* 41 (2008): 95–112.
85. Such is the convincing argument made by Dean A. Kowalski, "*Minority Report*, Molinism, and the Viability of Precrime," in *Steven Spielberg and Philosophy: We're Gonna Need a Bigger Book*, ed. Dean Kowalski (Lexington: University of Kentucky Press, 2008), 227–46.
86. Kowalski, "*Minority Report*," 238–39.
87. Lester D. Friedman, "*Minority Report*: A Dystopic Vision," *Senses of Cinema* 27 (July 2003), http://sensesofcinema.com/2003/steven-spielberg/minority_report/.
88. Bakewell, "The One-Eyed Man Is King," 111.
89. See Bakewell, "The One-Eyed Man Is King," 110.

CONCLUSION

1. This account is, for instance, given by Aleida Assmann, *Ist die Zeit aus den Fugen? Aufstieg und Fall des Zeitregimes der Moderne* (München: Hanser, 2014); and Harald Welzer, *Selbst denken. Eine Anleitung zum Widerstand* (Frankfurt: Fischer, 2013).
2. Günther Anders, *Die Antiquiertheit des Menschen. Über die Seele im Zeitalter der zweiten Industriellen Revolution* (Munich: Beck, 1961), 1:283.
3. See, for example, Daniel Wojcik, *The End of the World as We Know It: Faith, Fatalism, and Apocalypse in America* (New York: NYU Press, 1997); Immanuel Maurice Wallerstein, *The End of the World as We Know It: Social Science for the Twenty-First Century* (Minneapolis: University of Minnesota Press, 1999); Jared Diamond, "The Ends of the World as We Know Them," *New York Times*, January 1, 2005; Marc Steyn, *America Alone: The End of the World as We Know It* (Washington, DC: Regnery, 2006); Claus Leggewie and Harald Welzer, *Das Ende der Welt, wie wir sie kannten. Klima, Zukunft und die Chancen der Demokratie* (Frankfurt: Fischer, 2009).
4. *National Geographic Adventure*, http://adventure.nationalgeographic.com/survival.
5. Walter Benjamin, "Central Park," trans. Lloyd Spencer, *New German Critique* 34 (1985): 50.
6. See the bestsellers by Malcolm Gladwell, *The Tipping Point: How Little Things Can Make a Big Difference* (New York: Little Brown, 2000); and Nassim Nicholas Taleb, *The Black Swan* (New York: Random House, 2007).

7. Poul Harremoës et al., eds., *Late Lessons from Early Warnings: The Precautionary Principle 1896–2000* (Copenhagen: European Environment Agency, 2001), http://www.eea.europa.eu/publications/environmental_issue_report_2001_22.
8. E.g., Philippe Bourseiller, *365 Ways to Save the Earth: New and Updated Version* (New York: Abrams, 2008); Harald Welzer: *Selbst denken. Eine Anleitung zum Widerstand* (Frankfurt: Fischer, 2013).
9. Bruno Latour, "Si tu viens à perdre la Terre, à quoi te sers de sauver ton âme?" http://www.bruno-latour.fr/sites/default/files/109-ECOTHEO-FR.pdf. My translation.
10. Bruno Latour, "Agency at the Time of the Anthropocene," in *New Literary History* 45 (2014): 1–18; Bruno Latour, *Facing Gaia: Eight Lectures on the New Climatic Regime* (Hoboken, NJ: Wiley, 2017).
11. Slavoj Žižek, "The Interpassive Subject," http://www.lacan.com/zizek-pompidou.htm; Slavoj Žižek, "Die Substitution zwischen Interaktivität und Interpassivität," in *Interpassivität. Studien über delegiertes Geniessen*, ed. Robert Pfaller (Vienna: Springer, 2000), 18.
12. Don DeLillo, *White Noise* (London: Picador, 1985), 114.
13. Žižek, "Die Substitution," 15–16.
14. Jean Paul, "Speech of the Dead Christ," in *Jean Paul: A Reader*, ed. Timothy Casey, trans. Erika Casey (Baltimore, MD: Johns Hopkins University Press, 1992), 182.
15. Herman Kahn, *Thinking About the Unthinkable* (New York: Horizon, 1962), 143.
16. Jean-Pierre Dupuy, *Pour un catastrophisme éclairé. Quand l'impossible est certain* (Paris: Seuil, 2002), 141–42, 144–45. My translation.
17. Jorge Luis Borges, "The Creation and P. H. Gosse," in *Selected Non-Fictions*, ed. Eliot Weinberger, trans. Esther Allen, Suzanne Jill Levine, and Eliot Weinberger (New York: Viking, 1999), 223.
18. Dupuy, *Pour un catastrophisme éclairé*, 193. My translation.

BIBLIOGRAPHY

Adorno, Theodor W. "Trying to Understand *Endgame*." Trans. Michael T. Jones. *New German Critique* 26 (1982): 119–50.

Agamben, Giorgio. *Homo Sacer: Sovereign Power and Bare Life*. Trans. Daniel Heller-Roazen. Stanford, CA: Stanford University Press, 1998.

Alexandrov, V. V., and G. L. Stenchikov. *O modelirovanii klimaticeskich posledstvij jadernoj vojny* [On modeling the climatic consequences of a nuclear war]. Moscow: USSR Academy of Sciences, 1983.

Anders, Günther. *Die Antiquiertheit des Menschen*. Vol. 1. Munich: C. H. Beck, 1961.

———. *Die atomare Drohung: Radikale Überlegungen*. Munich: Beck, 1981.

Aradau, Claudia. "The Myth of Preparedness." *Radical Philosophy* 161 (2010): 1–7.

Aristotle. *Poetics*. Trans. George Whalley. Montreal: McGill-Queen's University Press, 1997.

Assmann, Aleida. *Ist die Zeit aus den Fugen? Aufstieg und Fall des Zeitregimes der Moderne*. Munich: Hanser, 2013.

Atwood, Margaret. *Oryx and Crake: A Novel*. New York: Anchor, 2003.

———. *The Year of the Flood*. New York: Random House, 2009.

Bakewell, Geoffrey. "The One-Eyed Man Is King: Oedipal Vision in *Minority Report*." *Arethusa* 41 (2008): 95–112.

Balke, Friedrich. "Störungen im Bau." In *Signale der Störung*, ed. Albert Kümmel and Erhard Schüttpelz, 335–56. Munich: Fink, 2003.

Ballard, J. G. *The Drowned World*. 1963. New York: Norton, 2012.

Bartens, Werner. *Vorsicht Vorsorge: Wenn Prävention nutzlos oder gefährlich wird*. Frankfurt: Suhrkamp, 2008.

Bate, Jonathan. "Living with the Weather." *Studies in Romanticism* 35 (1996): 431–47.

Beck, Ulrich. "Risk Society and the Welfare State." In *World Risk Society*, 72–90. Cambridge: Polity, 1999.

———. *Risk Society: Towards a New Modernity.* Trans. Mark Ritter. London: Sage, 1992.
———. *World at Risk.* Trans. Ciaran Cronin. Cambridge: Polity, 2009.
Beckett, Samuel. *Endgame: A Play in One Act, Followed by Act Without Words: A Mime for One Player.* New York: Grove, 1958.
Beckman, Karen. *Crash: Cinema and the Politics of Speed and Stasis.* London: Duke University Press, 2010.
Benford, Gregory. *Timescape.* New York: Simon & Schuster, 1980.
Benjamin, Walter. *The Arcades Project.* Trans. Howard Eiland and Kevin McLaughlin. Cambridge, MA: Harvard University Press, 1999.
Benjamin, Walter. "Central Park." Trans. Lloyd Spencer. *New German Critique* 34 (1985): 32–58.
———. "Franz Kafka: On the Tenth Anniversary of His Death." In *Illuminations*, trans. Harry Zohn, 111–40. New York: Schocken, 1968.
Bickenbach, Matthias. "Der Alltag der Kontingenz: Crashing Cars. Über Autounfälle, Exempel und Katastrophendidaktik." In *Eigentlich könnte alles auch anders sein*, ed. Peter Zimmermann and Natalie Binczek, 117–39. Cologne: Verlag der Buchhandlung Walter, 1998.
Bickenbach, Matthias, and Michael Stolzke. *Die Geschwindigkeitsfabrik. Eine fragmentarische Geschichte des Autounfalls.* Berlin: Kadmos, 2014.
Birnbacher, Dieter. *Verantwortung für zukünftige Generationen.* Stuttgart: Reclam, 1988.
Bloch, Raymond. *La divination dans l'antiquité.* Paris: PUF, 1984.
Blum, Carol Blum. *Strengths in Numbers: Population, Reproduction, and Power in Eighteenth-Century France.* Baltimore, MD: Johns Hopkins University Press, 2002.
Blumenberg, Hans. *Shipwreck with Spectator.* Trans. Steven Rendall. Cambridge, MA: MIT Press, 1996.
Borges, Jorge Luis. "The Creation and P. H. Gosse." In *Selected Non-Fictions*, ed. Eliot Weinberger, trans. Esther Allen et al., 222–24. New York: Viking, 1999.
———. "The Garden of Forking Paths." In *Ficciones*, trans. Helen Temple and Ruthven Todd, 89–101. New York: Grove, 1962.
Bourseiller, Philippe. *365 Ways to Save the Earth: New and Updated Version.* New York: Abrams, 2008.
Brandstetter, Thomas. "Der Staub und das Leben: Szenarien des nuklearen Winters." *Archiv für Mediengeschichte* 12 (2005): 149–56.
Brians, Paul. *Nuclear Holocaust: Atomic War in Fiction.* Kent, OH: Kent State University Press, 1987.
Briese, Olaf, and Thimo Günther. "Katastrophe: Terminologische Vergangenheit, Gegenwart und Zukunft." *Archiv für Begriffsgeschichte* 51 (2009): 155–95.
Bröckling, Ulrich. "Dispositive der Vorbeugung: Gefahrenabwehr, Resilienz, Precaution." In *Sicherheitskultur: Soziale und politische Praktiken der Gefahrenabwehr*, ed. Christopher Daase et al., 93–108. Frankfurt: Campus, 2012.
Brodie, Bernard, ed. *The Absolute Weapon: Atomic Power and World Order.* New York: Harcourt, 1946.
———. *Strategy in the Missile Age.* Princeton, NJ: Princeton University Press, 1959.

Brunotte, Ulrike. "Die Bühne der Götter: Figurationen religiöser Meteorologie." In *Zwei Grad: Das Wetter, der Mensch und sein Klima*, ed. Petra Lutz and Thomas Macho, 44–49. Göttingen: Wallstein, 2008.

Buffon, Georges-Louis Leclerc, Conte de. "Epochs of Nature." In *Natural History, General and Particular*, 2nd ed., trans. William Smellie, 9:401–4. London: W. Strahan, 1785.

Burgess, J. Peter. *The Ethical Subject of Security: Geopolitical Reason and the Threat Against Europe*. London: Routledge, 2011.

Byron, George Gordon. "Darkness." In *Lord Byron: The Complete Poetical Works*, ed. Jerome J. McGann, 4:40–43. Oxford: Clarendon, 1980–1993.

Calabresi, Guido, and Philip Bobbitt. *Tragic Choices: The Conflicts Society Confronts in the Allocation of Tragically Scarce Resources*. New York: Norton, 1978.

Calhoun, Craig. "A World of Emergencies: Fear, Intervention, and the Limits of Cosmopolitan Order." *Canadian Review of Sociology and Anthropology* 41 (2004): 373–95.

Canaday, John. *The Nuclear Muse: Literature, Physics, and the First Atomic Bombs*. Madison: University of Wisconsin Press, 2000.

Canetti, Elias. *Crowds and Power*. Trans. Carol Stewart. New York: Farrar, Straus and Giroux, 1984.

Capelle, Wilhelm. "Μετέωρος—μετεωρολογία." *Philologus* 71 (1912): 414–48.

Carpenter, Charles A. *Dramatists and the Bomb: American and British Playwrights Confront the Nuclear Age, 1945–1964*. Westport, CT: Greenwood, 1999.

Cavell, Stanley. "Ending the Waiting Game." In *Must We Mean What We Say? A Book of Essays*, 115–62. Cambridge: Cambridge University Press, 1969.

Charles, Ron. "Apocalypse Now." *Washington Post*. October 1, 2006.

Chernobyl Diaries. Dir. Brad Parker. Los Angeles: Warner Bros., 2012.

Cicero, Marcus Tullius. *On the Ideal Orator*. Trans. James M. May and Jakob Wisse. Oxford: Oxford University Press, 2001.

Coetzee, J. M. "Time, Tense, and Aspect in Kafka's 'The Burrow.'" *PMLA* 96 (1981): 556–79.

Cohen, Alain J. J. "*12 Monkeys*, *Vertigo*, and *La Jetée*: Postmodern Mythologies and Cult Films." *New Review of Film and Television Studies* 1 (2003): 149–64.

Collingridge, David. *The Social Control of Technology*. London: Pinter, 1980.

Condorcet, Jean-Antoine-Nicolas Caritat de Condorcet. *Outlines of an Historical View of the Progress of the Human Mind*. Philadelphia: M. Carey, 1796.

Crutzen, Paul J. "Geology of Mankind." *Nature* 415 (2002): 23.

Crutzen, Paul J., and John W. Birks. "The Atmosphere After a Nuclear War: Twilight at Noon." *Ambio* 11 (1982): 114–25.

Cuvier, Georges. *Essay on the Theory of the Earth*. 5th ed. Trans. Robert Kerr. Edinburgh: William Blackwood, 1827.

D'Annunzio, Gabriele. *Forse che si, forse che no*. Milan: Treves, 1910.

The Day After Tomorrow. Dir. Roland Emmerich. Los Angeles: Centropolis Entertainment, 2004.

Deep Impact. Dir. Mimi Leder. Los Angeles: Paramount Pictures, 1998.

DeLillo, Don. *White Noise*. London: Picador, 1985.

Derrida, Jacques. "No Apocalypse, Not Now (Full Speed Ahead, Seven Missiles, Seven Missives." *Diacritics* 14 (1984): 20–31.

———. "Of an Apocalyptic Tone Recently Adopted in Philosophy." *Oxford Literary Review* 6/2 (1984): 3–37.

Diamond, Jared. *Collapse: How Societies Choose to Fail or Succeed*. 2nd ed. New York: Penguin, 2011.

———. "The Ends of the World as We Know Them." *New York Times*. January 1, 2005.

Dingley, R. J. "'I Had a Dream': Byron's 'Darkness.'" *Byron Journal* 9 (1981): 20–33.

Dowling, David. *Fictions of Nuclear Disaster*. Basingstoke: Macmillan, 1987.

Dr. Strangelove, or: How I Learned to Stop Worrying and Love the Bomb. Dir. Stanley Kubrick. Los Angeles: Columbia Pictures, 1964.

Dupuy, Jean-Pierre. *Pour un catastrophisme éclairé: Quand l'impossible est certain*. Paris: Seuil, 2002.

Edwards, Paul N. *A Vast Machine: Computer Models, Climate Data, and the Politics of Global Warming*. Cambridge, MA: MIT Press, 2010.

Ehrlich, Paul R. *The Population Bomb*. New York: Ballantine, 1968.

Esposito, Elena. "Die offene Zukunft der Sorgekultur." In *Gefahrensinn*, ed. Lorenz Engell et al., 107–14. Munich: Fink, 2009.

———. "Formen der Zirkularität in der Konstruktion der Zukunft." In *Prophetie und Prognose: Verfügungen über Zukunft in Wissenschaft, Religionen und Künsten*, ed. Daniel Weidner and Stefan Willer, 325–40. Munich: Fink, 2013.

Esposito, Roberto. *Immunitas: The Protection and Negation of Life*. Trans. Zakiya Hanafi. Cambridge: Polity, 2011.

Ewald, François. "The Return of Descartes's Malicious Demon: An Outline of a Philosophy of Precaution." In *Embracing Risk: The Changing Culture of Insurance and Responsibility*, ed. Tom Baker and Jonathan Simon, trans. Stephen Utz, 273–98. Chicago: University of Chicago Press, 2002.

Fail Safe. Dir. Sidney Lumet. Los Angeles: Columbia Pictures, 1964.

Fischer-Homberger, Esther. *Die traumatische Neurose: Vom somatischen zum sozialen Leiden*. Bern: Huber, 1975.

Flammarion, Camille. *Omega: The Last Days of the World*. New York: Cosmopolitan, 1894.

Fleming, James Rodger, and Vladimir Jankovic. "Revisiting Klima." *Osiris* 26 (2011): 1–15.

Fontenelle, Bernard le Bovier de. 1686. *Entretiens sur la pluralité des mondes*. Paris: Ménard et Desenne, 1828.

Fontenrose, Joseph. *The Delphic Oracle*. Berkeley: University of California Press, 1978.

Foucault, Michel. *The History of Sexuality*. Vol. 1: *An Introduction*. Trans. Michael Hurley. New York: Pantheon, 1978.

———. *"Society Must Be Defended": Lectures at the Collège de France, 1975–1976*. Trans. David Macey. New York: Picador, 2003.

Frank, Pat. *Alas, Babylon*. London: Constable, 1959.

Freud, Sigmund. "The Uncanny." In *The Standard Edition of the Complete Psychological Works of Sigmund Freud*, trans. James Strachey, 17:217–56. London: Hogarth, 1955.

Friedman, Lester D. "*Minority Report*: A Dystopic Vision." *Senses of Cinema* 27 (July 2003). http://sensesofcinema.com/2003/steven-spielberg/minority_report/.

Fuchs, Peter. "Prävention: Zur Mythologie und Realität einer paradoxen Zuvorkommenheit." In *Moderne Mythen der Medizin: Studien zur organisierten Krankenbehandlung*, ed. Irmhild Saake and Werner Vogd, 363–78. Wiesbaden: VS Verlag, 2008.

García Márquez, Gabriel. "The Cataclysm of Damocles (Ixtapa-Zihuatanejo, Mexico, August 6, 1986)." In *I'm Not Here to Give a Speech*, trans. Edith Grossman, 38–45. New York: Viking, 2014.

Geertz, Clifford. "Thick Description: Toward an Interpretive Theory of Culture." In *The Interpretation of Cultures: Selected Essays*, 3–30. New York: Basic Books, 1973.

Genette, Gérard. *Narrative Discourse Revisited*. Trans. Jane E. Lewis. Ithaca, NY: Cornell University Press, 1988.

Ghamari-Tabrizi, Sharon. *The Worlds of Herman Kahn*. Cambridge, MA: Harvard University Press, 2007.

Gladwell, Malcolm. *The Tipping Point: How Little Things Can Make a Big Difference*. New York: Little, Brown, 2000.

Glasstone, Samuel, and Philip J. Dolan, eds. *The Effects of Nuclear Weapons*. Washington, DC: United States Department of Defense, 1957.

Glavinic, Thomas. *Night Work*. Trans. John Brownjohn. Edinburgh: Canongate, 2009.

Godwin, William. *Enquiry Concerning Political Justice and Its Influence on Morals and Happiness*. London: G. G. J. and J. Robinson, 1793.

Gould, Stephen Jay. *Time's Arrow—Time's Cycle: Myth and Metaphor in the Discovery of Geological Time*. Cambridge, MA: Harvard University Press, 1987.

Graham, Stephen, and Nigel Thrift. "Out of Order: Understanding Repair and Maintenance." *Theory, Culture & Society* 24 (2007): 1–25.

Grandazzi, Guillaume. "Commemorating the Chernobyl Disaster: Remembering the Future." *Eurozine*, April 21, 2006. http://www.eurozine.com/commemorating-the-chernobyl-disaster-remembering-the-future/.

Grusin, Richard. "Premediation." *Criticism* 46 (2004): 17–39.

Gwinner, Donovan. "'Everything Uncoupled from Its Shoring': Quandaries of Epistemology and Ethics in *The Road*." In *Cormac McCarthy: All the Pretty Horses, No Country for Old Men, The Road*, ed. Sarah L. Spurgeon, 137–55. New York: Continuum, 2011.

Hamilton, John T. *Security: Politics, Humanity, and the Philology of Care*. Princeton, NJ: Princeton University Press, 2013.

Hampe, Michael. *Die Macht des Zufalls: Vom Umgang mit dem Risiko*. Berlin: WJS, 2006.

Hann, Julius von. *Handbook of Climatology*. Trans. Robert Ward. London: Macmillan, 1908.

Hansen, James. E. "Climate Change Is Here—and Worse Than We Thought," *Washington Post*, August 3, 2012.

Harremoës, Poul, et al., eds. *Late Lessons from Early Warnings: The Precautionary Principle 1896–2000*. Copenhagen: European Environment Agency, 2001.

Hegel, G. W. F. *Phenomenology of Spirit*. Trans. A. V. Miller. Oxford: Oxford University Press, 1977.

Heidegger, Martin. *Being and Time*. Trans. John Macquarrie and Edward Robinson. New York: Harper & Row, 1962.

Heinlein, Robert. *Time Enough for Love: The Lives of John Lazarus*. New York: G. P. Putnam's Sons, 1973.

Heise, Ursula. *Sense of Place and Sense of Planet: The Environmental Imagination of the Global*. Oxford: Oxford University Press, 2008.

Herder, Johann Gottfried. *Reflections on the Philosophy of the History of Mankind*. Trans. Frank Edward Manuel. Chicago: University of Chicago Press, 1996.

———. *This Too a Philosophy of History for the Formation of Humanity*. 1774. In *Philosophical Writings*, trans. and ed. M. N. Forster, 8:272–358. Cambridge: Cambridge University Press, 2002.

———. "Vom Wissen und Nichtwissen der Zukunft." In *Werke in zehn Bände*, ed. Günther Arnold et al., 8:283–96. Frankfurt: Deutscher Klassiker Verlag, 1998.

Herodotus. *The Histories*. Trans. Robin Waterfield. New York: Oxford University Press, 1998.

Herzog, Arthur. "Report on a Think Factory." *New York Times Magazine*. November 10, 1963.

Hippocrates. "Airs, Waters, Places." In *Hippocrates*, trans. W. H. S. Jones, 1:65–137. Cambridge, MA: Harvard University Press, 1923; repr. 1957.

Holm, Isak Winkel. "The Cultural Analysis of Disaster." In *The Cultural Life of Catastrophes and Crises*, ed. Carsten Meiner and Kristin Veel, 15–32. Berlin: Walter de Gruyter, 2012.

———. "The Frailty of Everything: Cormac McCarthy's *The Road* and Modern Disaster Discourse." In *The Cultural Life of Catastrophes and Crises*, ed. Carsten Meiner and Kristin Veel, 233–48. Berlin: Walter de Gruyter, 2012.

Honig, Bonnie. *Emergency Politics: Paradox, Law, and Democracy*. Princeton, NJ: Princeton University Press, 2009.

Horn, Eva. "The Aesthetics of Heat: For a Cultural History of Climate in the Age of Global Warming." *Metaphora* 2 (2017).

———. "Being in the Air." In *Breathe! Investigations Into Our Environmentally Entangled Future*, ed. Klaus Loenhart. Berlin: Birkhäuser, 2017.

———. "Klimatologie um 1800: Zur Genealogie des Anthropozäns." *Zeitschrift für Kulturwissenschaften* 10 (2016): 87–102.

———. "Krieg und Krise: Zur anthropologischen Figur des Ersten Weltkriegs." In *Konzepte der Moderne*, ed. Gerhart von Graevenitz, 633–55. Stuttgart: Metzler, 1999.

———. *The Secret War: Treason, Espionage, and Modern Fiction*. Trans. Geoffrey Winthrop-Young. Evanston, IL: Northwestern University Press, 2013.

Horn, Eva, and Urs Stäheli. "Nachwort: Eine 'soziologische Spekulation.'" In *Fragment einer Geschichte der Zukunft*, by Gabriel Tarde, 113–44. Konstanz: Konstanz University Press, 2015.

Houellebec, Michel. *The Possibility of an Island*. Trans. Gavin Bawd. New York: Vintage, 2007.

Hulme, Michael. "The Conquering of Climate: Discourses of Fear and their Dissolution." *Geographical Journal* 174 (2008): 5–16.

———. *Weathered: Cultures of Climate*. London: Sage, 2017.

Hume, David. *An Enquiry Concerning Human Understanding*. 1777. Ed. Tom L. Beauchamp. Oxford: Clarendon, 2000.

Hutton, James. *Theory of the Earth, with Proofs and Illustrations*. Edinburgh: Cadell, Davies, and Creech, 1795.
I Am Legend. Dir. Francis Lawrence. Los Angeles: Warner Bros. Pictures, 2007.
An Inconvenient Truth. Dir. Davis Guggenheim. Los Angeles: Paramount Classics, 2006.
Independence Day. Dir. Roland Emmerich. Los Angeles: Centropolis Entertainment, 1996.
Jaspers, Karl. *Die Atombombe und die Zukunft des Menschen: Politisches Bewusstsein in unserer Zeit*. Munich: Piper, 1962.
Jonas, Hans. *The Imperative of Responsibility: In Search of an Ethics for the Technological Age*. 1979. Trans. Hans Jonas and David Herr. Chicago: University of Chicago Press, 1984.
Jones, Frederick L., ed. *The Letters of Percy Bysshe Shelley*. Vol. 1: *Shelley in England*. Oxford: Clarendon, 1964.
Jungk, Robert. "Die Entwicklung sozialer Phantasie als Aufgabe der Zukunftsforschung." In *Ansichten einer künftigen Futurologie: Zukunftsforschung in der zweiten Phase*, ed. Dietger Pforte and Olaf Schwenke, 121–35. Munich: Hanser, 1973.
Kafka, Franz. "The Burrow." In *Selected Stories*, trans. Stanley Corngold, 162–89. New York: Norton, 2007.
———. "Jubilee Report: Twenty-Five Years of the Workmen's Accident Insurance Institute (1914)." In *The Office Writings*, ed. Stanley Corngold et al., 301–21. Princeton, NJ: Princeton University Press, 2009.
Kahn, Herman. *On Thermonuclear War*. Princeton, NJ: Princeton University Press, 1960.
———. *Thinking About the Unthinkable*. New York: Horizon, 1962.
Kaldor, Mary. *The Imaginary War: Understanding the East-West Conflict*. Oxford: Blackwell, 1990.
Kant, Immanuel. *Anthropology from a Pragmatic Point of View*. Trans. Mary J. Gregor. The Hague: Martinus Nijhoff, 1974.
Kaplan, Fred M. *The Wizards of Armageddon*. Stanford, CA: Stanford University Press, 1991.
Kapp, Ernst. *Grundlinien einer Philosophie der Technik: Zur Entstehungsgeschichte der Kultur aus neuen Gesichtspunkten*. Braunschweig: Verlag George Westermann, 1877.
Kittler, Friedrich. "Real Time Analysis, Time Axis Manipulation." Trans. Geoffrey Winthrop-Young. *Cultural Politics* 13 (2017): 1–18.
Koppenfels, Werner von. "Le coucher du soleil romantique: Die Imagination des Weltendes aus dem Geist der visionären Romantik." *Poetica* 17 (1985): 255–98.
Kornmeier, Uta. "Fit für den Ernstfall? Überleben als Hobby." In *Überleben: Historische und aktuelle Konstellationen*, ed. Falko Schmieder, 395–409. Munich: Fink, 2011.
Koselleck, Reinhart. *Futures Past: On the Semantics of Historical Time*. Trans. Keith Tribe. Cambridge, MA: MIT Press, 1985.
———. *The Practice of Conceptual History: Timing History, Spacing Concepts*. Trans. Todd Samuel Presner et al. Stanford, CA: Stanford University Press, 2002.
Kowalski, Dean A. "*Minority Report*, Molinism, and the Viability of Precrime." In *Steven Spielberg and Philosophy: We're Gonna Need a Bigger Book*, ed. Dean A. Kowalski, 227–46. Lexington: University of Kentucky Press, 2008.
Kreienbrock, Jörg. *Malicious Objects, Anger Management, and the Question of Modern Literature*. New York: Fordham University Press, 2012.

Kruse, Harald. *Überlebenstechnik: Lexikon für das Überleben in Wildnis und Zivilisation.* Stuttgart: Pietsch, 1986.

Kuhlmann, Albert. *Introduction to Safety Science.* Trans. H. Hermann. New York: Springer, 1986.

———. "Was muss die Sicherheitswissenschaft leisten?" In *Leben in Sicherheit: 1. Weltkongress für Sicherheitswissenschaft*, ed. Albert Kuhlmann, 23–42. Cologne: Verlag TÜV Rheinland, 1990.

La Jetée. Dir. Chris Marker. Paris: Argos Films, 1962.

Lacan, Jacques. "Psychoanalysis and Cybernetics, or On the Nature of Language." In *The Seminar of Jacques Lacan—Book II: The Ego in Freud's Theory and in the Technique of Psychoanalysis, 1954–1955*, trans. Sylvana Tomaselli, 294–308. Cambridge: Cambridge University Press, 1988.

Latour, Bruno. "Agency at the Time of the Anthropocene." *New Literary History* 45 (2014): 1–18.

———. *Facing Gaia: Eight Lectures on the New Climatic Regime.* Hoboken, NJ: Wiley, 2017.

———. "Si tu viens à perdre la Terre, à quoi te sers de sauver ton âme?" 2010. http://www.bruno-latour.fr/sites/default/files/109-ECOTHEO-FR.pdf.

———. "Why Has Critique Run Out of Steam? From Matters of Fact to Matters of Concern." *Critical Inquiry* 30 (2004): 225–48.

Lebovic, Nitzan. "The Biopolitical Film (A Nietzschean Paradigm)." *Postmodern Culture* 23 (2012).

Leggewie, Claus, and Harald Welzer. *Das Ende der Welt, wie wir sie kannten: Klima, Zukunft und die Chancen der Demokratie.* Frankfurt: Fischer, 2009.

Lemke, Thomas. *Biopolitics: An Advanced Introduction.* New York: NYU Press, 2011.

Lessing, Gotthold Ephraim. *The Education of the Human Race.* 1760. Trans. Fred W. Robertson. London: C. K. Paul & Co., 1881.

Lewis, David. "The Paradoxes of Time Travel." *American Philosophical Quarterly* 13 (1976): 145–52.

Lieb, Claudia. *Crash: Der Unfall in der Moderne.* Bielefeld: Aisthesis, 2009.

Lincoln, Kenneth. *Cormac McCarthy: American Canticles.* New York: Palgrave Macmillan, 2009.

Lovell, Ernest, ed. *His Very Self and Voice: Collected Conversations of Lord Byron.* New York: Macmillan, 1954.

Lovelock, James. *The Revenge of Gaia: Why the Earth Is Fighting Back, and How We Can Still Save Humanity.* London: Penguin, 2006.

Lübbe, Weyma. "Einleitung." In *Tödliche Entscheidung: Allokation von Leben und Tod in Zwangslagen*, ed. Weyma Lübbe, 7–28. Paderborn: Mentis, 2004.

Luhmann, Niklas. *Observations on Modernity.* Trans. William Whobrey. Stanford, CA: Stanford University Press, 1998.

———. "Risiko und Gefahr." *Soziologische Aufklärung* 5 (1990): 131–69.

Lyell, Charles. *Principles of Geology.* 3 vols. London: John Murray, 1830–1833.

Malthus, Thomas Robert. *An Essay on the Principle of Population.* Ed. Patricia James. Cambridge: Cambridge University Press, 1989.

———. *An Essay on the Principle of Population as It Affects the Future Improvement of Society.* Oxford: Oxford University Press, 1966.
Marbe, Karl. *Praktische Psychologie der Unfälle und Betriebsschäden.* Munich: Oldenbourg, 1926.
Marchetti, Cesare. "1012: A Check on the Earth—Carrying Capacity for Men." *Energy* 4 (1979): 1107–17.
Marshall, Eliot. "Nuclear Winter Debate Heats Up." *Science* 235 (1987): 271–73.
McCarthy, Cormac. *The Road.* New York: Knopf, 2006.
Meadows, Dennis L., et al. *The Limits to Growth.* New York: Universe, 1972.
Menke, Christoph. *Tragic Play: Irony and Theater from Sophocles to Beckett.* Trans. James Phillips. New York: Columbia University Press, 2009.
Minois, Georges. *Histoire de l'avenir: Des prophètes à la prospective.* Paris: Fayard, 1996.
Minority Report. Dir. Steven Spielberg. Los Angeles: DreamWorks Pictures, 2002.
Monbiot, George. "Civilization Ends with a Shutdown of Human Concern: Are We There Already?" *Guardian.* October 30, 2007.
Musil, Robert. *The Man Without Qualities.* Trans. Sophie Wilkens. New York: Knopf, 1995.
Myrone, Martin, ed. *John Martin: Apocalypse.* London: Tate, 2011.
Nell [O'Neill], Onora. "Lifeboat Earth." *Philosophy and Public Affairs* 4 (1975): 273–92.
Oakes, Guy. *The Imaginary War: Civil Defense and American Cold War Culture.* New York: Oxford University Press, 1994.
Olster, Stacey. "White Noise." In *The Cambridge Guide to Don DeLillo,* ed. John N. Duvall, 79–93. Cambridge: Cambridge University Press, 2008.
Oreskes, Naomi, and Erik M. Conway. *Merchants of Doubt: How a Handful of Scientists Obscured the Truth on Issues from Tobacco Smoke to Global Warming.* New York: Bloomsbury, 2012.
Osteen, Mark, ed. *Don DeLillo: White Noise. Text and Criticism.* New York: Penguin, 1998.
Paddock, William, and Paul Paddock. *Famine 1975! America's Decision: Who Will Survive?* Boston: Little, Brown, 1967.
Paul, Jean. "Speech of the Dead Christ from the Universe That There Is No God." In *Jean Paul: A Reader,* ed. Timothy J. Casey, 179–83. Baltimore, MD: Johns Hopkins University Press, 1992.
Paley, Morton. *Apocalypse and Millennium in English Romantic Poetry.* Oxford: Clarendon, 1999.
———. "Envisioning Lastness: Byron's 'Darkness,' Campbell's 'The Last Man,' and the Critical Aftermath." *Romanticism: The Journal of Romantic Culture and Criticism* 1 (1995): 1–14.
Perrow, Charles. *Normal Accidents: Living with High-Risk Technologies.* 2nd ed. Princeton, NJ: Princeton University Press, 1999.
Pidoll, Michael von. *Der heutige Automobilismus: Ein Protest und Weckruf.* Vienna: Manz, 1912.
Playfair, John. "Hutton's Unconformity." *Transactions of the Royal Society of Edinburgh* 5/3 (1805): 39–99.
Post, John D. *The Last Great Subsistence Crisis in the Western World.* Baltimore, MD: Johns Hopkins University Press, 1977.

Pötter, Bernhard. "Knapp am Untergang vorbei." *taz.de*. September 12, 2007.
Poundstone, William. *Prisoner's Dilemma*. New York: Doubleday, 1992.
Powell, James Lawrence. *2084: An Oral History of the Great Warming*. Kindle E-Book, 2011.
Rapoport, Anatol. *Game Theory as a Theory of Conflict Resolution*. Dordrecht: Reidel, 1974.
The Road. Dir. John Hillcoat. Los Angeles: Dimension Films, 2009.
Robb, John. "The Difference Between Resilience and 'Prepping.'" *Walden Labs: Solutions for Self-Reliance*, August 13, 2013. http://waldenlabs.com/the-difference-between-resilience-and-prepping/.
Robinson, James E. "Samuel Beckett's Doomsday Play: The Space of Infinity." In *The Theatrical Space*, ed. James Redmond, 215–27. Cambridge: Cambridge University Press, 1987.
Rockström, Johan, et al. "Planetary Boundaries: Exploring the Safe Operating Space for Humanity." *Ecology and Society* 14 (2009).
Röggla, Katrin. *Disaster Awareness Fair: Zum katastrophischen in Stadt, Land und Film*. Graz: Literaturverlag Droschl, 2008.
Rousseau, Jean-Jacques. "Discourse on the Origin and Foundations of Inequality Among Men." In *The Discourses and Other Political Writings*, ed. Victor Gourevitch, 111–88. Cambridge: Cambridge University Press, 2012.
Sagan, Carl. *Nuclear War and Climate Catastrophe: Some Policy Implications*. Ithaca, NY: Cornell University Press, 1983.
———. *Pale Blue Dot*. New York: Random House, 1994.
Schäffner, Wolfgang. "Das Trauma der Versicherung: Das Ereignis im Zeitalter der Wahrscheinlichkeit." In *Modernität und Trauma: Beiträge zum Zeitenbruch des Ersten Weltkriegs*, ed. Inka Mülder-Bach, 104–20. Vienna: Universitätsverlag, 2000.
Schmauß, August. *Das Problem der Wettervorhersage*. Leipzig: Becker & Erler, 1945.
Schmidt, Arno. "Schwarze Spiegel." In *Brand's Haide: Zwei Erzählungen*, 153–259. Hamburg: Rowohlt, 1951.
Schmitt, Carl. *The Concept of the Political*. Expanded ed. Trans. George Schwab. Chicago: University of Chicago Press, 2007.
———. "Total Enemy, Total War, Total State." In *Four Articles, 1931–1938*, trans. Simona Draghici. Washington, DC: Plutarch, 1999.
Schnyder, Peter. "Paläontopoetologie: Zur Emergenz der Urgeschichte des Lebens." In *Die biologische Vorgeschichte des Menschen*, ed. Maximilian Bergengruen et al., 109–31. Freiburg: Rombach, 2012.
Seeßlen, Georg, and Markus Metz. *Krieg der Bilder, Bilder des Krieges: Abhandlung über die Katastrophe und die mediale Wirklichkeit*. Berlin: Edition Tiamat, 2002.
Seitz, Russell. "In from the Cold: 'Nuclear Winter' Melts Down." *National Interest* 5 (1986): 3–17.
Serres, Michel. *The Birth of Physics*. Trans. Jack Hawkes. Manchester: Clinamen, 2000.
———. *The Natural Contract*. Trans. Elizabeth MacArthur and William Paulson. Ann Arbor: University of Michigan Press, 1995.
Seton-Watson, Hugh. *Neither War nor Peace: The Struggle for Power in the Postwar World*. New York: Praeger, 1960.
Shute, Nevil. *On the Beach*. 1957. New York: Vintage, 2010.

Simmel, Georg. *Der Krieg und die geistigen Entscheidungen*. Munich: Duncker & Humblot, 1917.
Sloterdijk, Peter, et al. *Das Raumschiff Erde hat keinen Notausgang*. Berlin: Suhrkamp, 2011.
Smith, Joe. "Murphy's Laws: Origin." 1978. http://www.murphys-laws.com/murphy/murphy-true.html.
Soddy, Frederick. "Some Recent Advances in Radioactivity." *Contemporary Review* 83 (1903): 708–20.
Sombart, Werner. *Händler und Helden: Patriotische Besinnungen*. Munich: Duncker & Humblot, 1915.
Sophocles. *The Oedipus Cycle: Oedipus Rex—Oedipus at Colonus—Antigone*. Trans. Dudley Fitts and Robert Fitzgerald. New York: Harcourt Brace, 1976.
Souriau, Étienne. "La structure de l'univers filmique et le vocabulaire de la filmologie." *Revue internationale de filmologie* 7/8 (1951): 231–40.
Soylent Green. Dir. Richard Fleisher. Los Angeles: MGM, 1973.
Spurgeon, Sara L., ed. *Cormac McCarthy: All the Pretty Horses, No Country for Old Men, The Road*. New York: Continuum, 2011.
Steffen, Will, et al. "The Anthropocene: Are Humans Now Overwhelming the Great Forces of Nature?" *Ambio* 36 (2007): 614–21.
Stewart, George R. *Earth Abides*. London: V. Gollancz, 1949.
Steyn, Mark. *America Alone: The End of the World as We Know It*. Washington, DC: Regnery, 2006.
Strowick, Elisabeth. "Epistemologie des Verdachts: Zu Kafkas Bau." In *The Parallax View: Zur Mediologie der Verschwörung*, ed. Marcus Krause et al., 123–36. Munich: Fink, 2011.
Süssmilch, Johann Peter. *Die göttliche Ordnung in den Veränderungen des menschlichen Geschlechts aus der Geburt, dem Tode und der Fortpflanzung desselben*. Berlin: Verlag des Buchladens der Realschule, 1761.
Swiss Re. *The Risk Landscape of the Future*. 2004. http://www.swissre.com/library/The_Risk_Landscape_of_the_Future.html.
Szondi, Peter. *An Essay on the Tragic*. Trans. Paul Fleming. Stanford, CA: Stanford University Press, 2002.
Take Shelter. Dir. Jeff Nichols. Los Angeles: Sony Pictures Classics, 2011.
Taleb, Nassim Nicholas. *The Black Swan: The Impact of the Highly Improbable*. 2nd ed. New York: Random House, 2010.
Taurek, John M. "Should the Numbers Count?" *Philosophy and Public Affairs* 6 (1977): 293–316.
Taylor, Charles. *Modern Social Imaginaries*. Durham, NC: Duke University Press, 2004.
Temkine, Pierre, et al. *Warten auf Godot: Das Absurde und die Geschichte*. Ed. Denis Thouard and Tim Trzaskalik. Berlin: Matthes & Seitz, 2008.
The Terminator. Dir. James Cameron. Los Angeles: Orion Pictures, 1984.
Thaler, Estelle Manette. "Apocalyptic Vision in Heartbreak House and Endgame: The Metaphor of Change." *Zeitschrift für Anglistik und Germanistik* 34 (1986): 343–51.
Theisohn, Philipp. *Die kommende Dichtung: Geschichte des literarischen Orakels, 1450–2050*. Munich: Fink, 2012.

Thüring, Hubert. "Der Unfall und das Rettungswerk: Narrative und Modelle bei Thomas Mann und Adolf Wölfli." In *Rettung und Erlösung: Politisches und religiöses Heil in der Moderne*, ed. Johannes F. Lehmann and Hubert Thüring, 149–67. Munich: Fink, 2015.

Tourneux, Félix. "Accidens." In *Encyclopédie des chemins de fer et des machines à vapeur*, 2–10. Paris: Jules Renouard, 1844.

Turco, R. P., et al. "Nuclear Winter: Global Consequences of Multiple Nuclear Explosions." *Science* 222 (1983): 1283–92.

———. "'Nuclear Winter' to Be Taken Seriously." *Nature* 311 (1984): 307–8.

12 Monkeys. Dir. Terry Gilliam. Los Angeles: Universal Pictures, 1995.

Vernant, Jean-Pierre. *Parole et signes muets*. Paris: Éditions du Seuil, 1974.

Vernant, Jean-Pierre, et al. *Divination et rationalité*. Paris: Éditions du Seuil, 1974.

Virilio, Paul. *The Original Accident*. Trans. Julie Rose. Cambridge: Polity, 2007.

Virilio, Paul, and Sylvère Lotringer. "Technik und Fragmentierung." In *Aisthesis: Wahrnehmung heute oder Perspektiven einer anderen Ästehtik*, ed. Karlheinz Barck, 71–81. Leipzig: Reclam, 1983.

Vischer, Friedrich Theodor. *Auch einer: Eine Reisebekanntschaft*. 1879. Stuttgart: Deutsche Verlagsanstalt, 1908.

Vondung, Klaus. *Die Apokalypse in Deutschland*. Munich: Deutscher Taschenbuch Verlag, 1988.

Vonnegut, Kurt. *Cat's Cradle*. New York: Dell, 1963.

Wallerstein, Immanuel. *The End of the World as We Know It: Social Science for the Twenty-First Century*. Minneapolis: University of Minnesota Press, 1999.

Weart, Spencer R. *The Discovery of Global Warming*. Rev. and expanded ed. Cambridge, MA: Harvard University Press, 2008.

———. *Nuclear Fear: A History of Images*. Cambridge, MA: Harvard University Press, 1988.

Weart, Spencer R., and Gertrud W. Szilard, eds. *Leo Szilard: His Version of the Facts*. Cambridge: MA: MIT Press, 1978.

Weber, Eugen. *Apocalypses: Prophecies, Cults, and Millennial Beliefs Through the Ages*. Cambridge, MA: Harvard University Press, 2000.

Weigand, Hermann. "Franz Kafka's 'The Burrow' ('Der Bau'): An Analytical Essay." *PMLA* 87 (1972): 152–66.

Weisman, Alan. *Countdown: Our Last, Best Hope for a Future on Earth?* New York: Back Bay, 2013.

———. *The World Without Us*. New York: Thomas Dunne, 2007.

Wells, H. G. "The Time Machine." In *Seven Science Fiction Novels of H. G. Wells*, 1–76. New York: Dover, 1950.

———. *The Time Machine: An Invention*. New York: Henry Holt, 1895.

———. *The War of the Worlds*. New York: Bantam, 2003.

———. *The World Set Free*. London: Macmillan, 1914.

Welzer, Harald. *Climate Wars: What People Will Be Killed for in the Twenty-First Century*. Trans. Patrick Camiller. Cambridge: Polity, 2012.

———. *Selbst denken: Eine Anleitung zum Widerstand*. Frankfurt: Fischer, 2013.

Williams, Keith. *H. G. Wells, Modernity, and the Movies.* Chicago: University of Chicago Press, 2008.
Wojcik, Daniel. *The End of the World as We Know It: Faith, Fatalism, and Apocalypse in America.* New York: NYU Press, 1997.
Wolf, Christa. *Accident: A Day's News.* Trans. Heike Schwarzbauer and Rick Takvorian. Chicago: University of Chicago Press, 2001.
Wood, Gillen D'Arcy. *Tambora: The Eruption That Changed the World.* Princeton, NJ: Princeton University Press, 2015.
Zalasiewicz, Jan. *The Earth After Us: What Legacy Will Humans Leave in the Rocks?* New York: Oxford University Press, 2008.
Zalasiewicz, Jan, et al. "Are We Now Living in the Anthropocene?" *GSA Today* 18 (2008): 4–8.
Žižek, Slavoj. "The Interpassive Subject." 1998. http://www.lacan.com/zizek-pompidou.htm.
———. "Die Substitution zwischen Interaktivität und Interpassivität." In *Interpassivität: Studien über delegiertes Geniessen*, ed. Robert Pfaller, 13–32. Vienna: Springer, 2000.
———. *Welcome to the Desert of the Real! Five Essays on September 11 and Related Dates.* London: Verso, 2002.

INDEX

abandoned city, 138, 207
accident, 15–16, 37, 58, 76, 121, 140–156, 168, 172, 176, 192, 194, 196, 201, 228–229; design-basis, 138; escalation of, 148, 153, 156; imagined or fictional, 143, 163–173; technical, 91, 134–140, 156–162. *See also* maximum credible accident
Accident: A Day's News (Wolf), 139, 163
Adorno, Theodor W., 124, 128
adventus, the future as, 22
affect, 4, 10, 15–16, 41, 144, 173
After Earth (Shyamalan), 6
Agamben, Giorgio, 101, 115
agency, 4, 80, 143, 149–150, 231–232
Akimov, Alexander, 135, 161
alarmism, 116, 120, 232–237
alien, 3–4, 19, 105, 108; invaders, 99, 102, 105, 106, 107, 108
ambiguity, 129, 182–183, 185, 187–188
Anders, Günther, 43, 122–123; apocalypse blindness, 46–8, 228, 232; naked apocalypse, 23
an 2440, L' (Mercier), 201–202

annihilation, 42–43, 66, 75, 77, 99, 102–107, 185, 227
Anthropocene, 4, 8, 15, 63, 80–81, 231–232
anthropology, 12–13, 24, 28, 30, 33, 37, 39, 41, 60, 75, 88; Enlightenment and, 26, 35–36; of catastrophe, 13, 24, 42, 53, 64, 128, 130
anxiety, 9–10, 23, 25, 98, 118, 167–168, 173, 191–192, 196, 198, 205, 218. *See also* safety; security; *Sorge*
apocalypse, 5, 6, 11, 13, 21–23, 30, 40, 43–44, 91, 96, 103, 123, 229; blindness, 47, 228, 232; classical, 13, 21–22, 24, 26, 30; etymology, 22; imagery, 4–5, 22–23, 26, 42, 46, 64, 72; nuclear, 14, 25, 49, 50, 52–53, 77, 124, 204; "naked" or "truncated" (Anders), 23; Romantic, 26–29, 39, 40–41, 53; without God, 23–24, 27–28, 30, 34, 39. *See also* end of the world
Apollo, 182–184, 187, 188
asbestos, 163–166, 204
Aristotle, 6, 37, 60, 88, 100, 140, 180
Armageddon (Bay), 108
Assmann, Aleida, 5

276 INDEX

Auch einer (Someone Too) (Vischer), 148–150, 156

Bacigalupi, Paolo, 5
Ballard, J. G., 86–88
Bate, Jonathan, 40
Beck, Ulrich, 5, 10, 95, 140, 163, 254n53
Beckett, Samuel, 25, 122–124, 130
Benjamin, Walter, 7, 13, 192, 230
Bert the Turtle (cartoon character), 91–92
Bhopal, 1984 dioxin disaster at, 167
Bickenbach, Matthias, 145, 147
bifurcation, 18, 184; time as garden of forking paths, 22, 179, 180, 237; future as garden of forking paths, 47, 190, 200, 214, 225
biopolitics, 37, 41, 75, 98; of survival, 14, 89–115, 122–133; of scarcity, 112, 115–122, 132
bios, 122–123
bioterrorism, 207
Birk, John W., 70–71, 76–77
blindness, 16, 47, 180, 184, 185–187, 189–191, 195, 200, 206, 207, 213–214, 219, 225–226, 228–229, 232; blind reflexivity, 232, 235–237. *See also* apocalypse, blindness
Blindness (Meirelles), 108–109
Blumenberg, Hans, 144
Bobbit, Philip, 114
Bomb, the, 15, 42–47
Book of Dave, The (Self), 81
Book of Eli, The (Hughes and Hughes), 6
Borges, Jorge Luis, 18, 22, 179–180, 237
Boy Scouts, 90, 132, 169
Brandstetter, Thomas, 73
Bröckling, Ulrich, 167, 176–177, 191, 201
Brodie, Bernard, 46, 49
Buffon, Georges-Louis, 61, 65
Bulletin of the Atomic Scientists, 43–44
bunker, 109–111, 113, 128–129, 192, 194, 197–199; private, 9, 91, 93, 123–126, 133, 250n56
Bureau Veritas, 158
Burgess, J. Peter, 178
"Burrow, The" (Kafka), 191–196, 200, 225

Byron, George Gordon, 13, 25, 37, 39–41, 57, 65, 130, 227. *See also* "Darkness"

Calabresi, Guido, 114
Calhoun, Craig, 178
Canetti, Elias, 122
Cannibalism, 13, 34–35, 75, 78, 119, 130–132
Carpenter, Charles A., 126, 250n56
catastrophe: climate, 14, 55, 57–58, 65–71, 74, 80–81, 86, 109; desire for, 52–53, 170–172; etymology, 6, 7, 53, 174, 227, 255n1; environmental, 58, 91, 98, 108, 116, 118, 205, 229; narrative, 97–100, 108, 121, 233, 235, 238; nuclear, 72, 135, 138, 140, 163; as revelation, 9–12, 22–24, 26, 41, 96, 140, 235; secular understanding of, 14, 25, 41, 53; technological, 138–140; as test, 33, 110; without event, 4, 8–9, 13, 15, 54–56, 74–75, 80–81, 88, 229–231. *See also* future as catastrophe; imaginary, catastrophic
cautionary tales, 57, 164, 166, 233
Cavell, Stanley, 127, 251n58
chain of unfortunate events, 139, 148–156, 158–159, 161, 173, 178, 230
Chernobyl, 1986 nuclear disaster at, 90, 134–140, 144, 148, 161–163, 167, 205
Chernobyl Diaries (Parker), 137, 138
Cicero, 22
climate, 7, 12, 40, 56–57, 59, 60–63, 65, 70, 76, 77, 79, 80, 85, 87–88, 201, 230;
climate change, 5, 8, 10, 14–16, 43, 54–57, 59, 61–62, 64–75, 80–86, 88, 95; anthropogenic, 57, 61, 63, 74, 86; Intergovernmental Panel on Climate Change (IPCC), 62, 86, 88, 245n18. *See also* global warming
climate disaster, 40, 57, 63, 109
climate research, 15, 62–63, 70–71, 74, 82, 84–86, 88
climate skeptics, denialists of anthropogenic climate change, 86, 232
climatology. *See* climate research

Club of Rome, 15, 115, 228, 249n36, 249n43
Cold War, 12, 14–18, 25, 42–54, 56, 70, 75, 77, 90–91, 98–99, 104–105, 108, 123, 133, 170, 172, 177, 205, 228–229, 232–233; as imaginary war, 46
complexity, 7, 8, 14, 18, 156, 158, 159, 177, 223; hyper-complexity, 14, 58, 59, 73, 85; technological, 138, 139, 144, 160, 161, 162
Comte, Auguste, 175, 255n5
Marquis de Condorcet, 35–36
Contagion (Soderbergh), 6, 108, 109
Countdown (Weisman), 120
Country of Last Things, The (Auster), 74
coupling, loose or tight, 159–161
crash, 140–148, 151, 156, 168–169, 173, 176, 196, 228
Croesus (figure), 182–183, 184, 188–189
Crutzen, Paul, 70–71, 76–77, 80–81
cura (Latin: care), 191, 194, 200. See also security; *Sorge*
Cuvier, Georges, 65–66, 88

D'Annunzio, Gabriele, 144
"Darkness" (Byron), 12–13, 26, 31–37, 39–41, 63–65, 68, 97, 119, 124, 128, 130, 132, 202, 227, 234
Darwin, Charles, 57, 103, 105, 228, 255n7
data friction, 85
Day After, The (Meyer), 72, 74, 98
Day After Tomorrow, The (Emmerich), 5, 55–56, 81–82, 108–109, 111–112
Day the Earth Stood Still, The (Wise), 99
Deane, Lucy, 164–165
Deep Impact (Leder), 108–114, 121
deep time, geological, 4, 69, 86–88, 245n34
degeneration, 67–69, 98, 228
DeLillo, Don, 167–173, 234–235, 254n53
dernier homme, Le (Grainville), 26
Descartes, René, 79, 166
destiny, 115, 145, 152–153, 183–185, 235
deterrence, 46, 48–53, 228, 233
Derrida, Jacques, 49, 205

Diamond, Jared, 5
Dick, Philip K., 219
diegesis, 19, 209, 241n33
disaster fiction, 12, 13, 97, 99, 100, 105, 117, 121, 172, 231–233, 235, 236
Dr. Strangelove (Kubrick), 46, 49–53, 99, 228, 233
Dolan, Philip J., 70
doomsday, 51, 91
Doomsday Clock, 43, 44
Drowned World, The (Ballard), 86–88
Dubos, l'Abbé Jean-Baptiste, 60
"duck and cover," 72, 91–92, 94, 127, 246n42
Dupuy, Jean-Pierre, 236–237
Dyatlov, Anatoly, 135, 139
dystopia, 81, 88, 117, 119, 201

Earth, carrying capacity of, 120, 249n43
Earth Abides (Stewart), 26, 77
Earthrise, photograph, 82–83
Edwards, Paul, 85
emergency, 11, 14, 95–97, 109–110, 113, 115, 121–122, 127–128, 134–135, 138–139, 161, 172, 178, 192–193
emergency, state of, 14, 97, 127, 172, 234
Emmerich, Roland, 5, 88, 107, 111, 233
Endgame (Beckett), 7, 72, 123–130, 132, 250n54, 250n56
end of human history, 21, 23, 53
end of humankind. See extinction, of humanity
end of the world, 6, 21–26, 28, 29, 34, 40–43, 47, 53, 67, 99, 106, 123–124, 227–228, 231, 234. See also apocalypse
end times, feeling of living in, 43
enemy, 47, 49, 51, 98–100, 102–105, 107–108, 121–122, 193–194, 196
Enemy of the People, An (Ibsen), 165
Enlightenment, 22, 26, 35–36, 39, 64, 202, 224, 227; optimist anthropology, 26, 35–36, 39
Entretiens sur la pluralité des mondes (Fontenelle), 33

environmental protection, 82, 83, 90, 141
epidemic, 1, 36, 38, 71, 90, 96, 98, 109, 164, 176, 207, 208, 214, 229
Epochs of Nature (Buffon), 65
eschatology, 21, 22, 26–27, 34; history and, 13, 25, 41, 227
Esposito, Elena, 189, 191
Esposito, Roberto, 101
Essay on the Principle of Population (Malthus), 35–39
Essay on the Theory of the Earth (Cuvier), 66
Ewald, François, 166
experiment, 16–18, 23, 45, 48, 58–59, 73, 75–76, 85, 88, 110, 113, 128, 132, 134, 139, 151, 162, 171, 203; thought, 4, 24, 28, 30, 33, 49, 64, 67, 97, 122. *See also* test
extinction, 66–65, 75, 80, 108; of humanity, 2–4, 6, 12, 24, 27, 30, 34, 39, 42–43, 46, 63, 68, 72, 75, 77, 99, 102, 123, 132, 227, 234; of life, 69, 101
extrapolation, 10, 15, 23, 37–38, 40–41, 45, 57, 80, 176

Fail-Safe (Lumet), 46, 49–50, 52–53, 99, 228, 233
fallout, radioactive, 72, 91, 94, 125, 134, 136
fallout shelter. *See* bunker
Fallout Shelter Handbook (West), 93
famine, 34, 36, 38–40, 71, 74–75, 77, 82, 90, 114, 116, 117, 119, 228
Famine 1975! (Paddock and Paddock), 116
fantasy, 1, 5, 9, 11–12, 14, 21, 42, 46–48, 53, 56, 68–69, 75, 88, 97, 99, 100, 122, 199, 207,
fate, 23, 25, 34, 131, 152, 156, 182–185, 188, 191, 206, 256n33
fiction, 4–5, 9–11, 15–16, 18–19, 25–26, 30, 41, 43–44, 46, 49–50, 53, 57, 74, 77, 81, 86, 88, 98, 113, 144, 172–174, 178–179, 196, 204, 228, 230–238; Borges's theory of, 179–180 epistemic function of, 10, 11, 15, 16. *See also* disaster fiction
Final Destination (Wong), 152–156

financial crisis of 2008, vii, 190, 197–198
Flammarion, Camille, 67
Flight Behavior (Kingsolver), 81
forecast, 37–39, 41–42, 58–59
foreknowledge, 14–16, 18, 163, 180–182, 184–185, 187–189, 199–200, 202, 206–207, 211, 215–216, 222–225, 235, 237, 256n26; antiquity's concept of, 181–182, 184–185, 187, 189, 200
foresight, 22–23, 167, 175, 200, 223, 230
Foucault, Michel, 37, 100–101
4:44: End of the World (Ferrara), 6
Frankenstein (M. Shelley), 40
French Revolution, 40
Freud, Sigmund, 151
Friend of the Earth, A (Boyle), 81
Fuchs, Peter, 178
future, 3, 11, 17, 21, 35–41, 45–46, 52, 57, 64–65, 67, 69, 81–82, 84, 94, 97, 116, 128, 130, 141, 143, 145–148, 153, 162–164, 166, 171–173, 181–190, 197, 203, 206–208, 211, 213–223, 225, 234; fictitious, 10, 15–16, 49, 68, 178, 201–205, 228, 235–238; loss of, 42; modern relation to, 4, 6, 7, 9, 10, 13, 22, 41, 47, 53, 167, 174–181, 190–192, 194–195, 198–202, 225–229, 231, 237; obscurity of, 22–23, 168, 178, 221; thick description of, 16, 18. *See also* narrative
future as catastrophe, 5–9, 12–14, 25, 41–42, 53, 90, 133, 139–140, 162, 167, 174, 178, 181, 227, 230
future perfect (futurum perfectum, accomplished future), 4, 24, 41, 167, 174, 221
futurology (futurologists), 17, 48–49

Gaia hypothesis, 5
game theory, 46, 50–52
García Márquez, Gabriel, 69
"Garden of Forking Paths, The" (Borges), 22, 179
Genette, Gérard, 19
geology, modern, 65

Gladwell, Malcolm, 7
Glasstone, Samuel, 70
Globalia (Rufin), 81
global warming, 8, 15, 63, 80–83, 85, 87–88, 229. *See also* climate change
God, 21, 181, 237; absence of, 26–28, 30; plan of, 21, 153,
gods, 22, 57, 181–187, 189, 185, 199, 226
Godwin, William, 35
Gore, Al, 82–84, 88, 233
Graham, Stephen, 138
Grandazzi, Guillaume, 139
grandfather paradox, 203, 205, 206
Grusin, Richard, 16, 217–218, 225

Hamilton, John T., 194
Hampe, Michael, 161–162
Hann, Julius von, 62
Hansen, James, 5
Heavy Weather (Sterling), 81
Hegel, Georg Wilhelm Friedrich, 150
Heidegger, Martin, 191–192
Heinlein, Robert, 55
Heise, Ursula, 254n41, 254n53
Hell (Fehlbaum), 6, 81
Herder, Gottfried, 35, 60, 61, 88, 255n12
Herodotus, 182, 189
heuristics of fear, 167, 168, 172, 177
hindsight, 24–25, 46, 53, 97–98, 140, 148, 166, 167, 175, 183, 188, 229–231, 235
Historia magistra vitae (Cicero), 22
homo homini lupus, 39
homo sacer, 101
Honig, Bonnie, 126
hope, 5, 11, 22–24, 41, 47, 53, 57, 59, 75, 96, 177, 179, 182, 192, 205–206, 219
hopelessness, 65, 74, 118, 133, 213
Houellebecq, Michel, 5
human factor, 61, 145, 148, 162
hunger riots, 40, 119
Hurricane Sandy (2012), 96
Hutton, James, 65, 245n34
Hyginus, Gaius Julius, 191

I Am Legend (Matheson), 26, 239n2, 239n2, 241n8
I Am Legend (Lawrence), 1–3, 9, 24, 26, 239n2
ice age, 55, 57, 64, 66, 81, 228
imaginary: catastrophic, 12–14, 23, 26, 30, 39, 42, 53, 64, 95, 116, 227–228, 233; collective, 10, 16
imagination, 23, 26–28, 47–49, 56, 63–64, 72, 88, 96–97, 116, 127, 143–144, 204, 227, 232, 237
immunization, 101, 103, 176–178, 201
Imperative of Responsibility, The (Jonas), 167, 204–205
Inconvenient Truth, An (Guggenheim), 82–84. *See also* Gore, Al
Independence Day (Emmerich), 99, 105–107
Industrial Revolution, 4, 228
infrastructure, 3, 90–92, 94–97
insurance, 6, 7, 9, 144, 147, 165, 174, 176, 190, 198, 255n2
interpassivity, 233–236
Introduction to Safety Science (Kuhlmann), 160
Invasion, The (Hirschbiegel), 99, 105
Invasion of the Body Snatchers, The (Kaufman), 99, 105
Invasion of the Body Snatchers, The (Siegel), 99, 105

Jaspers, Karl, 43–44
Jean Paul, 27–28, 30, 38, 227, 235
Jerusalem, New, 21, 27
Jetée, La (Marker), 209
Jonah (prophet), 237
Jonas, Hans, 167, 177, 203–205
Jungk, Robert, 48

Kafka, Franz, 191–192
Kahn, Herman, 17, 46, 48–49, 51, 52, 72–73, 90, 177, 179, 236
Kapp, Ernst, 150, 253n25
Kennedy, John F., 205

Kingsolver, Barbara, 81, 88
Kornmeister, Uta, 95
Kowalski, Dean, 223
Krakatoa eruption (1883), 57, 70, 242n28
Kreienbrock, Jörg, 150
Kruse, Harald, 89–90
Kubrick, Stanley, 46, 50, 228

Lacan, Jacques, 234
Lamentations of Zeno, The (Trojanow), 81, 88
Last and First Men: A Story of the Near and Far Future (Stapledon), 202
Last Judgment, 21, 23–24, 27, 29, 41, 53, 103, 190, 227
Last Man, 1, 9, 12, 16, 24–26, 28, 30, 39, 41–42, 53, 77, 99, 122, 128, 130, 133, 227–230, 232
"Last Man, The" (Campbell), 26
Last Man, The (Martin), 28–30, 39
Last Man, The (M. Shelley), 26, 77, 202
lastness, 24–25, 41, 53
Late Lessons from Early Warnings: The Precautionary Principle, 1896-2000 (European Environment Agency), 164, 167–168, 204, 233
latency, 60, 83, 172, 230; period, 140, 165, 166, 171, 230; lacuna, 165, 230
Latour, Bruno, 5, 231–232, 235
Laws of Imitation, The (Tarde), 67
Lebovic, Nitzan, 100
Leder, Mimi, 109
Lemke, Thomas, 101
Lessing, Gotthold Ephraim, 35
Life After People (History Channel), 3
Lifeboat Earth, 10, 15, 102, 108, 112–113, 115–116, 121, 126
Limits to Growth, The (Club of Rome), 115–117, 120, 205, 228
long-term effects, 90, 93, 139–140, 143, 163, 171, 177, 205, 228, 230. *See also* side effects
Looking Backward: 2000-1887 (Bellamy), 202
Lovelock, James, 5

Lübbe, Weyma, 115
Luhmann, Niklas, 191, 195
Lumet, Sidney, 46, 233
Lyell, Charles, 66

Mad Max series, 6, 74
malice of the object, 148–150, 152, 156, 158, 162, 166, 172–173, 228
Malthus, Thomas Robert, 15, 35–41, 53, 101, 116–117, 119, 120, 130, 201, 227–228
Manhattan Project, 46
Man Without Qualities, The (Musil), 140, 146
Marbe, Karl, 145
Martin, John, 26, 29, 31
maximum credible accident (MCA), 138, 139, 161, 173, 178
McCarthy, Cormac, 5, 25, 75, 128–129
media of foresight, 200, 202–203, 206–226
Melancholia (von Trier), 6
Menke, Christoph, 124, 188, 256n33
metacrisis, 8
metaphor, 7, 10, 16, 18–19, 46, 72, 116, 196, 236
meteorology, 58, 59, 62, 73–74, 85
meteors, 58, 79, 244n5
Metz, Markus, 99
Minority Report (Spielberg), 207, 215–226, 233
Monbiot, George, 129
Monk by the Sea (Friedrich), 28
Montesquieu, Charles de, 60, 88
Morton, Timothy, 5
Murphy's Law, 150–152
mutually assured destruction (MAD), 11, 49, 50–53, 71–72

narration, necessity of, 4, 10, 15, 18, 143–144, 148
narrative, 3, 4, 10, 16, 44, 121–122, 148, 179–180, 190, 199, 226, 229; epistemological functions of, 15–16, 83–84, 88, 121, 143, 158–159, 166–168,

226, 228–230; 234; of the future, 4, 10, 15, 181, 202; proleptic, 226; hindsight, 97, 167, 174, 178, 204; biopolitical, 98–108, 115; structures, 14–15, 18, 159; trick, 166, 168
National Geographic Adventure, 91
National Oceanic and Atmospheric Administration, 59
National Socialism, 104
Nichols, Jeff, 196, 200, 206, 215
Nietzsche, Friedrich, 27
9 (Acker), 6
9/11. *See* September 11 attacks
non-knowledge, 15; knowledge and, 15, 232
nuclear family, 94, 99, 100, 109, 125, 127
nuclear power, 95, 138, 160; accidents, 134–140; safety, 253n34. *See also* Chernobyl
Nuclear Safety (magazine), 159
nuclear strike, 72, 90, 98; war, 16, 17, 26, 48, 50, 52, 53, 56, 91, 93, 205, 207, 228. *See also* Bomb, the
nuclear winter, 15, 69–81, 88, 90, 108, 128

Oakes, Guy, 91
Oblivion (Kosinski), 6
Oedipus (figure), 180, 184–190, 200, 219–220, 225
Oedipus Rex (Sophocles), 184–190, 213, 218–219, 224, 225, 237, 256n33
oil crisis, 91
Omega: The Last Days of the World (Flammarion), 67–68, 87
O'Neil, Onora, 113, 115, 116
On the Beach (Shute), 72, 99
On Thermonuclear War (Kahn), 48, 90
Oppenheimer, Robert J., 42
oracle, 256n26; at Delphi, 182, 183, 184, 187, 188, 224
Outbreak (Petersen), 108
overpopulation, 116–118, 120. *See also* Malthus, Thomas Robert; population

paleohistory, 86
Parable of the Sower, The (Butler), 81
Pentagon, 51
Perrow, Charles, 159, 161
Philosophie der Technik (*Philosophy of Technology*) (Kapp), 150
pollution, 95
population, 36–40, 94, 98, 100–104, 110, 201; control, 120; growth, 115–120, 176. *See also* Malthus, Thomas Robert; overpopulation
Population Bomb, The (Ehrlich and Ehrlich), 116–117
postapocalypse, 2, 4, 6, 26, 72, 122–124, 128, 129, 207, 239n2
Powell, James, 82
precaution, 9, 25, 41, 175, 178, 194
precautionary principle, 166–167, 177, 203–204
predetermination, 222–223
prediction, 11, 175, 176, 178, 180, 187, 190, 215, 237
preemption, 14, 41, 175, 177, 207, 215, 217–219, 222, 224–225, 232–234
"Premediation" (Grusin), 16, 217–218, 225
preparedness, 94, 133, 228, 247n2
preppers, 89, 94–95, 133. *See also* survivalist movement
prevention, 11, 14, 23, 41, 47, 174–185, 191–192, 201–206, 207, 214–215, 255n54; of accidents, 141–144, 147, 148, 151, 158; politics of, 15, 177, 215, 225–232, 235, 237; of risk, 95, 100; tragic structure of, 188–190
Pripyat, contaminated zone after the Chernobyl accident, 136, 137, 138, 163, 171
probability, 57, 60, 111, 146–148, 150–151, 156, 166, 171, 173, 176, 178–179, 201
prognosis, 175, 190, 203
progress, 23, 36, 41, 53, 227

prophecy, 21, 57, 169, 175, 181, 183, 189, 237; biblical, 21–22, 237; self-defeating/self-fulfilling, 179, 187, 190, 237, 238
providence, divine, 28, 227

Quetelet, Adolphe, 201

radiation sickness, 90
RAND Corporation, 48, 49
Real, the, 11; irruption of, 97, 100, 122
reality effect, 98
Red Alert (George), 49
resilience, 89, 94–96, 130, 133; movement, 94–96. *See also* preppers; survivalist movement
resources, 38, 117, 119, 120
resource shortage, 16, 36, 40, 98; water shortage, 74, 90
revelation, 27, 41. *See also* catastrophe, as revelation
Revelation, Book of, 13, 21, 24, 26, 28
Revelle, Roger, 84
risk, 139, 147, 164, 177, 201
risk society, 5, 95, 163, 255n53
Road, The (movie, Hillcoat), 6, 75
Road, The (novel, McCarthy), 5, 6, 12–13, 19–20, 25–26, 74, 74–81, 88, 97, 128–133, 234
Robb, John, 94
Röggla, Kathrin, 100
Romanticism, 12, 14, 16, 26–42, 56, 75, 80, 130, 239n2
Rumsfeld, Donald, 177
ruins, 25, 29–30, 77, 124, 128–129, 132, 140, 220

safety, 9, 92, 109, 138–139, 165; devices, 257n55; discourse of, 168–173, household, 152–153; measures, 18, 139, 164; mechanism, 138, 161; science, 86, 141–143, 151, 156, 158–162, 252n9; technical, 14–15, 134, 141–143, 147, 150, 156–158, 172, 215, 228; workplace, 165–166. *See also* security
Sagan, Carl, 71, 82
scarcity, 116–117, 119

scenario, 9, 17–19, 45, 52, 69, 71–74, 80, 82, 83, 116, 118, 121, 132, 153, 201, 228, 229, 231; as aid to the imagination, 236; as alternative future, 17; apocalyptic, 41, 229; climate, 57, 63; disaster, 8, 90, 115, 231, 234, 238; scientific, 16, 178; of survival, 123, 124; threat, 91; worst-case, 33, 40, 50, 75
Schmitt, Carl, 104, 110
Schwarze Spiegel (Schmidt), 26
second-order observation, 195, 226
securitization, 47
security, 9, 13, 15, 74, 95–96, 143, 189, 234; Cold War doctrine of, 49, 51–53; desire for, 192–200, 217; etymology, 191; knowledge, 177–180; post-9/11, 215–218, 223, 225; social, 100. *See also* anxiety; safety; *Sorge*
seeing, as knowing, 175, 185–188
seeing the future, 204, 214, 219, 222–223
Seeking a Friend for the End of the World (Scafaria), 6
Seeßlen, Georg, 99
September 11 attacks, 105, 176, 217
Serres, Michel, 58, 244n5
Shelley, Mary, 26, 39–40, 77, 202
Shelley, Percy Bysshe, 39
side effects, 70, 74, 80, 140, 163–164, 168–169, 172–173, 225, 230. *See also* long-term effects
Signs (Shyamalan), 99
Silent Spring (Carson), 74
Simmel, Georg, 104
simulacra, 167, 170, 254n53
simulation, 44, 59, 73, 74, 86, 139, 158, 170, 201; models, 80, 85
Siebenkäs (Jean Paul), 27
Sketch for a Historical Picture of the Progress of the Human Mind (Condorcet), 36
Sleeper Awakes, The (Wells), 202
sleepers, 105
Sloterdijk, Peter, 5
Soddy, Frederick, 45

solidarity, 96–97, 99
Solon of Athens, 183, 188
Sombart, Werner, 104
Sophocles, 184–189, 207, 219, 224–225, 237
Sorge (care, concern, worry), 191, 194, 196, 200, 227, 231, 257n50
Souriau, Étienne, 19, 241n33
Soviet Union, 51–52, 72, 99, 136, 244n5, 246n41
Soylent Green (Fleischer), 117–119
Spaceship Earth, 10
"Speech of the Dead Christ down from the Universe That There Is No God" (Jean Paul), 27–28, 30–31, 34
speed, 43, 145, 147, 157
Spielberg, Steven, 99, 206-7, 215–226, 233
Staël, Germaine de, 27
statistics, 37, 38–39, 41, 146–147, 150, 164–165, 171, 176, 201; statistical risk assessment, 158
steam engine, 156–157
steam boiler inspection and review association (*Dampfkessel-Überwachungs- und Revisionsverein*), 158
Strowick, Elisabeth, 192
sublime, aesthetics of, 29–30, 43, 150
survival, 11, 12, 14, 24–25, 46, 89–133; handbooks, 89; lottery of, 38; in nuclear winter, 70–77
survivalist movement, 14, 89–98, 200. *See also* preppers
Süssmilch, Johann Peter, 37
sustainability, 94–95
Swiss Re, 6, 174, 255n2
Szilard, Leo, 46
Szondi, Peter, 185

Take Shelter (Nichols), 196–200, 206, 215, 225
Taleb, Nassim, 203
Tambora eruption (1815), 40, 109, 242n28
Taylor, Charles, 10
TEOTWAWKI (the end of the world as we know it), 90, 174, 229
Terminator, The (Cameron), 205, 206, 207, 208, 225

Terminator II: Judgment Day (Cameron), 205
Terminator III: Rise of the Machines (Mostow), 205
Terminator Salvation (McGinty Nichol), 205
test, 12, 17, 85, 98, 130, 178, 182–183; crash, 141–143, 147, 158; safety, 134–135, 139, 151, 158, 164; stress, 24, 33–34. *See also* experiment
thanatopolitics, 101–102
theodicy, 251n65
think tanks, 45, 48
"Thinking the Unthinkable" (Kahn), 25, 122, 177
This Is the End (Rogan and Goldberg), 6
"365 ways to save the earth," 231–232
Thrift, Nigel, 138
time-axis manipulation, 202–203, 206, 209, 226, 258n76
Time Machine, The (Wells), 68, 202, 203
Time of the Wolf (Haneke), 6, 74
Timescape (Benford), 202, 205
time travel, 68, 203, 206, 208–209
tipping point, 7–8, 81–82, 153, 229–230
Tiresias, 185, 200, 219
tragic choices, 112–115, 120–122, 126–128, 132, 228, 235
trauma, 46, 98, 131, 143–144, 146, 152, 209, 211, 214, 252n10
triage, 121
Trier, Lars von, 5
Trojanow, Ilija, 88
TTAPS team, 15, 76
Turco, Richard, 71, 73
TÜV (*Technischer Überwachungsverein*), 141, 158
12 Monkeys (Gilliam), 207–214, 225
2012 (Emmerich), 6, 100, 108–111

ultimate judgment. *See* Last Judgment
ultimate weapon, 45–46, 53. *See also* Bomb, the
Uncanny, The (Freud), 151, 156, 173

Underground Man (Tarde), 66
"unknown unknowns" (Rumsfeld), 177
utopia, 5, 11, 23, 48, 57, 66–67, 201

Vertigo (Hitchcock), 211
Virilio, Paul, 138, 140
Vischer, Friedrich Theodor, 148, 156, 158, 166
vision, 21, 24, 97, 216, 219, 221–223
visualization, 47, 83, 215

Waiting for Godot (Beckett), 123
Welzer, Harald, 5
Wall-E (Stanton), 6
War on Terror, 104–105, 121, 176–177, 215, 218
war of the worlds, as narrative/scenario, 102, 105, 107, 108, 112, 119, 121–122
War of the Worlds (Haskin), 99
War of the Worlds (Spielberg), 99
War of the Worlds (Szulkin), 99
War of the Worlds (Welles), 99
War of the Worlds (Wells), 99, 102–105
Water Knife, The (Bacigalupi), 5, 18

weather, 19, 40–41, 55–56, 62, 65, 70, 72, 74, 76, 79–82, 108, 130, 242n28
Weber, Eugen, 22
Weisman, Alan, 3–4, 77, 120, 207
Wells, H. G., 46
White Noise (DeLillo), 167–173, 234–235, 254n53
Winfrey, Oprah, 129
Wohlstetter, Albert, 49
Wolf, Christa, 167
World Set Free, The (Wells), 45, 46
world without people, 2, 5, 77–78, 120
World War I, 45–46, 98, 104, 211
World War II, 51, 98
World War Z (Forster), 6
World Without Us, The (Weisman), 77, 120

Year Without a Summer (1816), 39–40, 57, 64–65

Zalasiewicz, Jan, 4
Žižek, Slavoj, 11, 233–234
zoē (bare/naked life), 28, 37, 123

GPSR Authorized Representative: Easy Access System Europe, Mustamäe tee 50, 10621 Tallinn, Estonia, gpsr.requests@easproject.com

www.ingramcontent.com/pod-product-compliance
Lightning Source LLC
Chambersburg PA
CBHW021937290426
44108CB00012B/875